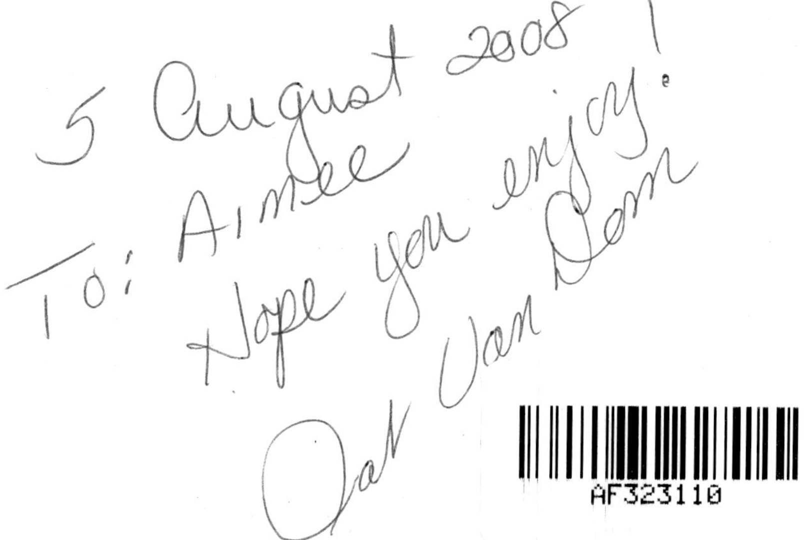

WHEN EVILS CONVERGE

BY

PAT VAN DORN

© 2007 by Pat Van Dorn

ISBN: 978-1-934666-06-7

Published and distributed by:
High-Pitched Hum Publishing
321 15th Street North
Jacksonville Beach, Florida 32250

Contact High-Pitched Hum Publishing at www.highpitchedhum.net

TO MY HUSBAND

FOR ALL HIS PATIENCE

WHEN EVILS CONVERGE

CHAPTER 1

It's 1957 ......

Robert Milhouse is the vice-president of the Bank of Florence in Florence Kentucky. He started as a bank teller and, due to his diligence and dedication, has been promoted into his present place of prominence in both the bank and the community. Robert is a very proud and very moral man. He and his wife attend church at least twice a week. Most of all, he wants nothing to tarnish or disrupt his comfortable way of life.

Josephine Milhouse is a housewife. She presides over the weekly bridge game that all the wives of the prominent men in town attend. She teaches Sunday school and leads the Tuesday night prayer meeting. She keeps an immaculate house and always makes sure dinner is on the table at the proper time.

Josephine enjoys being the wife of the vice-president of the bank and is careful to do nothing to sully Robert's image in the community. She likes their place of prominence in the community. The family isn't rich, but they are quite comfortable.

Robert and Josephine have one child, a daughter, Bobbie Jo. They succumbed to a southern tradition and named her after themselves. They are very proud of their child and have always been able to make sure she associated with all the right people. They even sent her to a private all-girls school in Cincinnati.

There is, however, a problem. When Bobbie Jo turned 15 she refused to attend the private school anymore. Actually, the school called Josephine and told her that Bobbie Jo would be allowed to finish out the summer semester, but her admittance application was not going to be renewed for the fall semester.

This would be a major blemish against the family name. Robert wouldn't allow that to happen and was in the process of contacting other private schools in the area when Bobbie Jo told him of her decision.

Robert did not react very well to this defiance, but after he and Josephine discussed the situation they were able to come up with an acceptable plan.

They decided to spread the word that Robert felt private school was too cloistered. He felt his daughter needed to attend public school for her last few years so that she would be ready for college and for the real world. He insisted the change from a cloistered private school to college would be so hard on any child they would not be able to concentrate and, therefore, be put in a position to fail.

If nothing else, Robert and Josephine were both very convincing. They were so good at telling the story, a number of the leading citizens of Florence decided to pull their children out of private school as well. After all, if one of the most prominent men of the community was doing it, how could it be wrong?

So in the fall of 1957 Bobbie Jo, now 16, was scheduled to enter public school for the first time.

This did pose some major problems for Robert and Josephine. Instead of wearing uniforms and being boarded at the private school, Bobbie Jo was home all the time. They soon found out that the cost of the private school was very reasonable in comparison to the increased costs for food and clothing, not to mention the additional wear and tear on Josephine and the house in general.

Before Bobbie Jo moved home, Josephine would rise at the seemly hour of 9am. This would give her plenty of time to make the plans for the day. Her household help, an old black lady called Sally, would have arrived at 7:30am. By the time Miss Josephine came downstairs, Sally would have prepared and served breakfast to Mr. Robert, cleaned the kitchen for the first time and would have started the daily laundry. When Miss Josephine appeared in the morning room, Sally would immediately stop what she was doing and fix Miss Josephine's morning tea. Mr. Robert always drank coffee, but coffee never passed Miss Josephine's lips.

While Josephine was drinking her tea and Sally was preparing her breakfast, she would carefully review her schedule for the day and glance at the items that needed tending the rest of the week.

After breakfast she would make up the lists for the day. According to Josephine, without lists, the world would crumble. She would hand one list to Sally and then carefully read it to her.

She felt Sally wasn't too bright and would steal from her if she didn't keep an eye on her.

She would never tell Sally if she'd be home for lunch just so she would be able to arrive home unexpectedly and, hopefully, catch her doing something wrong. Sally had worked for the best families in Florence for as long as anyone could remember and had never done anything wrong. Josephine didn't care. Deep in her heart she knew this old black woman couldn't be trusted. When she was satisfied her instructions were understood, she would prepare to go to town to accomplish the items on her list. This had been her daily routine for many years.

In the past Bobbie Jo only spent a week at home during the semester breaks and at holidays. This amounted in total to about six to seven weeks a year. The private school she'd attended provided a wonderful summer program that Bobbie Jo was always signed up for. All of this wonderful schooling, supposedly for the betterment of their child, was really because the two of them didn't want anything to disrupt their way of life.

Bobbie Jo was an unexpected surprise after they had been married 12 years. They didn't know what to do with her so they hired people to take care of her when she was a baby and shipped her off to private school as soon as she was old enough. It wasn't that they didn't love her; the child was just an inconvenience.

Bobbie Jo being at home was going to be a major change for everyone. Realizing this, Robert sat her down and dictated her schedule for school days.

"The bell for students to be in school rings at 8:15am. It's a 15-minute walk to the school from our home. If you're to have time to bathe, get dressed and eat, I feel you have to be up no later than 7:00am. Do you agree?"

Bobbie Jo just nodded her head to her father. It would have done no good to tell him what she really thought.

This schedule should have solved many problems but Robert overlooked a couple of issues. He forgot his comfortable home only had one bathroom. He had always commandeered the bathroom at 7:00am. Most importantly though, Bobbie Jo wasn't used to getting herself up (the boarding school rang a bell when it was time to rise) and no one in the house even thought about having to wake her.

The first school day after Bobbie Jo was back in their home; Josephine was sitting in the morning room drinking her tea when Bobbie Jo stumbled in.

Josephine was shocked to see her, "Why aren't you in school?"

"What time is it?"

"It's 9:30am. School started over an hour ago and you were supposed to be early today so Miss Marks, the principal, could go over the rules of the school and introduce you to your teachers."

Bobbie Jo replied, "Well, I guess she'll have to do it tomorrow cause I have other plans for my day." She then said to Sally, "Where's my breakfast?"

Poor Sally. No one thought to mention to her that the household duties were going to increase dramatically. Sally was a good soul though. All she said to the smart mouthed teenager was, "Tells me what you eat and I'lls fix it."

Bobbie Jo replied, "Never mind. I don't have time to wait for you to do your job. I'll eat out. Mother, I need some money."

Once again Josephine was caught off guard. She stumbled over to her handbag, found a dollar bill and handed it to her daughter.

"Mother! I said I needed some money, not a dollar. How about twenty?"

She had really been hoping for five but decided to see how much she could get.

Josephine didn't know what to say. She looked in her little handbag once again. All she had was ten dollars. She never needed much money as Robert had set up accounts all over town for her. "This is all I'm giving you. Make sure it lasts awhile."

"Yeah, yeah. Don't hold lunch for me. I won't be home til about 6pm."

"Bobbie Jo! We have dinner in this house at 5pm sharp. We always have and we always will", Josephine called after the girl who was walking out the front door.

"Well then, I guess Sally will just have to cook twice cause I won't eat leftovers", Bobbie Jo yelled as she slammed the door behind her.

Sally looked at Josephine. Josephine looked at Sally. Neither one of them could think of anything to say to each other. They both realized right then that their perfect little lives were in for a big change.

Three months later, Bobbie Jo came in after school and told her mother she wanted to talk to her. Josephine didn't know what to expect. She had been receiving calls from the school telling her Bobbie Jo was not attending. Robert had been receiving calls from shopkeepers saying that Bobbie Jo was loitering in their stores during school hours. She didn't arrive home for meals most of the time. She was totally out of control and they seemed to be able to do nothing.

"Mother, I think I'm pregnant", Bobbie Jo said matter-of-factly.

Josephine nearly fainted. She sat there with her mouth moving but no sound was coming out. Didn't Bobbie Jo know one did not get "that way" when one was so young? Didn't she know that if you had any breeding you didn't even say that word?

After regaining her ability to reason a little, she walked to the telephone and called her husband. After asking to speak with Mr. Milhouse in a very calm voice, she started to weep. When Robert came on the line, all he heard was his wife crying. He didn't know what was going on. "Talk to me. What's happened?" He kept saying those two things over and over with no response.

Finally, Bobbie Jo walked over to her mother and took the phone from her hand. "Father, I'm pregnant!" Then she hung up the phone.

Robert quietly hung up the phone. His secretary, who had taken the call from Josephine and who had heard him questioning his wife, asked if everything was all right at home. "Oh yes, just a minor problem that seems to have upset the dear. I can take care of it later. Thank you for your concern."

It was then nearly 3pm and the bank was closing soon. He'd be home by 4:45pm. There was nothing he could do about the situation right then so Robert figured he would simply go on as if everything were normal. Besides, he didn't want anyone at the bank to get an idea anything was really wrong. It was bad enough with all the things they did know. At times it was bad living in a small town. When something went wrong, everyone knew about it.

He managed to get through the rest of the day without incident. He had even begun to formulate a plan. On the way home, he was able to work out most of the details so when he walked into the house he felt he was once again in control. This child was not going to ruin his name in the community. He was sure of that.

Sally was surprised that the whole family sat down to dinner at the same time that evening. She knew Miss Josephine and that child were upset over something, but she didn't know over what. If Josephine had confided in her, Sally might have been able to help them take care of the problem. As it was they didn't tell Sally anything, and Sally didn't ask. She just served dinner and then went home for the evening, grateful for being able to leave a little early.

Soon after Sally left the house, Robert turned to Bobbie Jo and said, "Pack all of your clothes. Tomorrow you're leaving town to go visit your cousin in Crab Orchard. I haven't called her yet, but she owes me favors and will take you in. You'll have your child in her home and it will be put up for adoption. Do you understand?"

"Yes, Daddy", replied Bobbie Jo. She knew she was in a lot of trouble. She hadn't meant to get pregnant. She'd been told you couldn't get pregnant the first time. She thought that meant the first time with each boy. She just made sure she didn't do the deed with the same boy twice. She was sure that was the safe way to have fun and still not get "that way" as her mother would say.

Later Robert called his cousin, Ethel Lindsey. He was careful not to tell her what the situation was because the operator who put in the call or one of the people on the party line could be listening.

Ethel, a mid-wife, knew right away what the problem was. Her fancy cousin would never be calling her if it weren't that his little girl had gotten into big trouble. She had done this type of thing for other people. She had a friend who had an orphanage and handled adoptions. He was always willing to take a healthy baby and not ask any questions. He paid her pretty well for making sure the mother and the baby were in good health. Ethel would make sure her cousin Bobby, or Robert as he liked to be called now, would pay her well too.

Robert advised Ethel they would be over the next day. Inside he was very glad this all happened on a Friday. He could rid he and Josephine of the blemish immediately. Once he hung up the phone he turned to Bobbie Jo and said, "Pack all your things. You're leaving here tomorrow."

Early the next morning, Robert bundled Bobbie Jo and all her belongings into his Packard and drove off. He arrived at his cousin's house right around noontime. After unloading the car he talked with Ethel for a few minutes. Then he walked over to Bobbie Jo, who was sitting on the porch of the small house.

"Well, all right. It's all arranged. You'll stay here until it is time. You won't go anywhere until it is over. Once you're well, you can come back to my house where you will once again attend school. Do you understand?"

Bobbie Jo responded, "Yes, Daddy", but she was thinking about what a horrible place Ethel had. Robert nodded to Ethel and then drove off.

Once he arrived back at his home, he told Josephine Bobbie Jo was going to be staying with his cousin and her problem would never be mentioned in his home again. After that their lives went on as it did before Bobby Jo came home from the private school.

Robert didn't care that his daughter's life was going to be one of hard work and near-poverty for the next seven or eight months. She almost ruined what he and Josephine had spent a lifetime building. The child needed to learn a lesson. Robert felt all the money he had spent on her over the years was totally wasted. If she wanted to be a tramp then she needed to learn what the life of a tramp was really like.

Not once did either Robert or Josephine ever think about asking the identity of the baby's father. Not once did they consider taking the child into their home as their own. The well being of the child was never a consideration. Their only consideration was their standing in the community.

Bobbie Jo was not very happy with Ethel. She felt she should have been allowed to just sit around and do nothing while the baby was growing inside of her. Ethel, however, told her she needed to get off her butt and work. She was assigned duties and if they weren't done and done correctly, the belt came out. Bobbie Jo had never thought about her life, but she had always led a privileged one. She'd never been the one being abused. She was the one to do the abusing even if it was just verbally. Now she was to be on the receiving end of abuse. The first time she didn't make her bed in the morning, she found out just how verbally abusive someone could be. Later that day when she refused to go out to the garden and weed she found out how the sting of the belt felt. The next day when she didn't do the breakfast dishes she found out how it felt to be slapped hard in the face. Bobbie Jo was not happy about any of this and told Ethel she was calling her father to come and get her.

"Go right ahead honey", said Ethel. "You need to find out just what your Daddy thinks about what you gone and done. Call him right now. Call him at his fancy work. I dare ya!"

Bobbie Jo marched over to the phone sitting next to the front door. After giving the name of the town and the number she wanted to reach, she turned to Ethel and smirked. She knew her Daddy would come through. Her days there were numbered. She would be home by the weekend. Ethel would see.

Bobbie Jo heard the ringing of the phone and then Miss Marjory answered. Bobbie Jo turned on the charm. "Oh Miss Marjory, this is Bobbie Jo Milhouse. How are you? I haven't talked to you in so long."

Marjory didn't really know Bobbie Jo and her employer hardly ever mentioned her, but she was pleasant and replied, "I'm just fine, Bobbie Jo. How do you like your new boarding school? Your father said he had found a better school for you over in Coldwater."

Bobbie Jo was shocked. She hadn't thought about what her father and mother would have told anyone. Speaking in a stumbling voice she said, "Oh, I'm just getting used to it. I guess it will be fine. I just wish it was closer to home."

"Oh yes, I understand. It's hard making new friends, but from what I've heard about the school I'm sure it will be wonderful for you" said Marjory. "Do you want to speak with your father?"

"Yes, please," replied Bobbie Jo.

"Just a minute and I'll get him for you."

In the background Bobbie Jo heard her father's voice, but she couldn't make out what he was saying. The next thing she knew Marjory was back on the phone telling her, "Oh Bobbie Jo. I'm so sorry. I forgot your father's late for a meeting. He said he would call you tonight after he gets home."

"Oh! Okay. That'll be fine. Thank you."

"Take care, Bobbie Jo. I know you're just going to love the new school once you get over the homesickness" gushed Marjory.

Bobbie Jo hung the phone up and turned around. She had forgotten Ethel had been standing right behind her when she was talking. Ethel didn't say a word, she just laughed, turned and walked away. Bobbie Jo started to cry.

"Don't start with the blubbering. Get out to the weed patch that's supposed to be our garden. If them greens and corn don't grow, we don't eat. Get out there. I'll call ya when lunch is ready. Ya need to keep up your strength."

Bobbie Jo hung her head, picked up the hoe and walked out to the weed patch.

While this was going on at Ethel's house, Robert was walking out of his bank. He hadn't had a meeting, but he was not going to talk to Bobbie Jo at work. He didn't know what she wanted nor what she was thinking when she called him there. She knows enough not to call him at work. He got in his car and drove over to Nate Smeedy's farm. Nate had been thinking about buying some more equipment and had wanted to talk about getting a loan for it. Robert kept putting him off as he really didn't like the man and didn't care if he got more equipment or not. However, it gave him an excuse to leave the bank so he could escape taking the call from his daughter.

Robert spent most of the morning with Nate and successfully negotiated the requested loan. Nate thought it was wonderful that the banker came to see him. It made him forget that Robert had almost been rude when Nate tried to talk to him about a loan before. Now he felt like he was as important as some of the storeowners that always lorded it over him when he went to get supplies.

Robert, most of the time, would never have thought once to set foot on a farm. He had enough of that life when he was a very young boy; however, this time it allowed him some time to think as well as the opportunity to make money for the bank.

When lunchtime arrived Ethel, true to her word, called to Bobbie Jo to come into the house and eat. As Bobbie Jo walked in the door Ethel called over her shoulder for her to wash up. Then Ethel proceeded to put the food on the table. When Bobbie Jo walked into the kitchen Ethel said to her, "For heavens sake! Look what you've gone and done."

"What now?" cried Bobbie Jo.

"You've gone and got yourself sunburned. Don't you know to put one of them big straw hats on? Girl, what have you been doing all your life that you don't know enough to cover up from the sun?"

Bobbie Jo started sobbing. She was tired and hungry but most of all thirsty. She had been afraid to stop to get a drink for fear of being hit with the strap or slapped again and she had never worked in the sun before so she didn't know what could happen.

Ethel laughed. "You city girls think you know so much. Every time I get a city girl here I have to teach them just about everything. You think cause you know how to spread your legs you know it all. Well, you don't. You don't know nothing about getting by and getting by is what you have to do most of your life."

Bobbie Jo stopped sobbing. She picked up the glass of tea and drank the whole thing down and then asked if she could please have another.

"You didn't drink any water while you were out there did ya!"

Bobbie Jo just shook her head.

"Girl, girl, you don't know nothing, not nothing at all. Here have some more tea. Let's you and I do a little talkin' while we eat lunch." With that Ethel poured Bobbie Jo another glass of tea. Then she set the pitcher down between them so the girl could pour more for herself. Over lunch Ethel proceeded to tell Bobbie Jo about her being a mid-wife and how, for many years, she has made her living birthing babies and by taking in girls like Bobbie Jo. She told her about the birthing and about what happened to the baby after it was born. She also told her about how she needed to care for herself during and right after the baby was born.

Ethel noticed that Bobbie Jo wasn't eating much. "Girl, right now you don't need to be thinking about staying so skinny. There aren't any men to be interested in you right now anyway so you might as well eat so you and that baby are healthy. If that baby isn't healthy I don't get paid and neither do you.

As soon as Ethel said the word paid, Bobbie Jo's head popped up. "Did you say paid?"

"Yep. When that baby goes over to my friend and he finds a family to adopt it I get paid what's called a finder's fee. When I get the finder's fee I pay you some of it."

"How much?" asked Bobbie Jo?

"Depends."

"On what?" asked Bobbie Jo?

"On how much my friend can get for the baby. If the child's sickly, we don't get much and we wasted 6 or so months of our life. If the child is healthy we get more. If the family is rich we can get a lot for a healthy child. So I want you and that child to be healthy. Being healthy means you work to keep strong so the birthing goes easy and you eat so that baby is fat and sassy when it pops out. Are you starting to understand? This is a business for me and you're a part of it. If that baby you're carrying does good then we both do good."

After that lunch and discussion Ethel noticed that Bobbie Jo was much easier to get along with. Ethel knew the girl wasn't stupid; she was just uneducated in the way the world goes. That night Bobbie Jo went to bed early, exhausted. She never remembered that her father was supposed to call. Ethel remembered.

Robert never called. He never intended to. In fact, he had forgotten about receiving the call from his daughter until the next day when Marjory asked if he had been able to calm Bobbie Jo down. "She sounded so homesick. I know how it is to be away from home."

"Homesick? Oh yes, she's fine now. She talked with her mother and me and felt much better. I told her it would really be wiser if she called after I was home from work. I told her I'm so busy I don't always have time to stop and chat. Besides calling at night allows her to talk with both her mother and I."

"You are so right. I would never have thought of that. I'll bet she didn't either. She is so lucky to have such a smart father", chirped Marjory. Marjory thought her boss was the most perfect man in the world.

Robert was furious. He hated people knowing any of his business. Bobbie Jo is going to ruin everything, he thought.

Everything went along peacefully for the next few months. Robert and Josephine had settled back into their comfortable pattern. They had almost forgotten they had encountered any problem at all.

Life at Ethel's had changed some. Two more girls were dropped off for Ethel to care for. Much to Ethel's surprise Bobbie Jo was a great help in dealing with them. She actually was a pretty good teacher. In fact, Ethel told her she should think about becoming one.

"You would make a fine one, Bobbie Jo. You have a knack that not everybody has. Your Daddy has the money to send you so you don't have no worries there. You would be a respected member of any community you decided to teach in and the money is pretty good. It's sure better'n what I do."

"Maybe you're right. I'll think about it after this is over", replied Bobbie Jo. In reality, Bobbie Jo couldn't think of anything worse than being a teacher. It was too confining. She liked the idea of someone else working and her getting the money.

When Bobbie Jo's father dropped her off he told her she was not to go to school and she was not to go anywhere. She never disobeyed him. She didn't have to. Ethel was a very good teacher. She just didn't teach the same things that schools did. She taught important things. Plus she didn't have to go anywhere to have fun. Ethel had all kinds of relatives and friends that were always stopping by. Some were some very cute boys. More than once Bobbie Jo wished they could see her when she wasn't fat and in "that condition". She really missed being with all those fine boys. One day after supper she told Ethel how she felt.

"Wait until that baby is born. Then you can tell me how you feel about those boys."

Not long after that, Bobbie Jo went into labor. As usual Ethel called the man at the orphanage immediately. He didn't mind getting calls at any time of the day or night. Those calls meant money for him. He would usually have time for a leisurely meal and drive over to Ethel's. After all that, he would still wind up waiting for the birth. He sometimes had to wait hours but he was a patient man. However, this time the labor wasn't long and before he could arrive a healthy baby boy had been produced. Ethel took the child immediately into the back room, cleaned it up, diapered it and wrapped it in a plain receiving blanket. Once that was done she placed it in the small bassinette she had used for years. After that chore was finished, she went to tend to Bobbie Jo.

When Ethel walked back into the room, Bobbie Jo asked her if it was a boy or a girl.

"A little boy" responded Ethel.

"I'm glad. I might have wanted to keep it if it had been a girl."

Ethel noticed that Bobbie Jo never once asked to see the child. She thought it was unusual, but then she always felt this girl was a bit strange. In some ways she enjoyed having her in the house but in others she was unsure of what the child was going to do. It was like she was always planning something.

The man from the orphanage finally arrived. He was very pleased with the baby and said he thought he already had a family for the child. A rich couple from Louisville had been over to the orphanage several times but they were very picky about the child they wanted and always went away without one. He thought this baby just might do it. He said he'd be in touch with Ethel after he was able to finalize the arrangements. Then he picked up the baby, walked out to his car with the tightly wrapped baby in his arms, laid it on the front seat next to him and drove off. No one involved in the birth of the baby would ever see or inquire about the child ever again.

The next day Bobbie Jo seemed to be back to her original self again, only heavier. She didn't want to do any work around the house nor in the garden and she barely touched any food or drink. When Ethel and the other girls in the house asked her about it she just told them she needed to get her figure back as soon as possible. Ethel had expected her to give the normal response and say she was sad and just didn't feel like eating anything. This child was definitely strange.

Two weeks after the baby was carried away, the man from the orphanage called Ethel and asked her to stop by the next time she was in town. This meant that the deal had been finalized and he had her finder's fee. That night Ethel told the three girls that she would be going into town the next day and asked them if there was anything they needed. The two still pregnant girls nodded their heads no, but Bobbie Jo said she wanted to go with her. Ethel told her no. She said it was her personal business she had to take care of and didn't want anyone tagging along. She reminded her that her father had told her she was not to go anywhere while she was living here. Bobbie Jo wasn't happy about still being cooped up but she could do nothing about it.

The next day Ethel met with the man at the orphanage. He was so happy. "Ethel. I don't know, nor do I want to know where that baby came from, but I sure wish we could get them like that all the time. Your finder's fee is twice the usual amount. Whatever you did, do it again."

Ethel was astounded. She counted that money three times. Then she realized she couldn't put all of it in the bank like she normally did. It was too much money and people would know she didn't make that much birthing or selling her greens, corn and eggs. She decided to put some of it in the bank and hide the rest of it in her house. She had a little stash under the boards in her bedroom she used to hide things from the girls. She'd put it there.

Ethel never talked to Bobbie Jo about an exact amount of money but she knew that soon Bobbie Jo would be asking if the child had been disposed of yet. Bobbie Jo was getting itchy to move on and would want her money. Ethel knew she'd have to figure out how much she was going to give the child. She wanted to be fair, but she really didn't want to part with any of the extra. She hoped she would have a little time to figure that part out.

One month after the child was born, Bobbie Jo announced that she could fit into her clothes once again and that she was ready to go home. She demanded to know if the deal for the baby had been completed yet. Ethel said it had been, just the other day. Bobbie Jo then said, "I want my money and I want you to call my father to come and get me." With that said, Bobbie Jo announced she was going for a walk.

Ethel told the two girls who were just standing in the kitchen to get outside and go to work. "If those greens and corn don't grow, we don't eat. Now get."

Once everyone was out of the house Ethel put the call in to her cousin Robert. He was startled. He had forgotten that his daughter was not in a boarding school for fine ladies. He had forgotten that at some point she was going to want to come home. When his secretary told him that his cousin Ethel was on the line, Robert turned pale and dropped into his chair. Ethel apologized for calling him at work but explained she wanted to talk when there was no one around at her end to hear. Robert said he understood. Ethel explained what had happened over the past few months and told him that Bobbie Jo was ready to come home. She also told him about the money she had promised Bobbie Jo.

Robert didn't know that the girls received money. He had been sending money each week to Ethel for his daughter's care and had assumed that is how his cousin made her living. Ethel was concerned about what Bobbie Jo might do with all the money she was going to get and told Robert about her change in attitude since she'd gotten her figure back.

Robert agreed it could be a problem. Then he told Ethel not to give her any money. "Tell her you were given orders to send it to me for reimbursement for her care while with you. I'll talk to her when I pick her up Saturday. You can slip it to me while she is loading her things in the car."

Ethel agreed to do as he wished, but knew there was going to be some big trouble when Bobbie Jo was told her money had been given away.

Ethel heard Bobbie Jo before she saw her. Bobbie Jo was laughing and talking very loudly. When Ethel looked out she saw Bobbie Jo was walking with two boys. She was prancing around them like a female cat in heat. She was going to have to have another talk with that girl. Apparently she had not learned her lesson yet.

When Bobbie Jo walked in Ethel said, "I called your father."

"Good! When's he coming for me?"

"Don't know. He wasn't there. I just talked to that prissy that answers his phone," replied Ethel. "She said she'd have him call me back."

"That prissy is Marjory. You didn't tell her anything did you? She's such a gossip."

If there had been any doubt before, there wasn't now. Ethel knew that Bobbie Jo was back to herself once again. "Bobbie Jo. I may be from the country, but I'm not stupid."

"Yeah, yeah. Now I'd like my money. I worked real hard and I deserve it. Besides, I want to party some before I go back to the other jail."

"Bobbie Jo, do you think I keep money in this little place? Have you ever seen me with any money here? No, of course not. I'll have to go into town to the bank and get it. I figured I'd talk to your father first and then get you your money."

"When's that going to be?"

"After your father calls me back. I'll go as soon as he calls. Of course, the bank will have to be open. It shouldn't be any later than tomorrow."

"Tomorrow?" cried Bobbie Jo. "I have plans for tonight and I need money!"

"I was goin' to talk to you about your plans. I'm sure they include them two boys I saw you with a little while ago."

"Yeah, so what?"

"Them boys are your cousins."

That caught Bobbie Jo a little off guard, but to Ethel she said, "So what? We're just goin' to party together. No harm in that."

"Just remember the problem you just got rid of. I bet you were just having a party then too."

"That was different cause I wasn't related to them," Bobbie Jo said while hanging her head just a little.

Ethel caught the motion of her head, but said nothing about it. Instead she said, "If you insist on going with them boys, you tell them I said that they have money and they should spend it on you."

Bobbie Jo's head perked right up. She liked that thought. She had always spent her own money when she went to party. She had never thought about the boys or men spending money on her. She would definitely remember this lesson. "You're right." Then as she once again walked out the door she said, "Thanks Ethel."

Ethel was startled and wondered what she had said that had caused such a spark in that girl's eyes. Ethel didn't know what a devious mind Bobbie Jo had nor how her lessons would be twisted to become tools of laziness and greed.

Ethel watched Bobbie Jo leave. As soon as the girl was out of sight Ethel jumped in her beat up truck and headed to town. She had no reason to go, but she had told a couple of lies and had to pretend like she was going to the bank after talking with Bobbie Jo's father. There was going to be hell to pay tonight. Ethel hoped Saturday would come quickly. Ethel didn't like lies.

It was late when Ethel finally got home from her errands in town. The two other pregnant girls were just coming in from the garden. They were smart enough to stay away from Bobbie Jo now. They could see and hear the change in her and didn't want to get caught up in whatever she did.

"Sorry I'm late. I had to go to town to take care of some business for Bobbie Jo. I'll get dinner on the table while you two wash up. It won't be long, I promise."

The girls just said, "That's okay. It'll give us a chance to take a bath instead of just washing up."

Then Ethel felt really bad about dinner being late. These two girls worked hard and were no trouble at all. They were nothing like Bobbie Jo. No one had ever been like Bobbie Jo.

Finally Ethel and the two girls sat down to dinner. While the oldest girl said the blessing Ethel, in her mind, was saying one of her own. "Please help me get through this thing with Bobbie Jo." When the final amen was said to the blessing, Ethel's was said with a great deal of feeling.

Just as the dishes were being dried, Bobbie Jo came stumbling in. It was very apparent she'd been drinking. Ethel was not looking forward to this conversation.

"Where's dinner?" shouted Bobbie Jo.

"We finished dinner an hour ago", replied Ethel. "These girls worked hard today. They needed to eat to keep their strength up. We don't want them or their babies to get sick."

"They're so fat! They could go a couple of weeks without eating", laughed Bobbie Jo.

The two girls were shocked. Ethel looked at Bobbie Jo and then at the girls. "Girls, why don't you go to your room? I'm sure you're both tired. Bobbie Jo and I have some talking to do." Is that all right?"

Both girls just nodded to Ethel and started walking silently to their room.

"Bobbie Jo. This is still my house and you are still my ward. You can say what you like to me, but I will not have you treating my other charges so badly. They have done nothing to you."

"Yeah, yeah. But they are fat. I bet they always were. I could take any man from them if I wanted to. Wanna bet?"

"No. I don't gamble and I don't argue with drunks. Now do you wanna hear what your father had to say or not?"

"Fine. Tell me."

"He said he would be here Saturday to pick you up."

"Okay. Now how about my money? I don't need it to party anymore, cause you were right. Them boys had money and they spent it on me, but I want it so I can count it over and over", laughed Bobbie Jo.

"I went to the bank for the money and then I took it to Western Union."

Starting to sober up a little, Bobbie Jo asked, "What do you mean? I don't understand?"

"Your father told me to send your money to him."

Bobbie started screaming. "He has no right! I worked hard for that money. I even had to get fat to earn it. He can't do that."

Calmly Ethel replied, "Yes he can. You're still a minor. Really I don't even have to pay you anything because you were made my ward and I took care of you all this time. I pay you girls because I think it's the fair thing to do. Your father has the final decision. Now if you want some dinner, there's some stuff left in the fridge."

"I don't eat leftovers", Bobbie Jo screamed.

"Well then, I guess you don't eat tonight."

"Oh yes I will. I'm going out. I can get one of them boys to get me some dinner. They have money and they will spend it on me. I can make them."

As Bobbie Jo walked out the door, Ethel thought, "*Saturday cannot come too soon.*"

CHAPTER 2

It's August 1958 ......

When Robert told Josephine he'd be picking Bobbie Jo up on Saturday, she looked at him blankly. It was as if she didn't know who he was talking about. Both of them had done such a fine job of telling the new private school story that Josephine had really come to believe it. In actual fact, after the first week, no one mentioned Bobbie Jo again. All the ladies of the bridge club were actually glad to have her gone again. During Bobbie Jo's brief stay in the Milhouse home, their bridge club was disbanded. They had tried to play cards, but they were always being interrupted. When the day arrived that Josephine called them all and cancelled, everyone was relieved. None of them had children at home so the constant activities of a teenager irritated them.

Finally Josephine said, "Has the uh, uh, problem been dealt with?"

"Yes, it has."

"What are we going to do with her? Isn't she old enough to be out on her own? She is 17 now, you know. I was married at that age."

"Times are different now. Besides, what decent boy in town would have her now? The parents may not realize what's gone on with her, but I'm sure the young men do."

"Don't you know anyone who has a son? You know the kind."

"I know a lot of people who have sons, but I don't know what you mean by the kind."

"Oh yes you do. One who will eventually make a decent, honest living but he's the kind no girl will look at. There must be one boy in town who would make her a decent husband."

Then Robert got the point of what his wife was saying. She was looking for a man who would take Bobbie Jo off their hands, who would be able to take care of her and not embarrass them. To Josephine he said, "I understand you now. I'll start looking at the families who come into my bank." He would never admit to Josephine that she had a good idea, but this time she did. If he could find the right young man, their problems would be solved.

The next day he really started looking at and talking to the patrons who came in the bank. Most of the customers of the bank felt that Robert Milhouse was a cold, remote person. He might occasionally tip his hat to the ladies, but he would never utter a word to anyone unless he thought they were going to make his bank some money, until now. Little did they know he was prospecting for a husband for his daughter. If they had known, they probably would have been lining their sons up to be inspected. Most of them would have paid a dowager fee to have their offspring marry into such a prominent family.

By the time Saturday arrived, Robert had once again formulated a plan for his child. The last one he designed worked very well so he had all the reason in the world to believe this one would too.

The latest story to be circulated was that Bobbie Jo had completed the courses at the school she attended and now she was ready to be presented to the community. This would mean, to everyone who heard it, Robert and Josephine were ready for the child to be married. Bobbie Jo was apparently not going to college and they were all set for her to move out of the house.

Saturday arrived and Robert once again made the long trip down to Crab Orchard. He'd already forgotten about the money issue. All he could think of was getting Bobbie Jo home so he could find her a husband and move her permanently out of his home. He realized the latest plan would cost him some money. They'd have to host some expensive parties and both she and Josephine would need some party gowns. He didn't like parting with his money for frivolous things, but these expenditures were necessary in order to find the right person.

Bobbie Jo was anxious for her father to arrive. She wanted out of the hovel Ethel called home. She was tired of the farm boys that always were hanging around, but most of all she was angry that her father took her money. She had packed the night before and had started pacing the floor at the first light of day.

Ethel told her, "Girl. Ya know your father won't be here til noon. It's a long drive all the way from Florence. Y'all should've slept in today like you have every other day since that baby was born."

Bobbie Jo hadn't really been paying to much attention to what Ethel had been saying, but when she heard the word baby she wheeled around and snarled, "Don't you ever mention that word again around me or you'll be very sorry."

Ethel was astounded. "Girl. What are you talking about? You had a baby. There's no takin' that back."

"No I didn't. I didn't have any such thing. I come from a prominent family and I would never do such a thing. So don't you be spreading lies or, as I said, you'll be very, very sorry. I have friends who'll do anything for me. They *will* silence you if I ask them to. So, for the last time, I'm telling you to stop lying about me."

Ethel stood there saying nothing. She had thought this girl was strange, but not this strange. To Bobbie Jo she just said, "My mistake, Bobbie Jo."

"That's better. Just remember what I told you and everything will be fine."

Ethel turned back to her stove and tending to breakfast. She was wondering if she should tell Robert about the child's threat. She also wondered if she should tell him the hours she'd been keeping and that she had been hangin' out with her cousins. She finally decided she'd leave well enough alone. He was gonna have a hard enough time with answering the child's demands for her money.

Ethel had made a lot of money helping her cousin out, but she was not at all sure that it wasn't the biggest mistake of her life. She made a promise to herself to screen her clients a little better. In all her years of birthing and boarding girls til their time come, she had never had problems like with this child.

Right around 11:30am Robert arrived. He too had been anxious, but for different reasons than Bobbie Jo.

When Bobbie Jo heard the car coming, she brought her bag out to the little porch and sat on the steps. She didn't want to spend another second in that place or with that hick of a woman.

By the time Robert stopped the car and got out, Bobbie Jo was already putting her bag in the trunk. Then she got into the car without saying a word to anyone. Robert was a bit startled, but thought perhaps this unfortunate incident had taught his daughter a lesson.

At the sound of the car stopping, Ethel walked out her front door and said to Robert, "I'm just about to put lunch on the table. Wanna eat with us?"

Bobbie Jo hollered out of the car, "No. We don't have time to eat. We have to get back."

Robert, however, said, "No, thanks. I could stand to wash up and then perhaps a drink of tea would be nice."

"That's fine. You know where it is. I'll pour us all some tea and we can talk a bit."

Hearing that, Bobbie Jo just fumed to herself. She wanted out and they wanted to talk. She resigned herself to the wait, relaxed and laid her head back on the seat.

When Robert came out of the bathroom, the tea had been poured and some country biscuits placed on the table. He sat without being asked, and helped himself to a biscuit.

Ethel sat down and handed him a yellowing envelope.

"What's this?"

"That's her money."

"Oh you keep it", as he pushed it towards his cousin. "It can't be that much and I know she must have cost you more than I was sending you. Besides, she doesn't need money. She'll be getting married soon."

Ethel's eyebrow raised just a little bit. To herself she said, *Who'd have her?* To him she said, "It's quite a bit of money. It's $500."

It was Robert's turn to raise an eyebrow. "How did you get that?"

"Let's just say it is her share of the fee paid for the work she done."

Robert was astounded. "That much was her share?"

"I trys to be fair when I split it", Ethel said. She felt bad lying to her cousin, but he had lied to her. Ethel did try to be fair, normally. This time she was just giving the girl the normal share and nothing of the extra she received. "Here, take $200 of it back", said Robert as he counted the money out. "She won't know the difference or did you tell her how much she was getting?"

"I'm country, I'm not stupid. I didn't talk about how much she would get. I normally don't even mention money til they're done with the problem. I've found it's usually best not to mention it until they are feelin' sad and are being sorry about givin' the problem up. Bobbie Jo was different. I had to tell her up front so she'd take care of herself and the problem."

"Sure sounds like her."

Just then Bobbie Jo appeared at the door and said, "Aren't you done yet? It's getting hot out here."

"Have some tea and cool down", said Ethel.

"No. If you drink too much you have to go to the bathroom too much. I just want to leave."

"I was just thanking Ethel for her help. I'm ready to go. Thanks for the tea and the fine biscuit, Ethel. If you're ever up my way, stop in and see us. You'll always be welcome."

Ethel replied, "Thanks. I just might surprise you and do that one day." Ethel knew Robert never wanted to see or hear from her again, but he had been generous both now and for the past few months. She could afford to be pleasant to him one last time.

Robert and Bobbie Jo got in the car and without saying another word to Ethel, drove off. Once they were off the dirt road and back on the paved highway, Robert said to Bobbie Jo, "Your mother and I have a surprise for you."

This caught Bobbie Jo off guard as she had been trying to figure out how to ask her father for her money. "What?"

"We've decided you don't need to attend anymore school."

"Wonderful", said Bobbie Jo. She hadn't planned to go anyway so she was pleased they saw it her way.

"We have another surprise."

Bobbie Jo didn't respond so Robert continued, "We're planning a coming out party for you."

Bobbie Jo was still quiet. She was wondering what her father had up his sleeve. She just knew it wouldn't be good. She spent the rest of the ride home figuring out how she could use her father's plan to her advantage.

When they finally arrived at the family home in Florence, Josephine and Sally were waiting for them on the porch.

"Who does that nigger think she is", exclaimed Bobbie Jo?

"Bobbie Jo! Don't you talk like that. Sally's been a part of my family for more years than you can count", chastised Robert.

"Well, that may be but she has no right to be sitting on our front porch acting like she belonged there and I intend to tell her so."

Robert was shocked and shouted, "No you won't".

Bobbie Jo looked at him and bit her tongue to keep from saying just what she thought. She had no love for people of color. She truly believed they were just put on earth to serve her. Bobbie Jo was a very spoiled, prejudiced young girl.

As the car pulled into the drive, Josephine and Sally got up and walked over to it to greet them.

"Umm, uh, how was your trip dear", Josephine asked of Bobbie Jo?

"Just peachy mother. It was the best 6 months of my life" she replied sarcastically. "Just how do you think it was? I was stuck in that country bumpkin place and had no contact with my friends. It was terrible and I hated it. Don't ever send me to a place like that again."

Poor Josephine, she hadn't known what to say to her daughter and was just trying to make small talk. She hadn't really expected a response. Now instead of replying to her daughter's outburst, she just hung her head.

Sally had walked to the rear of the car to assist Robert. She couldn't help but overhear Bobbie Jo's comments. "Don't appear she's larned too much these past months."

"Oh, Sally. She's learned a lot. I'm just not sure what she learned is what we intended for her to she learn. Has Miss Josephine talked to you about the parties we have planned?"

"Yep. I understands what needs to be done. I has family that'll help with the cooking and serving. Just have Miss Josephine give me the list of days and I'll makes sure everything's perfect."

"You're a good friend, Sally. I hope Bobbie Jo isn't too hard on you before we can get her married."

"Don'ts you worry none, Mr. Robert. I was here before Bobbie Jo and I'll be here after she's moved on."

Robert just nodded his head at the old black woman. He did catch the subtle change in Sally's voice when she spoke of his daughter. He also caught that she no longer called her Miss. Sally was angry with Bobbie Jo and was showing it the only way she could.

Just then Bobbie Jo shouted, "Sally, take my bag up to my room and unpack it."

Robert answered, "Sally will do no such thing. She was kind enough to stay here so we would have a nice dinner when we arrived. She's certainly not going to take care of your bag for you. I'll carry your bag to the house then you can take it to your room."

Bobbie Jo just stomped her feet and turned to walk into the house. "Well, I hope she's fixed something good. I haven't had a decent meal in months." She just had to get the last word in.

Once again, Robert apologized to Sally.

Sally laughed and said, "Mr. Robert, you'd best not be apologizing every time that child says or does something nasty to me. You won't have time for anything else ifs you do."

"I'm sorry to say I think you're right, but I believe you are. How about I say I'll make it up to you when this is all over."

"Just havin' peace in the house again will be enough for me", said Sally as she laughed and walked to the house to put dinner on the table.

The next few months were busy ones. Robert and Josephine first had a coming out party for their daughter at the country club. They invited everyone in the area who had an eligible son. It was their thought that perhaps Bobbie Jo would catch someone's eye and immediately take her off their hands. It didn't happen at the initial party. Everyone had a good time. Bobbie Jo danced and talked with every young man there. Robert and Josephine talked with all the parents, but not one possible deal was struck. So the next step in the plan was to have smaller and, hopefully, cheaper parties held at their house. They felt that perhaps in the more intimate setting a deal could be made.

After they had a series of those types of parties and nothing had transpired, Robert realized he was going to have to go outside of the more prominent families of Florence to find a husband for his daughter. He had been correct when he thought the young men knew about Bobbie Jo and may have wanted to take her out but certainly did not want to marry her. What Robert didn't know is that most of the young men of the county knew Bobbie Jo's reputation.

Those that hadn't known it before were finding out about it quickly, as she was back to her old ways.

Robert and Josephine really were thinking that their daughter had finally changed her ways. She showed up for dinner each and every night. She was on time and she was nearly almost pleasant to them. What they didn't realize was that Bobbie Jo had finally figured out how to have her cake and eat it too. She wasn't dumb. In the past she had gone out with guys who had little or no money. She now had a source of men that had money. She had no intention of getting married, but was just using the parties to meet all the young men in the area. When dancing or talking with them, she was arranging to meet them later in the week. Her date book was always full. Her parents would throw her a party about twice a month. They usually invited ten families. If she played her cards right, she would then have a different date for each day of the next two weeks. Her parents didn't object as they thought this was a very good way for them to get to know each other. They were correct. They were getting to know each other, but not in the way her Mother and Father thought.

Perhaps one of the meetings could have led into a relationship, but Bobbie Jo wanted nothing to do with marriage. She had it too good at home. Her parents provided a nice house with household help, meals were provided and now, they had no objections to her buying or having clothes made. Why in the world would she want to get married?

In addition to her daytime dates, that Robert and Josephine thought were safe, Bobbie Jo had dates after dinner. These were not with anyone her parents would approve of. These were her old friends and their associates. These were people that made their living on the side of town where the prominent families never went. Bobbie Jo loved it over there. She hung out with some street girls at one of the pool halls. The girls worked the men while they were playing pool and when the game was finished they'd take them into the alley or around the corner to the fleabag hotel and turn a trick. This is how they made their money. Bobbie Jo didn't need money. She did it for the attention and for the excitement. She thought it was a kick to tell them who she had been with earlier in the day. She was playing a dangerous game, though, because she was starting to cut into the action and was costing the working girls money.

As far as her parents knew, the evenings out were spent with girl friends. They were so happy with the way their daughter was behaving. They just wished she would find a suitable young man and marry him.

Just as the working girls were planning to have a talk with Bobbie Jo, something happened. One night a somewhat familiar looking young man walked in the pool hall where Bobbie Jo was. After looking hard at Bobbie Jo he walked over to her and said, "You look a lot different than you did over at Ethel's."

Bobbie Jo's jaw dropped. She looked at him and then whispered, "Bobby Ray? I didn't think I'd ever see you again. Especially over here."

"Well, I got me a job over at Union Carbide in Covington and I thought I might try and look you up."

"How did you find me here? No one knows I come here."

"You told us enough about what you had done and where you had done it that I figured I could eventually find the area. It didn't take too long."

"Why'd you come?"

"I told you. I wanted to look you up."

Bobbie Jo just looked at him. Bobby Ray was one of the men Ethel told her to stay away from. She said he was a cousin. Bobbie Jo didn't want to get down with a relative so she asked him, "Ethel said you were a cousin. Are you?"

"Yep. I'm her brother's son. I'm her nephew. That makes me your cousin."

Bobbie Jo looked at him again. "Cousin's aren't really relatives, are they?"

"Nah. It's just somebody's idea of having a hold on people", replied Bobby Ray. "I don't like people having a hold on me."

Bobbie Jo smiled. She liked Bobby Ray. "I don't like that either. My parents are always trying to keep track of me. They think they own me, but I do what I want."

"Wanna beer?"

"No, thanks. I think a Coke would be fine. I have aspirin I can put in it. If I drink anything alcohol, my parents will smell it and then I'll have a hard time getting out."

"Okay, for now, but I think I can find something that will solve that little problem for you. Let me go get the drinks."

The working girls never had to have the talk with Bobbie Jo, because with the arrival of Bobby Ray, she never again hustled any of their clients. Bobbie Jo never knew how close she came to finding out what happens when street girls get even. Bobbie Jo never new how lucky she was that evening. All she knew was she was having fun.

It's the fall of 1958 and the all parties given for Bobbie Jo had produced nothing. Robert and Josephine decide to stop giving them, but they also knew that Bobbie Jo needed to be doing something to keep her out of trouble. They decided she needed to go to work. They expected Bobbie Jo to throw a tantrum when they tell her their decision, but are surprised when she says she agrees. What they didn't know was she'd been seeing Bobby Ray every night and she didn't really want to have to pretend to be interested in those boys from the prominent families. She found them boring.

Robert arranges for Bobbie Jo to get a clerical job at an insurance company in town. She'll only be working part time, but it will keep her in the public view and, hopefully, busy so she stays out of trouble. It'll also give her some money of her own. Robert is very upset over having spent so much money on her and not finding a suitable husband. He thought any of them would have been acceptable, but Bobbie Jo didn't. He wanted to force the issue but Josephine would have none of it. She wanted her daughter to choose for herself. Her father had arranged her marriage to Robert. Robert was right. Things were different now, so she wanted her daughter to do the choosing.

Once the parties stopped and Bobbie Jo started working, the household settled down to a comfortable pattern again. Sally was able to get back into her routine of fixing breakfast for Mr. Robert at 7:30am and Miss Josephine at 9:00am. Bobbie Jo didn't eat before she went to work at 11:00am, as she didn't want to get fat like her mother, so for all intents and purposes things were normal. Lunch was fixed for Miss Josephine, if she arrived home, once again trying to catch Sally doing something she shouldn't be and dinner was put on the table at 5:00pm sharp. After dinner Sally was once again free to leave the Milhouse residence to go tend the needs of her own family. After dinner Bobbie Jo would say she was going to visit a girl friend and would leave for the evening so Robert and Josephine were once again able to spend the quiet evenings together.

This peaceful arrangement went on until November of 1959. It was a few days after Thanksgiving that Josephine commented to Bobbie Jo, "Dear, you are always criticizing other people for being too heavy. Have you noticed that you've put on a little weight yourself?" Quietly Josephine was happy to be able to say something a little unpleasant to her daughter. Normally Josephine was the recipient of such comments from her daughter.

"Yes, I *have* noticed, but there's nothing I can do about it. I'm pregnant again", Bobbie Jo replied coldly. "I guess father will have to call that Ethel again.

"I'd better go. I'll be late for work again. Let me know what he arranges", said Bobbie Jo as she walked out the front door.

Poor Josephine. She just sat there with her tea cup suspended in mid-air. She looked around and saw Sally standing there. "Did you hear what she said?"

Sally replied, "Yes'm I did. That girls gone and done it again. Thought she'da learned something from the first time."

Now Josephine was really stunned. She had no idea that Sally ever knew about the first pregnancy. Putting her teacup carefully on it's saucer she said, "Well, I'd better call Mr. Milhouse and have him make the arrangements." Josephine rose from her chair and calmly called the bank. When he came on the line, he said sharply, "You know I don't like to be bothered at work. This had better be important."

Josephine started to laugh. "Robert, when was the last time I called you?"

Robert had no idea what she was talking about and was about to say something sharp to her when she interrupted him.

"You remember. After I called you with the problem, you called your cousin to have it handled."

"Oh yes. You don't call that often. I'm sorry I was sharp with you. What is it you need?"

"That's all right dear, because you have to make the call once again."

Robert reached over and closed the door to his office and then sat in his chair. Almost whispering he asked his wife to repeat what she had said.

Josephine laughed a little and repeated herself.

"This is not funny."

"No dear it isn't but I find lately when I'm nervous I laugh. I used to faint but now I laugh. I'm sorry, I just can't help it."

"We *will* talk to her tonight. In the meantime, I'll call my cousin and see if she's willing to take her in again."

Josephine, still laughing said, "Fine dear. See you then" and she hung the phone up.

"Sally."

"Yes'm?"

"I'll be working in the yard today so I'll be home for lunch."

"A'right Miss Josephine, but today is the day I usually works in the yard."

"It's a big yard. I'm sure there's room for both of us." Then Josephine went upstairs to put on her yard clothes. She would spend the rest of the day digging, weeding and planting. She needed to work off some nervous energy. She knew the evening was going to be stressful.

Robert called his cousin, Ethel, but she refused to have Bobbie Jo in her house again. She said the girl had caused too much trouble and was too strange. When Robert asked what she meant Ethel told him everything that had happened while Bobbie Jo was in her house. Then she went on to tell him how there were rumors around Crab Orchard about how Bobbie Jo had taken up with her cousin Bobby Ray who was now working over in Covington.

Robert was almost speechless, "I don't believe it."

Ethel replied, "Well you may not believe it, and it may not be true, but I can believe it cause I seen it with my own eyes. I tell you she was like a she cat in heat with them boys. I told her they was her cousins and nothing but trouble. She didn't listen."

"What am I going to do?"

"If'n it was me, I'd ask her who the father was. If it's Bobby Ray she better find a way to get rid of the child. I can't sell an inbreed child. I won't be any part of that kind of thing. She's a bad girl, Robert. Best you get free of her as fast as you can."

Robert was shaken. He thanked her for the information and hung the phone up.

That night, during dinner, Robert said to Bobbie Jo and Josephine, "We need to talk about this situation and we need to do it tonight". As soon as Sally left, the Milhouse family sat down for their talk. Bobbie Jo was expecting to hear she'd be leaving for Ethel's house soon and that she needed to give notice at the insurance company where she worked. She didn't care. She could put up with Ethel for 4 or 5 months. She was due in April and if she played her cards right and kept her weight down she could work another month or so.

She was startled when her father said, "Who's the father?"

"What?"

"I said who is the father?"

"Why?"

"Because I need to know."

"It's no one you know."

"Then you do know who fathered this one."

"Sure. I've only been with one guy for a long time now."

"How long is a long time?"

"Why?"

"Because I'm asking."

"About eight or ten months now."

Robert thought back to the conversation with Ethel. The time was about right so he took the chance and demanded, "Is it Bobby Ray Turnbull?"

Bobbie Jo was startled, "How do you know about him?"

"So it is him."

"Yes, it is. I thought we were being careful, but something must've happened."

"How far along are you?"

"What?"

"You heard me. How far along are you?"

"Why?"

"Because Bobby Ray Turnbull is your cousin, your first cousin. and if this child is born it may not be right."

"No he isn't. He's the son of Ethel's brother. He's a second or third cousin. That's okay. I checked in the library."

Josephine had just been sitting there not saying a word. She had never known who Robert sent Bobbie Jo to. She hadn't wanted to. Now she knew and now she was very concerned because of something that had happened long ago. "No Bobbie Jo. He's your first cousin."

Bobbie Jo looked confused.

Robert softly said, "You think I was an only child. I wasn't. I had a brother who was two years older than I. He got married and had a child, a son. He and his wife were killed in a fire. My mother and father felt they were too old to raise another child, so they gave the baby to Ethel's brother and his wife. They had never been able to have children and were only too happy to get the baby. Bobby Ray is my brother's son. The man he calls father is his cousin."

"What your father is saying is that Bobby Ray Turnbull is really Bobby Ray Milhouse," said Josephine. "He's your first cousin and you're carrying his child."

"If this gets out, you and he can be arrested. Did you know that?"

Bobbie Jo hung her head, "No. I had no idea. I really didn't. Can't Ethel take me in and take care of the problem for me once again?"

"No, she can't and she won't. I don't blame her. She could get in trouble as well."

"What am I going to do", cried Bobbie Jo?

"How far along are you?"

"About five months" answered Bobbie Jo.

"But you're barely showing" responded Josephine.

"I've been watching what I eat very carefully. It took me so long to lose the weight the last time, I swore it wouldn't happen again."

"I think she's too far along to get rid of it, but I have someone I can ask," said Josephine to Robert.

"You do?"

"Yes, I do. I'll ask tomorrow what can be done."

"All right. We'll talk again tomorrow night after dinner."

Bobbie Jo said, "Can I use the phone? I need to call Bobby Ray so he doesn't drive over here for nothing. I don't feel like seeing him tonight."

"Sure, go ahead. At some point he'll need to come here to talk as well, but not tonight."

"Okay, daddy", said Bobbie Jo as she walked towards the phone in the hall.

Robert and Josephine picked up their tea glasses and walked out onto the back stoop. Neither one said anything to each other. Neither one knew what could be said. Josephine was thinking she should have let Robert arrange a marriage for Bobbie Jo. Robert was thinking he should have found out who the father of the first child was and made them get married.

The next day, after Robert and Bobbie Jo had left the house, Josephine called to Sally to come into the breakfast room.

When Sally walked in, she knew something was wrong.

"Sally, you know Bobbie Jo is pregnant."

"Yes'm."

"You remember the fire that killed Mr. Robert's brother?"

"Yes'm."

"You remember there was a baby boy who was sent to live with another family?"

"Yes'm."

"Somehow Bobbie Jo has managed to have relations with him."

"She can't do that. Everybody knows the child wouldn't be right in the head."

"Yes, but because the family kept it a secret all these years, the boy doesn't know who his father was. They thought they were second or third cousins."

"Still ain't right."

"Yes, but it wouldn't be as bad. However, it is bad. They're first cousins and there is a baby started."

"Yes'm."

"How can we rid her of this burden?"

"How far along is she?"

"Five months."

Sally rolled her eyes. "Miss Josephine, you knows I'd do anything for this family. But I can't help you with this. I know someone who coulda helped, but the girl's too far along. There's too many things could happen."

"Thank you. I thought that was the case. Bobbie Jo has always been so sneaky and kept things from us. She always waits until the problem is a big problem and expects us to fix it. What can we do?"

"Make her marry the boy and have the baby. I'd talk to the midwife and tells her that the mother is to be fixed so's she can'ts have any more. Thems midwifes are smart. If'n she knows the problem before the birthin', she can fix it so's the child's born dead."

"Can they do that?"

"Yes'm and in this here case I think it should be done."

"Thank you Sally. You really are a good friend."

Robert made sure he was home early that night. He wanted a chance to talk to his wife without Bobbie Jo around. After Josephine explained what she had found out Robert walked out onto the back stoop. He didn't like not having options, but Bobbie Jo was not going to ruin his life.

After dinner the family once again gathered to talk. For the first time Bobbie Jo could remember, Josephine started the conversation. She explained in detail what she had found out. Bobbie Jo was horrified.

"What can I do?"

Then Robert started talking. "You're going to call Bobby Ray and tell him to come here tonight. We need to talk with him before any more decisions are made."

Actually, Robert had already decided, but he wanted Bobby Ray to hear what he had to say.

Bobbie Jo went to the telephone, called Bobby Ray and asked him to come to the house. She gave him directions, hung up the phone and sat down on the living room couch to wait. About an hour later there was a knock at the door. Bobbie Jo knew who it was. She opened the door and asked a very nervous Bobby Ray to come in and have a seat. Waiting in the living room were Robert and Josephine.

"Young man, I have a story to tell you. I am sorry this is the way you're finding out, but the family has always been one to keep secrets."

Bobby Ray interrupted, "I already know we are second or third cousins. I know this probably upsets you, but I do love Bobbie Jo. I looked it up. It's okay if we are second or more cousins."

"Shut up and listen", yelled Robert. He then proceeded to tell the whole story of the Milhouse family and the fire to Bobby Ray. At first, Bobby Ray kept trying to interrupt, but as the story progressed he started to make the connection. He'd overheard bits and pieces of this story over the years but didn't know who his mother and father had been talking about.

When Robert finished, Bobby Ray was very still. Finally Bobby Ray said, "What does this mean?"

Robert started out calmly, "What this means is you two are first cousins. What this means is the two of you could be arrested if anyone found out." The more he talked the louder he got. "What this means is my daughter is carrying an illegal child. What this means is she is too far along for the child to be dealt with." Finally he was shouting. "What this means is the two of you are getting married, having this child and my daughter will be fixed so she cannot have any more children."

When he finished everyone in the room was very quiet. Then, as quiet as a mouse, Bobbie Jo said, "No. I won't be fixed so I can't have more children."

"You have no choice. As long as you are living under my room and I'm paying the bills, you will do as I say."

With that Bobby Ray stood up and said, "Fine. She'll come with me. We don't need your permission to get married. You can't tell us what to do. I'll marry her and she *will* have my child. I'll be the one paying the bills, not you."

"Bobbie Jo. Is this what you want to do," asked Robert?

"Yes it is."

"Fine then, leave tonight. Remember though. Once you leave with him, you are no longer my daughter."

"That's fine with me", yelled Bobbie Jo. "Wait right here, Bobby Ray. It won't take me but a few minutes to finish packing. I've already started."

An hour later, Robert and Josephine were sitting alone in the living room. Josephine looked at her husband of many years and said, "Did we do the right thing or did we allow fear and emotions to get the best of us?"

For the first time ever, Robert said, "I don't know. I was just trying to do what was best for all of us. This baby would have ruined me. Bobbie Jo has always been such an inconvenience."

Josephine didn't disagree but she wondered where they went so wrong. They had always given her the best of everything. Then she thought, *"Oh well, things will be quiet again."*

Neither Robert nor Josephine would ever see Bobbie Jo or Bobby Ray again. They would never even know if or when the baby, their first grandchild, was born.

CHAPTER 3

It's April 1960 ……

Each day the hospital in Covington listed all births in the local newspaper. Under the date of April 29th appeared the following: *Arriving at 2:34am was a baby girl, Leah, to the proud parents of Bobbie Jo and Bobby Ray Turnbull.*

The Covington Gazette was delivered to the home of Robert and Josephine Milhouse. It always had been. It probably always would. Neither Robert nor Josephine read the birth announcements, but Sally did. Sally had family in Covington and, even though her reading ability was limited, she liked to hear about people having babies. She read the obituaries too, as she wanted to know when people died. You see she kept up the family bible. Sally considered telling Miss Josephine about what she'd read and then decided not to, but she did make her entry in the family bible. Silently she said a little prayer for the baby called Leah Turnbull. She was born a dark soul and, if she was normal in the head, she would cause a lot of pain for the people around her during her life. Sally would remember to say prayers for this child often.

The pregnancy had been pretty easy for Bobbie Jo. She'd remembered.what Ethel made her do during the last one so she made sure she kept her muscles in shape. She didn't, however, want to get fat like she did before so she didn't eat as Ethel had insisted. She remembered how she looked the last time and she didn't ever want to look like that ever again.

The doctor Bobbie Jo had been going to didn't believe she was as far along as she was because the baby inside her was so small. At every visit he would tell her she had to try to eat a little more. "For the sake of the child", he would say.

Bobbie Jo would always tell him that she was eating like a pig and couldn't possibly put another bite in her mouth or she'd throw up. In fact, she ate from a saucer rather than a full sized plate and measured her food out with a teaspoon. She felt the baby growing inside of her would just have to take care of itself.

Bobby Ray loved Bobbie Jo but he didn't understand her fear of getting fat because she was so thin you could almost count her bones. He thought the pregnancy would help fatten her up a little. Just like the doctor, he was concerned for the baby. If he tried to talk to his wife about eating more, she would get angry and refuse to eat the little bits of food she had put on her saucer. He never thought of talking to Bobbie Jo's doctor and telling him how she was acting.

Bobby Ray would say, "Baby, you have to eat more. That child inside you needs more'n you're eating. Remember, you're eatin' for two now."

Bobbie Jo would scream at him, "I'm not getting fat just for a kid. This kid needs to learn up front that no one will ever love you if you get fat!"

Poor Bobby Ray would gently reply, "Baby, that's not true. I'd love ya any way ya're."

Bobbie Jo would just stomp her feet and walk off.

As a result of Bobbie Jo's starving herself, when Baby Leah was born she was a very tiny baby. She only weighed a little over four pounds.

Bobby Ray was such a proud daddy. He paced in the hospital waiting room for the 2 hours it took for the baby to be born. Once he was told his wife had delivered a baby girl, he couldn't wait to see the child. When he did see her, he was shocked. The doctor was at the viewing window with Bobby Ray and took note of the look on his face.

"Mr. Turnbull, the child is very thin."

"Thin? She looks like a little skeleton. What's wrong with her?"

"Starvation, as best as we can tell. Other than lacking in nourishment, she appears to be fine. I've been concerned about this and have been talking with your wife about it at every one of her visits."

"She has this thing about being fat."

"What did you say?"

"Bobbie Jo has this thing about being fat. She believes if she gets fat, no one will love her."

"I wish I had known. She kept telling me she was eating like a pig and didn't know why she wasn't gaining weight."

"She lives mainly on sweet tea and hard candy. The only meal I ever see her eat is dinner and that ain't much."

"How much does she eat?"

"Well, if'n I don't say nothing to her she might eat a bite or two of what ever meat there is and a bite or two of potatoes."

"What about vegetables? Does she eat any vegetables?"

"Not that I've ever seen. She calls lettuce and any kinda greens rabbit food."

"God, I wish I would've known. I would have been more insistent."

"Wouldn't done any good. When I talk to her about it, she stops eating and leaves the table. Ya know, when I was growin up, dinnertime was a time for everybody to tell what happened durin' the day. It was a fun time. Lotsa laughs, ya know?"

"Yes, I do."

"Well, dinner time in our house is just one big pain. She can't understand why I expect her to have some food ready for dinner. More'n once she's told me to fix myself a bologna sandwich if'n I was hungry."

"Really?"

"Yes'r. Usually she tells me I ate lunch so why'm I asking for dinner too."

"What?"

"Yes'r. That's her way. She has something against food, I guess."

"Why? Was there a problem with her mother and father?"

"Don't think so. I only met them once. They were normal sized and the house smelled like a nice meal'd just been cooked. I dunno what the problem with Bobbie Jo is."

"Well, what's done is done. We're going to keep the baby at least a week. We have to get some weight on her before we'll allow her to go home."

"That's okay with me doc. I'm ashamed of the child looking that way. I make enough money to keep food on the table. There's no reason for her to be that way."

"Once she's gained two pounds she can go home with you. But, before I release her I want to have a meeting with you and your wife. It has to be with the two of you because I want you to know what this child is going to require if she's going to grow up normal."

Bobby Ray thought to himself, *"Normal. Yes, I'm concerned if she's going to be normal too. But I'm not concerned about weight. Maybe her parents were right. God, I hope not."* To the doctor he said, "No problem. I work at Union Carbide and they're allowing me to off shift so I could be around to see the baby born. They're real good about doctor's appointments and such."

"Good because I think you're going to have to watch your wife and make sure the baby is fed properly."

"I will, I promise."

"Your wife can go home tomorrow. You can pick her up at 11:00am."

"Good. I'll be here in plenty of time. Thanks Doc."

"Try to get your wife to eat a little more. Don't fight with her, but encourage her. Okay?"

"I'll try. I have been, but I'll try harder."

"See you tomorrow at 11:00."

It only took Bobbie Jo about five days at home to get tired of being a housewife and then she started her old ways again. The fact that she was now married with a child didn't slow her down much.

Bobbie Jo was tired of being at home alone and would go to the neighborhood social club. There she found a new source of entertainment. She'd look for a couple seated at a table for four. She'd approach them asking if a chair was vacant and then sit down. Once she was at the table she'd slowly join their conversation, usually letting them do most of the talking. This is how she'd find out about where the men worked, the hours they worked and where they lived. She especially watched to see how the couple reacted to each other. If they had a close relationship, she would remain quiet, not ask a lot of questions and let them control the conversation.

If the couple seemed distant with each other, she would become the leader of the conversation and try to draw the man's attention to her.

Bobbie Jo was bored. She was bored with Bobby Ray, bored with being a housewife and bored with not having any money. She wanted to change that.

Bobby Ray worked the day shift at the plant. When his shift was over he'd go to the hospital to see his daughter. He'd talk to the nurses on duty and pray over his baby girl. He so wanted the baby to be healthy and to come home. He also worried about his wife. He didn't know what Bobbie Jo did during the day when he was gone, but she certainly didn't stay at home. The apartment was dirty, laundry wasn't done and she never had a meal waiting for him. Those things didn't bother him as much as the fact that she never asked about the baby.

At first Bobby Ray would drive from Union Carbide back across town to the apartment to get his wife so they could go see their baby together. He would have gladly taken the bus to work, but Bobbie Jo didn't drive. No matter what he said or did, she had no interest in learning how. So each day for a week he'd made the trip to get her. Each day he'd arrive home and ask her to go with him. Each day she refused. She never really had a reason; she just didn't want to go.

After a week, Bobby Ray stopped going home before he went to the hospital. He would go alone and spend a couple of hours sitting next to the scrawny baby in the incubator.

The nurses commented on his devotion to his daughter and on the fact they never saw the mother. Every time they would see him praying over the small child, they would silently add their prayers as well. They had no way of knowing that the parents were first cousins and he was praying his child would grow up normal. He would pray *"We made a terrible mistake, God, but please don't take it out on the child."*

As for Bobbie Jo, she liked having the extra time at the club. The decent wives and devoted couples would have left the club to do have dinner and the party people were free to let loose and have some fun. The hard-core social club patrons would become very social with each other. Bobbie Jo was in her own element then. She was no longer bored.

There's a lizard called a chameleon. This lizard is able to change colors to match his environment. His normal color is what he prefers to be, but he can adapt so he isn't noticed.

Bobbie Jo is like that lizard. She was really a party girl, but she could change so she blended in with the people who came to the social club to talk and visit with their neighbors.

Bobbie Jo never mentioned the fact that she had a baby to anyone at the South Side Social Club. Whenever anyone would comment on how much time she spent at the club, she'd tell them her husband was so abusive she had to get out of the apartment when he was home from work. She would make the story even more believable by saying he had lady friends that he'd see after work, when he worked days.

She never talked to Bobby Ray about the baby but he thought she was just sad and didn't know how to talk about the possible problems. She had already had one baby, he knew, when she stayed with cousin Ethel. He felt the new baby just opened up all that sadness too. He felt she just needed time to heal.

Bobby Ray was happy with Bobbie Jo. He loved her. No she wasn't the best housewife he'd ever seen, but she was always willing to take care of his physical needs. He'd always heard from the guys at work that once a baby came, that part of your life stopped. He was happy they were wrong and was happy to brag a little about it.

He just knew once the baby came home, everything would be all right. Maybe some day he could get Ethel to tell him where her first child was and he could get that child back for Bobbie Jo. *"Funny,"* he thought, *I don't know if it was a boy or girl Bobbie Jo never told me."*

Bobby Ray and Bobbie Jo's routine stayed the same during the week with him going to work and, unknown to him, her going to the South Side Social Club. Weekends were a different story. He liked to get up early so he could enjoy a full day. She liked to sleep til noon or later. This would always start a fight. He liked to go for a drive out in the country. City life was all right, but he longed for a house and some land. He hated being in an apartment, but it was cheaper and by staying there they could save up for the down payment on a house and land. Each week he would sign his check and tell Bobbie Jo to cash it. She was to keep enough out to cover the rent, utilities and food. The balance was to go in the savings account he'd opened when he first moved to Covington. He was proud to put her name on it when they got married. He never checked on what Bobbie Jo was doing with the money. He just assumed she was saving it as she was supposed to be.

One evening two months after Leah was born, the doctor saw Bobby Ray sitting next to his daughter.

"The nurses say you come every day."

"Yep."

"They also say they don't see the missus."

"Nope."

"Why"

"Dunno? She's sad, I guess. She can't even talk about the baby."

"Is she eating?"

"Dunno? She's never hungry at night when I'm around. But she eats on the weekends if we go out to the local social club. She seems to perk up a little after that."

"Well, you can take the baby home any time now. She's almost gained the weight we wanted and she's doing fine. I think it's about time she got to know her mother."

"Can I take her now?"

"Sure, if you're ready to have her home."

"Absolutely!"

"Fine. I'll have the nurse get her ready. I'd like your wife and baby to both come in for a check up in a week or so. We can talk then. Can you arrange that?"

"Sure. Thanks Doc."

Bobby Ray was so happy when that baby was put in his arms. He carefully carried her to the car and laid her on the front seat. The nurse had given him what she called "a starter pack". There were a couple cans of formula and a package of twelve diapers. He put the package on the floor on the passenger side of the car. All the way home he kept touching the baby and mentally pinching himself. In some ways it seemed so long since she'd been born, but in other ways, it seemed like just yesterday. He could hardly wait to see the surprise on Bobbie Jo's face.

Arriving at the apartment building, Bobby Ray parked in his normal spot. Walking to the passenger side he picked up his daughter and then the starter package. He used his foot to shut the car door as he had run out of free hands. As he walked up the steps to the apartment, he wanted to shout to the world that his daughter was home now and he finally had his family. When he got to his door, he didn't have a free hand to get his key from his pocket so he used his foot to lightly kick the door a couple of times. He expected Bobbie Jo to answer the door and yell at him for being too lazy to put the groceries down just as she had a hundred times before, but she didn't. He kicked the door again, only a little louder. Still no response. Finally he dropped the package, fished his keys from his pocket and opened the door. The apartment was dark and silent.

"Bobbie Jo? You sleeping already? Get up, sleepyhead. I've gottta surprise for you." There was no response. "Bobbie Jo", he said as he walked to the bedroom. It too was dark. Bobbie Jo wasn't home. He was disappointed, but felt she was just at a neighbor's, like usual.

He laid the baby in the bassinette he'd bought at the used furniture store in anticipation of her arrival. Leah stirred a little, but never fully woke up. Then he put the diapers on the changing table he'd found on another trip to the second hand store. The formula he put on the counter in the kitchen.

No dinner was started, so he fixed a sandwich of lunchmeat, poured a glass of milk and sat down to wait for his wife.

After an hour had passed and she hadn't arrived, he decided to take his shower. When he'd finished he went to check on the baby and found Bobbie Jo asleep on the bed.

Just then the baby started to fuss a little. He picked her up, changed her diaper, put her on the bed next to her mother and went to the kitchen to fix a bottle. Suddenly he heard a loud scream from the bedroom. He ran in just in time to see Bobbie Jo jump off the bed and back up against the dresser.

"What's that", she cried?

"Our baby, of course", responded Bobby Ray.

"What's it doing here?"

"The doctor said she could come home."

"Get rid of it."

"What?"

"You heard me. Get rid of it."

"It's our baby and we have her home now. Aren't you happy?"

"Hell no! I did my part already. I carried that thing for nine months. I'm through. I'm not doing any more."

"Honey, you have to. It's your baby."

"No, it's your baby not mine. You take care of it if you want it so bad. I told you I did my part." With that said she ran into the bathroom, shut the door and latched it closed.

Bobby Ray didn't know what to do. Now Leah was crying and his wife was locked in the bathroom. He didn't know what was wrong with either one of them. Finally he picked his daughter up, brought her to the kitchen and gave her the bottle he had fixed for her. After she finished eating, he once again changed her and put her back in her tiny bed. While he stood there watching his daughter fall asleep he thought, *I shouldn't have surprised her that way. I should have called her and talked with her before I brought the baby home. It's my fault she reacted that way. She'll be fine once she gets used to the baby.*

In the bathroom Bobbie Jo was thinking, *how do I get rid of this kid? It's Ethel's fault. She should have taken this one too. Daddy probably didn't pay her enough. No one can say this is my fault. It's all because of them. Bobby Ray shouldn't have gotten me pregnant to begin with and if Daddy had paid Ethel enough, she'd have done what she's supposed to do. Boy, you just can't trust anyone...not even so called family.*

The next morning Bobby Ray got up earlier than normal so he could care for Leah. He just knew once Bobbie Jo had her sleep she'd take care of her own child like she's supposed to. He'd fixed enough bottles for the baby for the day, so Bobbie Jo just had to change the baby and hold her. He was positive all would work out so he didn't worry a bit as he wrote his wife a note and stuck it in the side of the bathroom mirror where she'd be sure to see it.

Once that was all done he hurried off to work. He couldn't afford to be docked any wages now that he was a family man. "Family man", he said out loud. *Boy,* he thought *those words sound real good to me.*

Bobbie Jo had heard her husband moving around and talking to his brat. She didn't know what she was going to do with the child, but she had a couple of friends she could call and talk to. They'd have some ideas for her.

When she finally got out of the bed, she couldn't help but look in at the sleeping child. To herself she thought, *Last time I was glad it was a boy cause I thought I'd been tempted to keep a girl child. Well, here's the girl child and I don't want this one either.* She walked out of the bedroom, shutting the door behind her and went into the small kitchen to make her some fresh sweet tea. When she opened the refrigerator to see what there was for her to eat she saw three baby bottles filled with milk. Her stomach churned at the sight of them and she shut the door without another thought of food.

As the water was heating to make her tea she walked to the bathroom to do her morning routine. There she found Bobby Ray's note.

> "Honey, the doctor said the baby needs to be fed about 3 ounces of formula every couple of hours. I fixed enough bottles for the day. I'll show you how to mix the formula tonight. Diapers are on the changing table."
>
> Love you
>
>   Bobby Ray

As she read the note, Bobbie Jo thought, *Feed her every couple of hours? Is he nuts? And he expects me to fix that stuff - no way! He can get up early like he did today and do it. It's his kid so he can do it!*

After fixing her tea and eating a small piece of dry toast, she started calling all her friends from the social club. She stated with Mary Lou. After saying hello and asking how she was doing Bobbie Jo said, "You can't believe what happened last night?"

"Did he beat you up again" was the reply?

"Oh no, he hasn't done that in awhile."

"I'm so glad. Whenever I don't see you or hear from you I think he's been beating on you again."

Bobbie Jo smiled, but in a quiet, sad voice said, "This is much worse."

"What do you mean? What could be worse than that?"

"He brought home a kid."

"What?"

"A baby. A small baby and listen to this note he left me." Then she read her the note word for word.

"Didn't he tell you he was bringing a kid home for you to take care of?"

"No. He never said anything to me."

"You mean he just brought it home?"

"That's what I said. Can you believe it? And now he expects me to spend my time caring for it."

"The nerve of him. Whose baby is it anyways?"

"His."

"His? You mean it's his baby."

"Yep", replied Bobbie Jo smiling. She couldn't believe how easy this was. She hadn't told a single lie and listen to this girl just carry on. This was so easy.

"What're you goin' to do?"

"Dunno. That's why I'm calling you. You're my best friend and I thought you could help me."

"Wow! I've gotta think about this."

"Really. I understand that myself. I've just been sitting her thinking since he left for work."

"I'll talk to you at the club this afternoon. I should have some ideas by then."

"Dunno if I'll be there. I can't just go off and leave this kid alone. Not like he did today."

"What a terrible person he is."

"I've always told you about his awful temper and how I thought he'd been running around on me."

"Yes, you have."

"What do ya think now"?

"Boy howdy. How've you put up with him for so long"?

"He used to be a nice person, but he's changed so much. Oh, must go. I hear the baby starting to fuss."

With that she hung up. She smiled and again thought how easy that had been. After a minute of thought, she picked the phone up again. She repeated this same call with all the other women from the social club. She was hoping someone would come up with a plan for her because other than planting more disinformation about

Bobby Ray with all the people she knew, she had no idea what she was going to do next.

Bobby Jo had heard the baby fussing at times when she was on the telephone, but had ignored her. Now Leah was screaming in earnest. Bobby Jo looked at the clock. It was nearly 1:00pm and she was a little hungry. As she opened the refrigerator to get the fixings of a sandwich she once again saw the bottles. She pulled one out, walked into the dark bedroom, shoved it in the crying child's mouth, propped it up with a dirty shirt of Bobby Ray's and walked out of the room to eat her lunch, being sure she shut the door behind her. She didn't want her lunch ruined by the sound of the kid crying. To be sure she didn't hear anything, she turned her radio up a little louder than normal.

After Bobbie Jo finished her lunch, she went in to the bedroom to change her clothes to go to the club. She had to talk to her friends, at least for a little while. She looked in the bassinette and saw the bottle had fallen out of the kid's mouth and was dripping on the bed. She also saw the child was asleep. She quietly changed her clothes, slipped out of the apartment and headed for the club. She told herself she wouldn't be gone long. Besides the kid was asleep and no one would even know the difference.

When she walked in the club, the only person there was Mary Lou. She had her usual glass of Mogen David Blackberry sitting in front of her.

"Whew. What a day I've had and it isn't over yet", said Bobbie Jo to no one in particular, but loud enough so everyone in the club could hear her.

"What's been happenin," asked Mary Lou.

"Oh, it's just that kid. Always needing something. I hardly had anytime to get all my house work done!"

"Who'd ya get to watch it", asked Mary Lou?

Bobbie Jo had to think fast as she hadn't expected anyone to ask that question and didn't want to be tripped up. "Do ya know that Mexican family that lives across the hall from me?"

"Can't say's I do. I make it a point of not socializing with people the likes of them."

"Well normally neither do I, but I had to get out of that apartment cause I'm so worn out. I just had to get some air and talk to somebody about my problem. I knows she has lots of young'ns so I knocked on her door and asked her if she would like to make a dollar."

"A dollar? You got her to sit for a baby for a dollar?"

"Yep. She don't know nothing about our money so she jumped at it."

"Wow. Are you smart or what?"

"Yeah, well I'm smart, but I don't know what to do about all that's happening. Did'ja come up with anything?"

"To tell you the truth, Bobbie Jo, no. If ya had a job and had your own money, you could just leave him, but without any money or nobody to take care of ya, I think ya're stuck."

"Yeah, that 's what I thought too." Then in a louder voice she said, "Of course, if I could get one of these fine gentlemen to take care of me, my worries would be over."

From across the room a voice said, "I'd like to take care of you Bobbie Jo, but I think my wife might get a bit upset at me." With that all the men at the bar started laughing.

"Bobbie Jo", whispered Mary Lou, you can't go talking like that. People might get the wrong idea.

"Just having a little fun, Mary Lou. Can't a girl have a little fun", she asked as she looked around the room at the men who were there. She didn't bother to lower her voice. She was looking for a good time and didn't care who knew it. She saw all the fooling around that happened in the club and she knew what went on inside the club stayed inside the club. She wasn't worried in the slightest about talk getting back to Bobby Ray.

As time passed, a couple more girl friends came in and joined the girls at their table. No one had any ideas of how Bobbie Jo could get out of her situation. After awhile Mary Lou said to Bobbie Jo, "How long did you tell that Mexican woman you would be gone?"

"I didn't. I just said I had to go out. Why?"

"Just wondered. Baby sitters usually ask how long they are going to have to watch a kid. I just realized it was 5 o'clock and I'm late getting home to fix dinner."

Bobbie Jo hadn't realized how late it had gotten. She'd better be home with the kid when Bobby Ray gets home or there will be hell to pay. To her friends she said, "Oh well. I guess I'll have to cut my fun short again. Between a man who beats me and now taking care of his kid, I never have any fun. I'll walk to the corner with ya." With that she said her good byes to the men sitting at the bar and walked out the door with Mary Lou.

"Bobbie Jo, I don't know how ya put up with all that you do. I do believe you must be a saint."

"Life has dealt me a rough hand, that's for sure. But I'll find a way to make it better."

The girls had been walking slowly towards the corner, but as soon as Mary Lou was out of sight, Bobbie Jo started running. She had to get home and look like she's been taking care of the kid all day before Bobby Ray got there.

As soon as she turned the corner of the apartment building, she started looking for his car. *Nope,* she thought, *he's not here yet. I have time to get there and take care of things.* As soon as she got to the top of the stairs she heard the kid crying. She almost felt bad that she had left it so long. She unlocked the apartment and ran to the bedroom. She picked little Leah up and put her on her shoulder to try and calm her down. She had to get the crying stopped before her husband got there. Everything else would have to wait. She thought, *he can fix himself a bologna sandwich if he's hungry.*

Within minutes of Bobbie Jo picking Leah up, Bobby Ray arrived home from work. For him, the day had dragged by. He really wanted to stay home with Leah and Bobbie Jo, but he had to work to put food on the table and a roof over their heads. When he got to the base of the stairwell he heard a child crying uncontrollably. *That couldn't be Leah, could it,* he thought? There were a lot of children in the apartment building and you could always hear crying, but he'd never heard anything like this before. He rushed up the stairs and into the apartment, just in time to see his wife and baby coming out of the bedroom.

Bobbie Jo looked at her husband and started crying. "She's been crying for hours. I can't get her to stop no matter what I do. You have to do something. She's your kid and I'm a wreck from listening to her all this time." Bobbie Jo was always so careful not to tell a lie. She just never told the whole story.

"Here. Let me take her." Bobby Ray threw down his lunch bucket and jacket so he could take his baby from Bobbie Jo. "Sh.

Sh. Sh. What's wrong little girl? You hungry? Hmmm?" As he was patting his baby gently on her back he realized she was soaking wet from head to toe and she smelled. Then he realized the baby had on the same clothes as when he brought her home from the hospital the night before.

"Bobbie Jo?"

"What?"

"Didn't you give Leah a bath and change her clothes this morning?"

"You didn't tell me to do that in the note you left me."

"I didn't tell you to do a lot of things, but you still know you have to do them."

Bobbie Jo didn't answer him. She just picked up the telephone and dialed a number.

With that, Bobby Ray took the baby into the bedroom to get a clean outfit to put on the baby. As he laid the baby on the changing table, he noticed that there were no diapers gone from the pile he had laid out for the day. He also noticed that an empty bottle was laying in the bassinette and that the bed was soaking wet from pee and from formula. Instead of just changing the baby he picked up the still crying child and walked with her to the kitchen. The two other bottles of formula were still in the refrigerator. He just shook his head and pulled out a small pot so he could warm up one of them. He also pulled out the dishpan he had bought to use as a bathtub for his daughter. As the bottle was warming up, he peeled the totally soaked garments off his child and threw them in the sink. Leah's crying had slowed somewhat by now and as he put her in the warm water, he could feel her relax a little. As he gently washed her he could feel her relax a little more. When he finished, he wrapped her in a little towel and put her on his shoulder so he would be able to test the formula to see if it was the right temperature. He thought it was about right so he went into the living room to sit down and feel the child. As soon as the nipple touched the baby's lips she started sucking.

"Bobbie Jo? Leah is starving. When did you feed her last?"

"What?"

"When did you feed her last?"

"I'm on the phone. Stop interrupting me all the time. You are so rude!"

Bobby Ray stood up, walked over to his wife and said, "Rude? I'll show you rude" and he grabbed the phone out of her hand and hung it up.

"Now answer me. When did you feed Leah last?" With that, Leah started crying again so Bobby Ray sat back down and put the bottle back in her mouth.

"See how she is. She's a pig not a normal baby."

"Answer my question. When was the last time you fed her?"

"I don't know when the bottle ran out. I wasn't watching."

"What do you mean you weren't watching? How can you not watch your own baby that you are holding?"

"I didn't hold her. She had the bottle in that little bed with her, so I left it there."

"What? I can't believe you. Are you telling me you didn't hold her or check on her the whole day?"

"You make it sound terrible. I had things to do and you had that bottle all propped up so I went about my business. When I heard her crying, I picked her up."

None of this was a lie, of course. She just failed to tell her husband that she had been out of the apartment half the day.

At first Bobby Ray was speechless. He finally said, "I guess you don't know anything about being a mother even though this is your second baby."

Bobbie Jo screamed, "What kind of lies are you telling now? I don't have any other kids. I never wanted kids. This is the only kid I've had to take care of and it's yours not mine. I have to take care of it for you cause I'm your wife. Don't start telling lies just because that kid has you upset."

Once again, Bobby Ray was speechless. He had never seen Bobbie Jo like this before. He thought he knew her, but it was becoming clear to him that he didn't.

"Okay, okay. You're taking care of my child. Fine. Yes you are my wife and this is my child. Does that make you happy?"

"That's better."

"Since you were busy doing things in the house all day, when will dinner be ready?"

"I haven't had time to fix anything. When would I have had time to fix anything? Besides, I'm too upset and couldn't eat anyway."

"Fine. I'll fix me a sandwich or two."

"You sure eat a lot."

"No, Bobbie Jo, I don't. I just want something to eat when I come home from work. I'm tired and hungry, just like the baby was."

"If ya eats lunch, that should hold ya for the day."

"Well, I'm not saying that's right or not, but it doesn't so I expect dinner when I get home."

By now Leah had finished her bottle. Bobby Ray burped her and held her until she fell asleep. As he went to put her in her bassinette he remembered the bed was soaking wet.

"Bobbie Jo?"

"What?"

"Come here please. I need some help."

Much to Bobby Ray's surprise Bobbie Jo came into the little bedroom.

"What?"

"Pull all the blankets and the sheet off this bed and put some clean ones on so I can lay Leah down. You'll need to wash them all tomorrow cause we only have two sets."

Bobbie Jo grumbled some, but did as Bobby Ray asked.

When she had finished, Bobby Ray laid his little daughter down and rubbed her back so she would go back to her deep sleep.

After he had fixed his sandwiches he walked into the living room. "Bobbie Jo, we need to get some things straight."

His wife looked at him, but said nothing. She knew he was going to lay down the law. She knew her days of freedom were over. She was right.

Over the next few months Bobbie Jo turned into a good housewife and mother. Bobby Ray had forced her into it. He'd threatened her with being sent home to her parents. He was so angry; Bobbie Jo knew he wasn't kidding.

CHAPTER 4

It's July 1960 ……

Not out of choice, Bobbie Jo learned how to change diapers, how to bathe the baby and how to take care of the house a little. Bobby Ray would call the house several times a day to make sure she was home and to tell her what else she needed to do in the house. He didn't call at the same time each day so Bobbie Jo had to stay there to get the call.

One day in September, she had the radio so loud, she didn't hear the phone ringing. She found out what would happen when she didn't answer the phone. Bobby Ray couldn't leave work, but he could call the police and he did. When the police arrived at the apartment, they pounded on the door. Bobbie Jo thought it was her husband being lazy and kicking the door so she started screaming at the door for him to stop being such a lazy bum and open the door himself. When the pounding continued, she finally decided to open the door. She was still screaming while she walked over to it. "You lazy mother fucker! Open the damned door yourself. I'm not your nig…" She cut her words off as she opened the door because she saw two very large policemen standing there. One officer was black.

She didn't know what to say to them so she said nothing. Finally one of the officers asked her. "Are you Bobbie Jo Turnbull?"

"Yeah", she answered in a questioning manner.

"Are you all right?"

"Yeah", she answered again. "Why?"

"We received a call from your husband. He told us you'd been sick and he couldn't reach you by phone. He said he worked clear across town and it would take him so long to get here to check on you, so he asked if we could. He was very concerned, ma'am."

"Oh yeah?"

"Ma'am. Maybe if you turned that radio down a bit, you could hear the phone when it rang. Your neighbors would probably appreciate it too."

"Screw the neighbors. I pay rent here and can do as I like and I like the radio loud so I can hear it."

"Well ma'am, let's put it this way, turn your radio down or we will write you a ticket for disturbing the peace." The black officer had been trying to be nice to this woman, but it was very apparent that nice didn't work with her.

Bobbie Jo walked over to the radio, turned the volume down and then walked the couple of steps back to the door. She was no longer afraid of the cop. "That better, officer?" she asked with a sarcastic tone in her voice.

"Yes'm it is. Now I bet you can hear that phone if it rings."

"Sure, like I want to answer it."

"Well, that's your choice. Just keep it turned down. Besides, now you can hear your baby crying."

"That's why I turned it up in the first place. All that kid does is cry, cry, cry."

"What's wrong with it."

"Spoiled, that's what."

"Excuse me", said the white officer that was now standing in the background?

"You heard me. Spoiled. That hospital spoiled her when she was in there and now my husband spoils her. Then he goes off to work and expects me to do the same. Well, I ain't gonna do it."

"How old is the baby, ma'am?"

"Dunno."

"What?"

"Not mine. It's his so I dunno. Don't you understand what dunno means?"

"Yes'm but it seems strange that you would be taking care of a baby and not know how old it is."

"Oh I kinda know, just not exactly", she said smiling at the white officer. She thought he was kind of cute. "As I said, it's his, not mine."

"Guess we'll leave you to take care of her before she hurts herself with all that crying."

"Oh, she won't hurt herself. She cries like that everyday."

"Is she sick?"

"No. Probably wants to be spoiled again."

"What do you mean by spoiled?"

"You know, like wanting to be picked up, or fed or changed. You know, something like that. That kid always wants something."

"Well, maybe you should see what needs to be done?"

"Suppose so."

"Actually, we'll wait to see if the child is all right. If we feel you can't take care of the child, we'll take it in protective custody."

"I can take care of it just fine. I just ain't gonna spoil it anymore than it is now, that's all."

"Well ma'am. Go take care of the child. If we ever get another report of disturbance from here, we'll take the child from you."

"You can't do that."

"Yes we can and we will if we get any more calls."

When Bobby Ray got home, there was no dinner on the table, but the baby was clean, fed and dry. His wife, however, was furious.

"Whad'ja call the cops for", she screamed at him?

"I was worried when I couldn't get hold of you."

"Where could I go? I have no money. I don't drive. I don't have any friends anymore because of you and I have this kid to take care of all the time."

"You have no money because I don't give you my check anymore. You were supposed to be putting the extra money in the bank to save for a house."

"You don't earn enough to have any extra to put in the bank."

"Now that I'm taking care of the money, we have extra. You just don't have access to it. And you don't have friends because you don't pay their way at the club. None of this is my fault."

"Yes, it is. I need money of my own."

"So get a job."

"A job?"

"Yes, a job. You could get a part time job and then you would have your own money. I'm sure Mrs. Torras could watch Leah each day for not too much."

"Who's Mrs. Torras?"

"She's the lady across the hall."

"You mean that Mexican?"

"Yes. She's a very nice lady."

"How do you know her?"

"I see her with her children when I'm doing the laundry."

"You been spending time with her?"

"Sure, while the laundry is washing and drying. She's a very pleasant person."

Bobbie Jo was furious. First Bobby Ray tells her to get a job and then he tells her that he has been talking to that fat foreign woman. *I'll never understand men*, thought Bobbie Jo. *Here I am thin and young and who does he spend time with but a fat, old woman with five kids.*

The next day, Bobbie Jo couldn't wait to call Mary Lou.

"Bobbie Jo. I haven't heard from you in ages. I thought you must have moved."

"No. Just been busy with this kid."

"Oh no. You kept the child?"

"Didn't have any choice. The baby had no where else to go."

"You are such a wonderful person taking care of his child like that. I don't think I could be that nice."

"Well being nice hasn't got me anywhere. Do ya know what happened yesterday?"

"No, what?"

"Ya know how he always said, *The wife's place is in the home, not out working.*"

"Yes, that's what you told me."

"Well that's what he always said, until last night."

"Really? What did he say last night?"

"He told me I should get a part time job."

"Really. Why?"

"I told him I wanted some pocket money cause I never have any."

"You always did before."

"Yes I did, but since that kid came into the house he's taken to keeping all the money for his self."

"Really?"

"Yes, really. I don't even have money to buy my personal stuff and he won't buy them for me."

"Oh no. That's terrible."

"Sure is. Plus, you'll never guess what else."

"What?"

"He told me he knows a Mexican lady who will take care of the baby so I can work and I have to pay her to watch the kid."

"It's his child and you are supposed to pay?"

"Yep. And he's been spending time with her."

"No!"

"Yep. I asked him outright if he had been spending time with her and he said yes."

"You poor thing. Does he still hit you?"

"Not since the baby came into the house. But can you believe him? Here I am. I'm young. I'm thin. This here Mexican is fat and old. Plus she has a half dozen kids or so. Maybe that means she's good in the sack."

"Bobbie Jo I'm shocked to hear you talk like that."

Quickly Bobbie Jo apologized, "I'm sorry. I never talk like that. It's just that I'm so upset. I just don't understand any of this."

"I know, dear, I know. But you just have to put up with the way men are. That's just the way things are. They make the money and we have to put up with sharing their beds and letting them always have their way. Be grateful you don't have any children of your own."

"I guess you're right. I just feel better having someone to talk to."

"You call anytime you want."

"I'd better hang up now. He calls here every couple of hours checking on me and gets really mad if the line is busy or if I don't answer. That's another reason why I haven't been to the club in a long time. He gets so jealous and then he gets mean. I'll talk to you soon."

"Bye."

Right after Bobbie Jo hung up the phone, it rang. It was Bobby Ray calling.

"Everything all right?"

"Yep. Why?"

"The line was busy."

"I was calling on a couple of ads I saw in the paper."

"That's good. I talked with your doctor and he thinks it would do you some good to go to work. He thinks it would help build your self esteem."

"Good for him. I got good esteem. I just don't got a job."

"You have a fancy education so that shouldn't be a problem. We can talk about who you called today when I get home tonight. See you then."

"Yeah. See you then." After hanging up Bobbie Jo ran to find the newspaper. She had to find a couple of ads for employment. *That Bobby Ray is always so nosey. And why'id he call my doctor? What's he got to do with it?*

She spent most of the afternoon circling ads in the paper. She even called a couple of them so she would have something to say to her husband when he grilled her after dinner.

Things went on like this for the next few weeks. Bobby Ray believed his wife was happier and seriously looking for a job. Each night she told him of the places she had called or the places she was going to interview with the next day. Each week when he was paid, he made sure he paid Mrs. Torras for babysitting his daughter while his wife looked for work. Each week he would tell Mrs. Torras, "Remember, when Mrs. Turnbull finds steady work we still want you to watch little Leah."

Mrs. Torras always responded that she understood, but she never told him she didn't think his wife was really looking for work. If he had ever asked her she would have shared her feelings with him but he didn't ask so she kept quiet.

Then one night, just as Bobby Ray walked into the apartment from work, Bobbie Jo started screaming at him. "You've gone and done it again!"

"What?"

"You bastard. You've gone and got me pregnant again."

"How can that be? You're on that pill from the doctor. Remember? We decided we were lucky with the one baby and weren't gonna have any more, remember?"

"Yeah, well it didn't work."

"Have you been taking it every day like the doctor said to"?

"Pretty much."

"How often is pretty much?"

"Oh, all right. I don't like taking it cause it makes me fat. Are you happy now?"

"That's a stupid reason for not taking it. It's even more stupid that you didn't say anything to me or the doctor. Didn't he ask you how you were doing on the pill?"

"Yeah."

"So what did you tell him"?

"I didn't tell him anything. He's a quack. He said it was in my head. It ain't in my head, it was that pills fault."

"Bobbie Jo. I am trying to save for a house for us. You were trying to get a job to help out. I've spent money for your job hunting and now you turn up pregnant. Why did you lie to me and the doctor?"

"I didn't lie."

"You did!"

"He never asked me if I was taking the damn pill. He just asked how I was feeling and I told him fat. Then he told me that sometimes the pill does that to some women. So I stopped taking it. I didn't lie. I never lie."

"Bobbie Jo you know better. You have all that education and you keep doin' stupid things. We ain't never gonna have anything."

"That's not my fault. If you would leave that stupid plant and find a good paying job, we'd be fine."

Bobby Ray knew better than to get in an argument with her in the mood she was in so he just walked in the kitchen and washed out his lunch bucket. He saw there was nothing started for dinner and knew he was in for many months of hell

CHAPTER 5

It's May 1961 ……

The hospital in Covington still automatically lists all births in the local newspaper. Under the date of May 12th appeared the following:

Arriving at 4:56pm was a baby girl, Misty, to the proud parents of Bobbie Jo and Bobby Ray Turnbull.

At the Milhouse residence, Sally dutifully cut the notice out of the paper and made the notation in the big bible.

Once again Bobbie Jo had given birth to an under weight child. Bobby Ray and the doctor had done their best to get her to eat more during her pregnancy but it did no good. She was obsessed with the thought of getting fat and refused to eat. This child would also have to spend extra time in the hospital to gain weight.

Just before the baby was born Bobby Ray hired Mrs. Torras to come in three days a week to do some cooking for them so there would be food in the apartment. Mrs. Torras even took care of Leah and did some cleaning. On the days she worked he came home to the most wonderful smells. On the days she was off the smells in the apartment were not so pleasant. One day the smells were particularly foul and he couldn't keep quiet.

"Bobbie Jo how come this place smells so bad?"

"I dunno what ya're talking about."

"The smell in the apartment is terrible."

"It's not my fault."

"Why not? You've been home all day not me. Who's fault could it be?" By now Bobby Ray knew that it was always the fault of someone else. His wife would never take responsibility for anything wrong.

"It is too ya're fault."

"How do ya figure that?" He could never figure how her brain worked and was always interested in what her answer would be. She was so good at twisting things around. Sometimes he almost believed what she said.

"If ya had your Mexican lady friend come in every day, it wouldn't smell in here. It's her job to clean this place, not mine. I'm doing my job by carrying your kid. I shouldn't have to do any more than that."

Bobby Ray just nodded his head. He figured she would find a way to make it his fault.

"Bobbie Jo. I'm working six days a week so you can have help three days a week. I would think you could empty a diaper pail once in awhile."

"Sally only gets one day a week off."

"Your parents live in a big house. Your father is the president of a bank. He can afford to have a full time housekeeper. We live in a three room apartment and I work on the line at a plant."

"I deserve to have a housekeeper too."

"Well after you have the baby and go to work perhaps you can afford to hire one."

"If'n I do, it shur won't be that Mexican friend of yours."

"Mrs. Torras is a nice lady who works very hard to keep food in our fridge and clean up our messes."

"And ya're sleeping with her. I know it. I got proof."

"I work 12 hours a day, six days a week. The rest of the time I'm here. When do I have time to do anything besides eat and sleep?"

"I know what you two are doing in that laundry room."

"I'm not talking to you about this any more. You're talking crazy." Bobby Ray just walked away and into the small bedroom to visit with his daughter. He knew she would need changing and a bath. He also knew she probably hadn't been fed since he fed her before he went to work. Leah was a good baby. She didn't cry like she used to. He guessed she had gotten used to being wet, dirty and hungry when she was with her mother. He knew it was a big expense, but he had to find a way to keep Mrs. Torras.

After the baby was born, the doctor saw Bobby Ray each evening in the hospital just like he had with the last child. He always wondered why Bobby Ray looked so concerned. He remembered that same look on the man's face with the last child. Finally one night he stopped to visit with Bobby Ray.

"You have another fine baby girl."

"Hope so."

"Sure you do. Just because the mother didn't eat well, that doesn't mean the child will suffer too much. Actually, the baby takes what it needs from the mother's reserves so if anyone suffers from not eating it's mainly the mother. We need to get her on vitamins and we need to get her to eat."

"Doc. It really isn't all about how skinny the baby is and I really don't care anymore if Bobbie Jo eats."

"What is it then?"

"I shudda told ya this before, but I was ashamed."

"Nothing to be ashamed about. You can always tell me."

"This could get me in trouble, but I have to tell ya cause I can't go through this anymore."

"Come now. You won't get in trouble. Tell me what you can't go through."

"We can't have any more children."

"Children are expensive to raise but I have pills to fix that."

"She won't take no pills. She says they make her fat. But the expense isn't the problem".

"Well......"

Bobby Ray cut him off. "The problem is that we're first cousins."

The doctor took a deep breath and quickly looked around to see if anyone could have heard what was being said. "We'd better discuss this in my office. Come with me."

Once in the office with the door shut the doctor started asking questions. "Who knows about this?"

"No one but you and us."

"You have no family?"

"Oh yeah. They all know, but they disowned her when they found out she was pregnant."

"What were you thinking?"

"We didn't know we was first cousins. It's a long story and the family had never told any of us kids. When her father found out she was pregnant he spilled the beans. When he decided she had to get rid of the baby she refused. They disowned her. We moved here and got married. We, well, I thought we decided not to have any more kids. I thought she was taking the pills ya gave her. Didn't find out she wasn't until after she got pregnant again. That's why I spend so much time here with the babies. I been praying over them. It ain't their fault for what me and their mom done."

"Well, I won't turn you in. What I will do is run some tests we don't normally run to see if both the girls are all right. But, be sure you get her to take those pills. If you're fortunate enough to have two normal children, you'd best not push your luck."

"Thanks doc. You have to believe me, I had no idea she wasn't taking them pills."

"I do. But remember if you're going to continue having relations with her, she has to take those pills and she has to take them according to the instructions."

"Can I put them in her food?"

"Yes, but is there something she always eats?"

"Yep. Sweets. She always eats sweets."

"That would be good. They do taste a little bitter when crushed, so the sugar would hide that."

Bobby Ray thought *I'll have to talk to Mrs. Torras. She'll help me out.*

On the way home, Bobby Ray stopped at a drug store he hadn't been in before and had the prescription the doctor had given him filled. He didn't want to take a chance of having the pharmacist mention the pills to Bobbie Jo. He would talk to Mrs. Torras in the morning before he left for work.

It wasn't long before baby Misty was able to come home from the hospital. When the nurses were getting her ready, the doctor and he talked some more.

"I ran the tests on this child, Bobby Ray, but I need to see your other one."

"I asked Bobbie Jo to make an appointment. Didn't she?"

"No. I haven't heard from her at all."

"Well, she still doesn't drive so I'll be bringing her and the babies in for Misty's first check up. You can run the test then."

"All right. Does your wife know we're doing this?"

"No. I never told her. I didn't think she'd care one way or the other."

"Hasn't she gotten over her sadness yet? It's been a long time."

"No and now that there are two babies in the house, she's worse. If'n it wasn't for having day help I don't know what would happen to the kids."

"Day help? Can you afford day help?"

"Not really. I'm putting in as many overtime hours as I can, and the lady only comes in 3 days a week. I need to get me another job, but with me taking care of the kids and cooking when Mrs. Torras isn't there plus all the extra hours I put in I don't have the time."

"Your wife is strong and healthy. She should be helping with the children."

"Yep she should, but she won't. She says she done her job by carrying them for nine months. All she can talk about is not having any money and not being able to go to see her friends at that neighborhood social club."

"I've heard about clubs like that."

"Anything good?"

"Not really."

"Didn't think so. Bobbie Jo's latest thing is that she's goin' to work."

"It might be good for her."

"Probably, but it's all talk. The last time she was talking like that I bought her clothes so she'd look nice going on interviews. I spent all kinds of money on her and paid for lots of babysitting. Come to find out she was doin' no such thing. She was just talking on the phone to her friends and going to the social club to visit."

"Really?"

"Yep. Then when I started asking too many questions about her so called interviews, she turns up pregnant again."

"That shouldn't happen this time."

"Better not."

Bobby Ray didn't expect Bobbie Jo to be happy about having another child in the house, but he didn't expect her to become so violent. When he opened the door to the apartment, Bobbie Jo was sitting on the couch talking on the telephone. When she saw that he had a baby in his arms she started screaming.

"Oh no. He's done brought another child into my house. I can't believe it. Mary Lou, did you hear me? He's brought another child into my house."

Mary Lou didn't know what to say to her friend and even if she did, she wouldn't have been able to say it anyway as Bobbie Jo was ranting, raving and screaming at the top of her lungs. As she was trying to say something that might calm her friend, the line went dead. Someone had hung the phone up. Mary Lou didn't know what to think. This was the second time she'd been told that a strange child was being brought into the Turnbull home without her friend knowing where it came from. Over the time since she met Bobbie Jo, she'd never known her to lie but this was getting a little hard to believe. First there were the stories of the beatings. Then there were the stories of his hard drinking and smoking. Then there was a strange child brought home and now a second child. Mary Lou's head hurt from just thinking about it all. When she talked to her husband about Bobbie Jo's strange life he advised her to stay away from the family. He thought they both sounded crazy and he didn't want anything to do with them. Mary Lou liked Bobbie Jo, as she was fun to talk with even if she didn't see her in person any more. Mary Lou didn't know what she would do when Bobbie Jo called tomorrow. She knew the call would come, it always did.

When Bobbie Jo started screaming, Bobby Ray calmly walked into the bedroom with Misty and laid her in the bed next to her sister. He hadn't had any extra money to buy her a bed of her own and even if he did, there wasn't room in the tiny bedroom for anything else. When he was sure his two babies were all right, he went back to his screaming wife. He could only imagine what the neighbors thought and was surprised someone hadn't called the cops on them. He walked over to Bobbie Jo, reached around her and, without a word to her, took the phone from her and hung it up.

"Bobbie Jo. Why do you tell that lie?"

"I didn't tell no lie. I said you brung another baby into the house and you did. Ain't no lie."

"Maybe not, but the way ya say it people might get the wrong idea."

"Whadda mean, the wrong idea?"

"Like it wasn't your child. That's what I mean. This is your baby too, ya know. No matter what you say, both babies belong to both of us."

"No-o-o", screamed Bobbie Jo as she picked up the telephone and threw it at her husband.

As he ducked out of the way Bobby Ray said, "Yes it is and things have to change around here. You need to start being their mother."

"No-o-o! Stop saying those things! I've done my part. I'm never goin' ta be their mother." Then Bobbie Jo started throwing everything she could pick up at her husband. When she ran out of items to throw, she started tearing the curtains. When they were totally shredded she started ripping at the clothes she had on.

Bobby Ray finally got hold of her and forced her down on the floor. As he sat on her to keep her from doing any more damage, he picked the phone up and placed a call to the doctor. Once he reached him, Bobby Ray explained his wife had gone crazy and explained what she had done.

As he was trying to talk to the doctor, Bobbie Jo started screaming again.

"What are ya doin' to me. Stop beating me. Somebody help me. He's trying to kill me."

"Don't move. I'll be right over with an ambulance."

Bobbie Jo was still screaming but Bobby Ray was talking to her very quietly. "Honey, look what you gone and done. You can't be doin' this all the time. I told ya that before."

Before long, the doctor and the attendants from the ambulance were there. When Bobbie Jo saw them she started screaming again. When the men picked her up and started putting her in a straight jacket, she became violent. She couldn't move her arms or hands, but she could move her head, feet and legs. She kicked and bucked and screamed until the doctor finally gave her a shot to quiet her. The attendants were then able to put her on the gurney and tie her down. As they were wheeling her out to the ambulance, the doctor told them he would meet them at the hospital.

"Bobby Ray, does this happen all the time?"

"Not all the time, but a lot. This is the worst she's been. Usually I can handle it, but she really went off this time."

"What caused it this time?"

As Bobby Ray told the story the doctor just shook his head. Then the doctor said, "It sounds like she's just having temper tantrums."

"What?"

"I don't think there is anything physically or mentally wrong with your wife."

"There has to be. Ever since we had the first baby she's been this way. And now with the second one look how she's got."

"Is she an only child?"

"Yeah. Why?"

"Does she always want to be the center of attention?"

Bobby Ray thought a little about when Bobbie Jo was living with Ethel. Then he thought about the few times they went to the social club together. Finally he said, "Yeah. I believe that to be true cause whenever we went out if'n a girl come in the place and men stopped talking to her to go talk to the new one, well she'd just up and leave."

"She's not the center of attention any more. When you come home do you ask about her or the baby?"

"Baby, of course, cause she never takes care of it."

"You told me she was upset over not having money."

"Right."

"Did she have money before the babies came?"

"Sure. I just turned my check over to her to take care of everything."

"You don't do that now?"

"No, cause she never saved anything. I don't know where she spent it. She says I spent it all, but that ain't true. Now that I'm paying the bills, I can even put some aside for a rainy day."

"I'll keep her for a couple of days and I'll run some tests, but I think I'm right."

"What if ya are? I can't go back to the way we were. We'd all starve and be thrown on the streets cause the bills wouldn't be paid."

"I don't know the answer to that, but you said she wanted to get a job."

"Yeah. You wouldn't know it, but she went to good schools and finished them all."

"Perhaps you should help her find a job."

"Where?"

As the doctor was walking towards the door to leave he said, "I can't help you there, but it might be the answer. It sure wouldn't hurt the situation any."

Bobby Ray just nodded his head in agreement. As he was shutting the door he saw Mrs. Torras and a couple of her children looking out their door. "Evening, Mrs. Torras. Can I talk to you a minute?"

Mrs. Torras said something to her children in Spanish. The children went inside the apartment and their mother walked to the Turnbull door.

"Did ya hear the commotion?"

"Si."

"We have two babies now. Two girls."

Mrs. Torras didn't respond.

"Mrs. Turnbull is going to be in the hospital for awhile."

Still no response.

"We're gonna need ya even more now. Can you come every day? At least until my wife is out of the hospital?"

"Si."

"Does my wife ever act this bad when you're here with her?"

"No. She just talks on the phone to her friends and gives me orders to do things."

"Did she ever help with the baby?"

"No."

"Thank you Mrs. Torras. I'll find someway to pay you."

Mrs. Torras nodded her head and walked back to her apartment door. "Mr. Turnbull?"

"Yeah, Mrs. Torras?"

"I think you and your family would be better off without your wife."

"I think so too, but what can I do?"

Without responding, Mrs. Torras walked into her apartment and Bobby Ray turned and shut his door.

He didn't get much sleep that night caring for his two babies, but he was still up ready for work and in the kitchen fixing bottles for his girls when Mrs. Torras softly knocked at the door. He told her he was going to stop at the hospital after work but he should be home by 6:30pm. She just nodded her head. Bobby Ray went in the bedroom to take one last look at his babies before leaving for work. Even though his wife wasn't home, it really wasn't any different than other mornings other than being very quiet. He had to admit that life with Bobbie Jo was never quiet since the babies came along. When he thought a little more about it, he realized it had never been quiet. She had always been pitching a fit about something the whole time he'd known her. Then he thought about what the doctor had said and decided he would ask around work and see if there was something she could do at the plant.

On his morning break he called home to see how everything was going. Mrs. Torras told him everything was fine and not to worry. He felt better just hearing everything quiet in the background. Then he called the hospital to talk to Bobbie Jo. The nurse told him she was sleeping. He asked her to tell his wife he called and that he would be by after work to see her. The nurse assured him she would. Bobbie Ray went back to work feeling better than he had in a long time. Everything was quiet.

During his lunch break Bobby Ray went to the front office and talked to the man in the personnel department. The man was very nice, but explained to Bobbie Ray the company didn't want couples working in the same plant. He offered to see what he could do to get her in the plant near Louisville, if Bobby Ray was interested. Bobby Ray explained Louisville was too far away, but thanked him for his help. As Bobby Ray was walking out the door the personnel man said, "If she's interested in working in an office here in town, I can ask around some of my friends."

Bobby Ray turned and said, "Would you do that for me?"

"Sure. I go to business meetings a couple times a month in town. I always hear when people are looking for help. I'll keep my ears open for something for you."

"Thanks. I really appreciate that", said Bobby Ray. He shut the door to personnel and walked with a happy heart back to the lunchroom to quickly down his bologna sandwich.

After work he drove directly to the hospital to see his wife. When he walked into her room, he thought she was sleeping so he tip toed over to the chair next to the bed and quietly sat down. He wanted to stay with her a few minutes, even if she was asleep.

Just as he sat down Bobbie Jo growled, "Whadda doin' here?"

"I came to see you."

"Why bother? You and that damn doctor put me in here for no reason. I'm forced to eat awful food, ya don't call me all day and then ya come in like nothings wrong."

"I bother cause I love ya."

"Ha. Ha. That's funny. If ya loved me ya would 'a called."

"I did call. The nurse said ya was asleep. She said she'd leave a note."

Now Bobbie Jo started getting louder. "Note. Smote. Ya didn't talk to me so ya didn't call."

"Bobbie Jo, don't be that way."

Then Bobbie Jo started yelling. "I'll be any way I like. Ya didn't call and now you sneak in here trying to make nice to me and ya don't even bring me flowers."

"Bobbie Jo, keep your voice down. People are sick in here."

"No-o-o-o I won't", screamed Bobbie Jo. "If ya loved me, you'da brung me flowers."

"Bobbie Jo, I just got off work. I didn't have time to - - -"

Before he could finish, the doctor and two orderlies burst into the room.

"Bobbie Jo", the doctor said, "You know what I told you. You have to keep quiet and if you don't I'll have to give you a shot to keep you quiet."

Bobbie Jo responded by screaming louder. "No-o-o. Let me go! Help! Somebody help me!"

"Okay, guys hold her so I can give her something to calm her down."

As ordered, they held her down while the doctor gave her a shot. When she was calm, they pulled straps from under the bed to tie over her.

"Is that necessary?" asked Bobby Ray.

"I'm afraid so. I don't want her having one of her tantrums and hurting herself nor anyone else. What set her off?"

"She said I didn't call."

"Sure you did. I saw the note."

"Well, she said since I didn't talk to her it was like I didn't call. Then she was upset that I didn't bring her flowers. That's what really set her off. I tried to quiet her, but she only got louder."

The doctor just nodded his head and motioned for Bobby Ray to follow him to the hall. Standing in the hall with the door to the room shut, the doctor said, "The tests I ran today show everything is normal."

"Then what's wrong with her?"

"I want a doctor friend of mine to see her. That is if your insurance will pay for it."

"What kind of doctor?"

"A psychiatrist."

Bobby Ray slumped against the wall. Then he said, "Ya think she's crazy?"

"No. I think she's a spoiled brat, but I also think she needs some help growing up and maybe this would help her."

"Okay then. Do I need to do anything?"

"No. I'll check with your insurance and let you know if there is a problem. If not, I'll set up the appointment to be here in the hospital."

"I'll see ya tomorrow night then", said Bobby Ray.

"No. Just call me when you get off work. I think it's best if you don't visit her for awhile."

Tears came into Bobby Ray's eyes as he said, "Don't know if I can do that doc. I do love her ya know."

"I believe you Bobby Ray. I just don't think she loves anyone right now, even herself. So just stay away until I tell you otherwise."

Bobby Ray just nodded his head then turned and walked away. He was so worried about his wife but there was nothing he could do. The doctor was right, Bobbie Jo didn't act like she loved anyone right now. She sure didn't love the two beautiful babies they had at home. Thinking about his daughters cheered him up so by the time he got to the apartment he was in a brighter mood.

It was 5:45pm when Bobby Ray opened the door to the apartment. Mrs. Torras was sitting on the couch, holding baby Misty and had Leah lying next to her. She was talking quietly in Spanish to them. As usual, the house smelled clean and dinner smelled wonderful.

"You home early", said Mrs. Torras.

"Yep. The wife isn't doing too good so's the doc told me it'd be best if'n I stayed away for awhile."

Mrs. Torras looked at Bobby Ray kind of strange, but to him she only said, "I'll fix your plate."

"Thank you. How were the girls today?"

"They be so beautiful and they eat everything."

"I'm glad they didn't give you any trouble."

"No, señor, babies not give trouble. When they get older they give trouble, but not as babies. When they babies they just be beautiful."

Bobby Ray thought about what his friend had said and how it was so different than what his wife always said. He had taken baby Misty from Mrs. Torras and was now sitting on the couch with his two children. All he could think about was how peaceful the apartment was. It was clean. It smelled good. The children were peaceful. They were clean and had full bellies. They were awake and looking around. Mrs. Torras was right. They were beautiful. How different this evening was from all the other evenings when he walked in from work, even when Mrs. Torras was helping Bobbie Jo out during the day. *Maybe the doc was right. Maybe Bobbie Jo was being the way she was just because she didn't have all my attention. Maybe she done all she's done just because she's mad.*

"Your dinner ready", Mrs. Torras called from the kitchen. "I go home now, okay?"

"Sure. I can take it from here. Thanks again. See you tomorrow", Bobby Ray said as he laid his daughter in the couch next to her sister.

"Okay. I be here." With that Mrs. Torras left the little apartment and walked the few steps to her own so she could put dinner on the table for her family and then do her own cleaning.

Life was very quiet and peaceful for Bobby Ray and the children for the next couple of weeks. Mrs. Torras had asked permission to bring the babies to the park when her children went. She didn't like them going alone and she said the fresh air would do the children good. Bobby Ray said it was a good idea. Then she asked if once she had finished the chores in his apartment, if she could bring the babies to her place so she could do some of her own chores. Bobby Ray didn't mind that either. In fact, he had been feeling guilty that she had to work so late into the night to keep her own place up because of taking care of his babies.

Things went along like this for about three weeks. Then the day came that the doctor called Bobby Ray and told him that the insurance was about to run out so he had to once again bring his wife home.

"Is she better, doc?"

"Some days have been good and some days haven't."

"What did you find out?"

"I didn't find anything medically wrong with her."

"What about the shrink you asked to see her?"

"He's been seeing her everyday."

"Good. Was he able to find out what is wrong with her?"

"No. Not really. You really should talk to him, but I believe he has come to the same conclusion that I did."

"What's that?"

"She's angry because she isn't the center of attention."

"So what can I do about that? I can't just get rid of the children."

"She'd like it if you would, but you're right. I'd suggest she get a job. She won't like having to abide by anyone's rules, but it would be the best thing for her, and for your family. At least, that's my opinion."

"Thanks doc. I'll pick her up after work today and I'll do my best to find her some work."

"Good luck", the doctor replied. To himself he thought, *this man is going to need a awful lot of luck to see this through. If it were me, I'd be thinking about getting rid of the wife and keeping the children.*

Bobby Ray called Mrs. Torras and explained he would be bringing Bobbie Jo home from the hospital that night, so he might be a little late.

Mrs. Torras just said, "Okay" and hung up. She didn't say anything to Bobby Ray but she wasn't looking forward to his wife being in the house. Mrs. Torras thought she was a very mean woman, who hated her own babies, but Mrs. Torras needed to work and this was so convenient for her. She just didn't look forward to being treated so badly again.

When Bobby Ray got off the phone after talking to the doctor and to Mrs. Torras, he went to the personnel office. He wanted to see if the man there had heard anything about a job for Bobbie Jo.

"As a matter of fact, just yesterday I heard about a part time job in an insurance office."

"Really", Bobby Ray said excitedly. "Where is it? What would she be doing?"

"Hold on, now. I don't have all the answers. I just heard about the job. Let me write the guys name down. You call him. Tell him I told you to call and explain the situation to him about your wife."

"Sorry. It's just that I pick her up from the hospital today and I think this would cheer her up. Ya know, thinking that she had something to look forward to."

The personnel man said, "Sure, I understand. No problem. Use the phone in the hall to call this guy." To himself he said, *If it was me just getting out of the hospital and being with my family again would be what I would be looking forward to. Oh well. Glad it's him and not me.*

Bobby Ray did just what the man in the personnel office said. He talked to Mr. Rayburn at the insurance agency. He explained the whole situation to him. After hearing where Bobbie Jo went to school, Mr. Rayburn told Bobby Ray he would like to talk to her in person. Arrangements were made for her to come to his office the following week. Bobby Ray was so happy. He could hardly wait to see his wife and tell her the good news.

Bobby Ray drove to the hospital right after work. He was so excited about her coming home and his news about a job for her, he almost ran to her room. When he got there he found her lying in bed.

"Bobbie Jo. Why aren't you dressed?"

"Who're you?"

"Bobbie Jo, you know who I am."

"I don't think I do. You couldn't be anybody important cause if'n you were I'da seen you here visitin' me from time to time."

"The doctor told me it would be better for you if'n I stayed away."

"You always have somethin' to say don't cha?"

"It's true. You kin ask him for yourself."

"He'd jest lie to protect ya."

"Com'on. Get ready so's ya can come home with me."

"I ain't goin'."

"Ya have ta."

"Why? I like it here. I don't have ta do anythin' I don't wanna do and I get to lay in bed all day long. Nothing wrong with staying here."

"Don't ya wanna come home to your babies and me?"

"No. Ya'll don't mean anythin' to me. Ya never did. I just needed a way to get away from the old folks."

"Now, Bobbie Jo. Ya don't mean that. We had some good times together."

"Sure we did. Now that ya brung them babies to my house we don't never have any fun."

Bobby Ray ignored what she said, knowing that she was just looking to start a big fight. Instead he said, "Ya know how ya said ya wanted a job of your own?" She did not respond. "Well I talked to the personnel manager over at the plant."

"I won't work in that dirty place. Besides I'd have to get up too early."

"Fine. He said ya couldn't work there anyways cause I already did." Still she did not respond. "He said he would keep an eye out for something for ya somewhere in town. Just today he told me about a job in an insurance company."

Bobbie Jo still didn't say anything, but she turned over so she could see her husband. Bobby Ray thought this was a good sign so he kept talking.

"He didn't know anything about the job, but he told me to call the guy and say I was sent by him. So's I called the insurance man and I told him about you and where you went to school."

"Yeah, so what?"

"So he'd like to talk to ya in person in a week or so. He said after you were feeling stronger."

"Ya didn't tell him I was in the hospital did ya?"

"Sure, why not?"

"He's gonna think I'm crazy."

"No he won't. I told him ya just had our second baby and needed a little rest."

With that Bobbie Jo started screaming. "You told him I had two babies? How could ya do that? That's personal business. Ya had no right. Them's your chilrin's and ya had no right saying they was mine."

As Bobbie Jo's voice got louder she could be heard all the way to the nurses station. The nurse on duty called to Bobbie Jo's doctor and told him what was going on. It wasn't but a couple of minutes until he walked in the door.

"Mrs. Turnbull", the doctor said loudly. "Aren't you ready for your trip home?"

"No-o-o-o", Bobbie Jo really screamed. "My name is Bobbie Jo Milhouse. Don't never call me that other name again."

"All right Bobbie Jo. I think that's enough of that. We all know you don't like the idea of having gotten married and then having children. We have heard all about it now for weeks; however, you did get married and you do have children. We talked about this just this morning. There is nothing wrong with you. Your insurance will not pay for any more time in the hospital and you have to leave here today. If you won't go quietly, I will call security and have you removed. Now, are you going to get dressed and be quiet or am I going to make that call?"

Bobbie Jo didn't say a word. She just threw back the covers, exposing her naked body, got out of bed and started putting her clothes on.

Bobby Ray was so startled to see his wife parading around naked in front of strangers he said nothing. He just stood there with his mouth open. When the doctor touched his arm, he jumped.

"Let's give her a little privacy. We can talk in the hall."

Bobby Ray followed him out to the hall.

"She has been doing this a lot. It's her way of getting attention. She waits until a young orderly is working outside her door and then she drops her tray on the floor. When he comes in to clean up the mess, she jumps out of bed naked as a jay bird, squats down so she's facing the poor young man and says she wants to help him."

"What?"

"She's just trying to get the attention of every man she sees."

"She ain't never been like this before."

"She's done worse things than that since she's been here, but this is what she does most frequently. I don't envy you. I really don't."

"Is she sick."

"Yes, but not with anything that we can cure. What started her yelling this time?"

"I think I found her a job."

"She was mad about that?"

"No. She was mad because I told the man she just had our second child and was in the hospital for some rest."

"So. Why did that make her mad?"

"She said that I had no right telling anyone her personal business."

The doctor said nothing. He just nodded his head. To himself he thought, *this woman is sick. I wouldn't want to be living in the same house with her and I really wouldn't want her caring for my children.*

To Bobby Ray he said, "Good luck. Call us if things get really bad."

Bobby Ray said he would.

Bobbie Jo came out of her room with her things in a paper sack. "Let's get outta here."

Once home things settled into somewhat of a schedule. In the morning Mrs. Torras would walk in just as Bobby Ray was walking out. During the day, Bobbie Jo would sleep late and after getting up she'd go out. She'd come home just moments before Bobby Ray would get there. Once he walked in the door Mrs. Torras would walk out. Bobby Ray longed for the days when Bobbie Jo wasn't there. Things were so much happier.

Time went by and finally, in August, Bobbie Jo went to work for the insurance company. She didn't have to be to work until 10am so she could still sleep in a little, plus she got off at 3pm so she had time to go to the social club once again. Part of the bargain of her going to work was that she would not ask her husband for any money. She would contribute a little money to buy groceries, but she got to keep the rest of her paycheck. Bobby Ray thought this was fair enough because she would finally have her own money.

The problem is that after her second week of working and getting a paycheck, she told him she wasn't giving him anything towards groceries because she never ate anything at the house. After the third week at work she informed Bobby Ray that he was to start calling her BJ instead of Bobbie Jo. She told him her boss, Mr. Rayburn, said BJ sounded more professional than Bobbie Jo.

Bobby Ray agreed to keep peace in the house and things seemed to smooth out a little. BJ was even starting to sleep in the same bed with him once again, instead of staying on the couch all night.

CHAPTER 6

It's January 1969 ......

BJ startles Bobby Ray by coming into the kitchen when he's eating his breakfast. Bobby Ray knows his wife. She's never up at 5:30am so he knows something's wrong.
"What's up?"
"Ya done it again."
"What did I do?"
"Ya done and got me pregnant again."
"Ya can't be."
"Well, I am so I guess I can be. Ya did this just cause I was doing so well at work. Ya done it so's I'd have to quit." She'd said her piece and didn't expect an answer. Not waiting for one she walked into the crowded bedroom and crawled back into bed.

Bobby Ray didn't know what to say to his wife so he was glad she'd gone to the bedroom without a fight. The one thing he did know was that he and his wife hadn't had relations in a very, very long time. He didn't believe the child was his. Bobbie Jo was right about one thing. She had done well working at the insurance company. Mr. Rayburn was more than generous and paid her well. However, Bobby Ray never saw any of the money. She cashed her checks each week at the social club and as far as he knew she never saved a dime. He didn't know what she spent the money on because she didn't have a lot of fancy clothes and she was skinnier than ever, so she couldn't be spending it on food.

Bobby Ray didn't know what to do. He finally decided he'd call the doctor who had been so much help before. Maybe he'd be able to give him some idea of what to do about the baby. He was positive Bobbie Jo wouldn't want this child either.

On August 9, 1969, the Covington Gazette listed the following announcement.

Arriving at 10:21pm was a baby girl, Edna, to the proud patents BJ and Bobby Ray Turnbull.

During the pregnancy BJ had taken care of herself. She drank milk, ate and actually gained the weight the doctor prescribed. Both Bobby Ray and the doctor were pleasantly surprised. Even more of a surprise was the fact the baby was able to go home when BJ was released.

BJ had worked until she was 4 months pregnant. Then she told her employer she was having medical problems and had to stay off her feet. Bobby Ray had been caught off guard when she told him she wasn't working anymore until after the baby was born, but didn't want to say anything to her for fear of what she might do that would hurt the baby.

He wasn't at all sure it was his child, but a child is a child and he didn't want to see it hurt. She was married to him, so he would accept it as his child. He prayed if it were his child, it would be normal like the other babies were. They were 8 and 9 years old now and doing pretty good. They didn't like school, but he thought that was normal. To him acting normal was a good sign.

Now that BJ was home Bobby Ray told Mrs. Torras they wouldn't need her help until his wife went back to work. BJ had other ideas. She told Mrs. Torras she wanted her to do their laundry and ironing. Bobby Ray had always done the laundry and what ironing that should have been done, never was. He'd hung the clothes on hangers and straightened them the best he could. He didn't understand why BJ had Mrs. Torras doing the laundry but once again didn't say anything because of how she might react.

Money was tight. BJ wasn't working and there was another mouth to feed as well as Mrs. Torras to pay each week, so Bobby Ray picked up a side job. He had run into a man who owned a small appliance repair shop where he needed help. Bobby Ray didn't know anything about fixing toasters and things like that, but the man said he would train him. At first he would have to work at the shop, but once he learned how to do the work, he'd be able to bring some of the things home to fix and bring them back when he was done. Bobby Ray liked the sound of that so right after BJ and the baby came home from the hospital he started working for "Moody's – We Do It Small – Repair Shop".

To Bobby Ray things seemed to be going along just fine. His wife was at home with the baby and the two older ones were in school. When he got home there was always a meal on the table. It wasn't like what Mrs. Torras used to cook, but it was a meal. The house was somewhat clean and it definitely didn't smell like it did with the first and second babies. The most amazing part was baby Edna always had a clean diaper on and had already been bathed when he got home. He really believed BJ had gotten over her fits and had finally become a mother. Work was going well at the plant and he was enjoying working on the small appliance repairs. He was content.

One night in January 1970, BJ announced at dinner that she was going back to work.

"What?" exclaimed Bobby Ray.

"You heard me. I'm going back to work. I start on Monday."

"Where? I thought Mr. Rayburn replaced you."

"I wouldn't work for that jerk anymore. I found me a full time job as a secretary."

"How can you be a secretary? You don't know how to type."

"They said they'd send me to school to learn how."

"Who's they?"

"Trammell Transport Company, that's who."

"Where're they located?"

"On the other side'a the river."

"How ya gonna get there?"

"I can take the bus. The number 15 takes me almost to the front door."

"When did all this happen?"

"It's been happening. You knew I was gonna go back to work. I've been looking, that's all, and I found me a good job. So's you'd better get aholt of your Mexican lady friend. I'm sure she's been missing ya with her having ta do the laundry for us and all."

"What are you talking about?"

"I know'd you and her were doing things when you were supposed ta be doing the wash."

"Are you crazy?" Bobby Ray yelled at her. "What could we possibly be doing when we're doing the wash?"

"I know and so do everyone else in this apartment building. I have friends who'll testify."

"Testify? Testify to who?"

"To them lawyers, that's who."

"Lawyers? Testify to lawyers about what? What are you talking about?"

"I called one of them free lawyers and told'm what was going on. He told me if I wanted to get a divorce you'd have to support me and the kids for all my life. Plus he said I would get everything."

"Get everything?" What do we have that you'd get?"

"Yeah sure, play dumb. I know'd how much you make. Where's all the money? I told that lawyer all this and he said you probably hid it somewheres, but that he could find it."

"I don't know what you're talking about. When did you start thinking about a divorce?"

All this shouting was going on at the dinner table with Leah and Misty sitting there. Right then Leah interrupted and said, "What's a divorce?"

BJ said to her oldest daughter, "That's when the daddy leaves the house and me and my little girls get to sit and play all day and daddy has to pay all the bills. Doesn't that sound like fun?"

The two girls shouted, "Yeah! We can play all day and not have to go to school! Yeah! Let's get a divorce!"

Bobby Ray started to say something, but realized no matter what he said he'd sound like the bad guy so he was quiet and just finished his dinner.

After dinner was over and the girls were in bed he quietly asked his wife, "What was that all about?"

"I've been sitting at home all this time. I ain't got no money. I can't go anywhere cause of your kids. I seen this ad on television about this free lawyer so I called him. He asked me a bunch of questions about you and I had to tell him honest."

"What did you tell him?"

"That you didn't give me any money and that you beat me up sometimes and that you made me go to work and that you were whoring around with your Mexican lady friend right here in the apartment building."

"I don't give ya any money cause ya don't need money. I buy you everything you need."

"Yeah, well, he says that if I got a divorce he could guarantee that I'd never have to work again cause of the special circumstances."

"What special circumstances?"

"All of them. So's what I'm telling ya is ya better watch out. If'n ya don't stop doing bad things to me, I'm getting a divorce and taking everything." With that she walked into the bedroom and slammed the door.

Bobby Ray had no idea what she was talking about. He decided he'd better call his insurance company in the morning to see if they would pay for some more visits with the psychiatrist. He just knew BJ had gone over the edge. He turned the television on and prepared to once again sleep on the couch.

The following Monday BJ was dressed by the time Bobby Ray was heading off to work.

"I don't get off work until 5:30pm and the first bus I can get home doesn't come until 6:00pm so don't expect me home until nearly 7:00pm", BJ called to her husband.

Bobby Ray just nodded. He thought that was a long time for her to be working but said nothing. He didn't want to set her off. Since she'd told him she was going back to work she had been in a pretty decent mood and he didn't want that to change for his children's sake. He saw Mrs. Torras on his way out. He stopped and told her that BJ was nearly ready to leave for work so she could go over any time. She looked surprised, but nodded an okay and went into her apartment to finish her chores.

A couple of minutes after she walked back into her apartment someone started banging on her door. Before she could get to the door, the person on the other side started yelling in addition to the banging. "Are ya gonna come watch these youngins' or not? I gotta get to work. I ain't no lazy Mexican."

When Mrs. Torras opened the door she saw BJ standing there. She had on skintight Levi's, a short tee shirt and high-heeled shoes.

"Are ya comin' or not? I gotta go or I'll miss my bus."

Mrs. Torras nodded and walked out her door and over to the Turnbull apartment.

Don't be feeding these girls too much. They're getting fat as it is. And I ain't givin' you a key either. Yer're bein' paid to be here, not somewheres else."

Mrs. Torras nodded and BJ sauntered down the stairs. BJ didn't know that Bobby Ray had given Mrs. Torras a key to the apartment a long time ago just in case something happened when he wasn't home.

Just as the door to the Turnbull apartment was closed; Leah and Misty came out of the bedroom.

"Is she gone?" asked Leah.

"Yes, she is," replied Mrs. Torras.

"Good, we didn't want to get in her way. She can get so mad. Are you going to be getting us ready for school and fixing our meals again?"

"Yes, I am," said Mrs. Torras.

The two girls yelled, "Yeah".

Mrs. Torras smiled, told them to go get ready for school and turned into the kitchen to see what was there to fix for the girls breakfast. She knew she could make a list for Mr. Turnbull and he would buy the things she needed for the house.

Once the girls were dressed and seated in the kitchen having their breakfast, Mrs. Torras went into the bedroom to get the new baby. When she walked in the room she couldn't help but notice that the missus had left clothes thrown all around and the big bed wasn't even made. She also noticed that the small bed the girls shared was at least pulled together. When she got to the bassinette she found baby Edna all cleaned and ready to be fed. This surprised her because in all the time she'd been working for the Turnbull's she had never found a baby clean in the morning. She wondered what was different about this child that the mother was taking care of her.

Mrs. Torras brought the baby out to the kitchen, fixed a bottle for her and sat with the children while they ate.

"Did ya notice mama cleaned the baby up before she left?" asked Misty.

"Yes, I did", replied Mrs. Torras.

"She likes this baby. I heard her say that to somebody she was talking to on the phone", said Leah.

"Me too. I heard her too", said Misty. "Does that mean she doesn't like us?"

"No. I don't think that. Some peoples just really love having babies. You girls are so big you hardly need your mama any more", explained Mrs. Torras.

Leah responded, "I heard her say that too. I heard her say that we were in school so she didn't have to do nothing for us no more. Then I heard her say that if it wasn't for the baby she'd be long gone."

Mrs. Torras didn't know how to respond, so she just nodded and continued feeding the baby.

After she walked the Turnbull girls and her children to the bus stop and saw them safely get on the school bus, she returned to the Turnbull apartment and started cleaning. It would take her most of the day to get the place almost clean. She only stopped to feed and change the baby and to go to her own apartment to get lunch. Late in the afternoon she started dinner for both her family and the Turnbull's. By the time Bobby Ray came home the hallway smelled heavenly.

When he walked in the door to his apartment he exclaimed, "I don't know how you do it, Mrs. Torras, but this whole building smells so good and this place is once again spotless. You're wonderful!"

Mrs. Torras just smiled and turned to stir the pot on the stove one more time and to turn the flame down to a simmer.

To Bobby Ray she said, "This can be turned off and reheated if you want to wait until your wife comes home."

"Thanks, but I stopped waiting to eat dinner with her years ago. The girls and I need to eat. She can reheat it if she wants anything when she comes home."

Mrs. Torras took off her apron and started walking to the door to leave. Just as she got to the door Bobby Ray asked her, "What time did my wife leave this morning?"

"Right after you did."

"What? She left that early?"

"Yes, she did. She came over banging on my door and yelling something awful until I answered the door and came over. She said she was going to miss her bus."

"Are you sure? I left at 6:30 this morning."

"Yes, I know. We talked in the hall. Remember? She came over right after you left. She was dressed in some tight pants, tee shirt and high shoes. I've never seen her dressed like that before. I was surprised to see her so early and dressed like that."

Bobby Ray just nodded his head. Then he said, "Thank you. See you in the morning. I'll talk to BJ tonight and see why she left so early. It's not right you having to come over so early."

"It's all right Mr. Turnbull. I don't want no trouble. I feed the girls and then we all walk to the bus stop. Your wife said I couldn't have no key. But I have one already. I didn't think I should tell her. She gets so mad about things."

"You did right. I'm just sorry she got you here so early."

"No problem. I'll see you tomorrow."

Then Bobby Ray called to his girls, "Ready for dinner?"

The two girls came running out of the bedroom where they'd been doing their homework. "Yes", they yelled.

"We could hardly wait cause everything smelled so good", said Misty.

"Yes, it does. Yes, it does", said their father.

With that, the three of them sat down and enjoyed a wonderful dinner. Not one of them mentioned the fact that BJ wasn't there. Not one of them suggested they should wait to eat until BJ got home.

After dinner, Bobby Ray told the girls to get their bath and to be sure and wash their hair. He always felt BJ was wrong in telling the girls they didn't have to take a bath if they didn't want to. He didn't understand why she was like that with the girls. She enjoyed taking a long bath herself.

After both girls had bathed, they came into the living room, sat on the couch and started watching television while their dad worked on a toaster he'd brought home.

About 7:30pm Bobby Ray heard a car screech its brakes out front. He looked out and saw BJ getting out of a pick up truck. She was staggering a little as she walked up the sidewalk. He didn't have to ask her where she had been. He knew she'd stopped at her social club. He wondered where she got the money this time, as he hadn't given her any. When she walked in the apartment she spotted the girls in the living room and immediately started shouting.

"What are they still doing up?"

"It's early, Bobbie Jo", Bobby Ray calmly replied not even looking up from his work.

Still talking very loudly BJ answered, "I go outta the house one time and ya let them get away with staying up late and I told you never to call me that. My name is BJ. Are ya trying to make me mad on purpose?"

Quietly Bobby Ray responded, "You don't need to shout. We're all sitting right here. Do ya want the whole neighborhood to hear what ya have to say? Ya know I keep the windows open for fresh air."

Now BJ was almost screaming, "I go out to earn some money so's we can get a little ahead and this is how ya treat me. Next think I know ya'll be hitting me again. Is that what ya're gonna do?"

Quietly Bobby Ray answered his wife, "BJ, I ain't never hit ya in ya're whole life. I don't think nobody's ever hit ya. I think that's part of the problem with ya."

"Whadda ya mean?"

A little louder Bobby Ray said, "I mean, ya probably needed to be smacked good a couple a times and nobody's ever done it."

With that BJ ran into the bedroom and slammed the door. Bobby Ray looked at his two daughters and smiled at them. "Don't worry. Mommy's just very tired. She worked hard today and she's a little mad at daddy."

"Okay, daddy", said Leah.

Just then the bedroom door opened a crack and BJ ordered the girls to come to bed.

Bobby Ray quietly said, "I guess ya better go. I'll try and talk to her tomorrow morning."

Both girls responded in a whisper, "Okay, daddy. Good night."

Once the bedroom was shut, Bobby Ray went back to repairing the toaster he'd been working on. He'd promised it would be ready to be picked up in the morning. He had to finish so he could drop it off at Moody's on his way to the plant.

After the girls were in the bedroom and the door was shut, BJ started talking very quietly to her girls. She was educating them in her way of doing things. She wanted them to know how all men were and she wanted them to know early so they didn't make the same mistakes she did.

"Do ya remember what I told ya about where babies come from?" BJ asked her 9 and 10-year-old daughters.

"Yes, momma, they replied in unison.

"Do ya remember what I told a about how they get put in ya're belly?" BJ asked.

Once again they replied in unison, "Yes, momma."

"Good. Now did ya hear how he was talking to me?"

"Yes, momma."

"And ya know what I told ya about him making me go ta work if's I want to buy ya pretty things."

"Yes, momma."

"Well, now ya heard him talking about hitting me and all. Before my babies came, he used to hit me all the time. But he don't want ya to see him hitting me cause then ya could tell what ya saw. But ya heard him say I deserved to be hit, didn't ya?"

"Yes, momma."

"That's what men do. They screw ya and put babies in ya're belly and then they hit ya. That's all men want."

"Yes, momma."

"So's ya have ta be smarter then them. And we girls have ta stick together. Remember, ya don't ever tell him anything we talk about. Ya don't ever tell him all the things I'm teaching ya. Ya gotta be sneaky. Ya gotta listen to all he says with that Mexican lady and tell me everything. Ya gotta listen to what she says during the day and tell me everything she says too. Okay? But remember, ya don't be telling anybody what we talk about. It's family business."

"Yes, momma."

Satisfied that her girls had learned another valuable lesson, she told them to go to bed. When they said they hadn't brushed their teeth yet, she said, "Don't matter if ya do that. Just go ta bed and don't make any noise."

The girls did as their mother said and before long, they heard the window to the communal bedroom opening. Not moving, Leah opened her eyes to see what was going on. She saw her mother crawling out of the window onto the fire escape. However, she must have moved her head a little because BJ looked at her and hissed, "If ya know what's good for ya, ya won't tell. Understand!" Leah nodded her head and shut her eyes. She knew this would be the next night's lesson.

Out in the living room, Bobby Ray heard the fire escape creak and walked to the living room window to see what was going on. What he saw surprised him. His wife was walking out to that same truck that had dropped her off earlier that evening. He wondered if it had waited for her and he wondered where she was going. In some ways he didn't care, but it hurt just the same. He decided he would wait and see if she would continue to sneak out each night. He also decided he needed to find out more about the place where she worked.

After watching her drive away, Bobby Ray went into the bedroom to tuck his children in. He knew neither one of them was asleep, but he also know they wouldn't let him know they were still awake. When he tried to hug them, they stiffened their little bodies. He didn't know why, but it made him sad.

The next morning BJ was coming out of the bedroom just as Bobby Ray was packing his lunch. "Want me to make ya a sandwich for you're lunch?" he asked her.

"Yuck! I wouldn't eat that stuff. I buy my lunch", she replied with distain.

"Well, I eat this stuff to save a little money."

"Fine. I gotta make me some tea. Ya need to tell ya're Mexican lady friend she needs ta make tea in the afternoon so's the girl and I can have some that's already cold in the morning. I don't like it when it's warm."

"I'm surprised to see ya up so early."

"I gotta go ta work."

"Kinda early."

"Trucking companies start early ya know."

Bobby Ray just nodded. Then he asked, "Sleep well?"

"Like a baby. Fell asleep as soon as my head hit the pillow."

Bobby Ray just nodded. He decided not to tell her he knew she didn't get in until after 1am. "Well, I'm off."

"Ya're leaving early."

"I gotta drop this toaster of at Moody's. The lady wants to pick it up first thing this morning."

"Whatever!"

"What do ya mean by that?"

"Nothing. Just that I want ya to know that I know what ya're up to", responded BJ.

"I ain't up ta nothing. I'm working two jobs so's we can get ahead. I ain't got time for nothing else."

"Right."

"BJ are ya trying to pick a fight so early this morning?"

"Nope. Just telling it like it is."

Bobby Ray shook his head then asked, "What time ya gonna be home tonight?"

"About the same time as last night."

"Them's long hours ya're working. Ya getting paid over time?"

"What's it to ya. This's my business, not ya'res."

Bobby Ray responded sadly by saying, "I gotta go or I'll be late."

After he left, BJ sat down with her warm tea, which she hated, and wrote a list of things for Mrs. Torras to do during the day. At the top of the list was making a big pitcher of tea with three cups of sugar in it. She underlined the words three cups of sugar. The only thing she hated more than warm tea was tea without enough sugar in it.

Having completed writing the list, she went into check on baby Edna. The baby was sleeping so she left her alone and got dressed to go to work. When she finished dressing she once again checked on baby Edna. Seeing she was still asleep she picked up her handbag and went to knock on Mrs. Torras' door to tell her to come to work. When the knock was answered, BJ told Mrs. Torras she'd left the door to the apartment open so she could get in and that she'd left a list of things to be done on the kitchen table.

It was then she said, "The baby was still asleep so you'll have to give her a both and feed her. I have some special soap for her bath that I keep in the kitchen. It's behind the trashcan so them older girls don't ahold of it. Be sure and keep them away from it. It's expensive and I don't them wasting it. Ya understand?"

"Yes, I understand", replied Mrs. Torras. As she watched Leah walk away she thought, *No. I don't understand. I've known you since you started having babies. This is the first baby you've ever cared about. I wonder why the older girls can't have bubble baths, but the baby can have special soap. I wonder why the older girls have to dress themselves and comb their own hair. I wonder why you don't care for those girls, but the new baby you do. No. I don't understand anything about you.*

Instead of saying anything, she checked on her children to be sure they were up and getting dressed and then went to her neighbor's apartment to wake the older girls up. She always knocked very quietly on the door before she started opening it. As usual she started her little sing-song voice to wake them, just as she did her children.

"Sandman's gone. Time to wake up now. Beautiful children, are you waking up?"

Both girls always woke with a smile after hearing their caretaker. They both felt mornings were happy times. Leah said, "We're getting up right now. We heard momma leave and we was waiting for you to call us."

This warmed Mrs. Torras heart. She smiled at them and said, "I made some extra biscuits last night and I warmed them up this morning so all my children could have them with honey and a big glass of milk. Does that sound good?"

The girls looked at each other and then back to Mrs. Torras. Misty said, "Will they make us fat?" Then Leah said, "Momma said milk is for babies and it's too expensive so we can't drink it anymore."

Mrs. Torras didn't quite know what to say to them. Looking at Misty, who was very thin, she said, "No. They won't make you fat. That is unless you're gonna eat all that I made and you can't do that because we're all going to share."

Hearing that, Misty seemed a little less nervous.

Then looking at the older girl, Leah, who was so thin you could almost count her ribs Mrs. Torras said, "Well in my house everyone drinks milk, even me. But if your momma said you can't drink milk, okay. What are you supposed to drink? Water?"

"Momma said we're supposed to drink tea. She said it has to have lots of sugar and we're supposed to drink two full glasses before meals. She says we can have all we want to eat after we drink all our tea."

Mrs. Torras was shocked. "I wouldn't have any room for food if I drank two glasses of anything before I ate. Do you have any room for food after drinking all that?"

Leah hung her head and said, "Not usually."

"If you don't eat anything, don't you get hungry after awhile?"

"Yes, but momma says I can always have more tea."

"Well, biscuits with honey don't taste very good with tea. Do you think she'd mind if you had milk this one time? I did go to a lot of trouble to bake all those biscuits."

"She'd know if too much of the milk was gone. She'd know Edna didn't drink that much", said Misty who really wanted the milk and biscuits.

"How about I go get some milk from my house?"

Misty thought would be okay, but Leah was still very nervous. However, Mrs. Torras went to her apartment and got a pitcher of milk for the Turnbull children. She also picked up a tiny glass that she used for measuring out medicine for her children. When she got back into the Turnbull apartment the girls were getting dressed. She called them to come to the table to eat. Misty bounded right into the kitchen but Leah held back.

"Leah, I know you have to do what your momma says to do, but I have a question for you. Did your momma say how big a glass of tea you had to drink before you could eat?"

Leah thought for a minute and then said, "No, she didn't say how big, she just said it had to be full."

"All right then, here's a glass you can drink your tea from" and she put the tiny glass on the table.

Leah looked at the glass and her eyes flashed just for a moment. "Is that a real glass, like one you drink from?"

"Yes, it is. All my children have used it at one time or another."

"Okay. I guess it would be all right, but I have to have two full glasses of tea before I can have a biscuit."

Mrs. Torras smiled and said, "Fine, you just sit down and drink your tea while I get the biscuits, honey and milk on the table." Then she poured the little glass full of the warm tea their mother had made that morning.

Leah drank first. She made an awful face once it got in her mouth.

"Don't you like tea, Leah?"

Leah swallowed and said, "No. But momma says I have ta learn to cause that's all we can afford."

Then Misty drank her first full glass of tea. She, too, made a face.

Mrs. Torras filled the little glass for the third time and watched Leah still make a face when she drank. Finally she filled the glass for the fourth time and watched Misty drink.

"Well, now that you both have had two full glasses of that awful, sweet tea, are you ready for some biscuits and honey?"

In unison, both girls said they were. Then Leah quietly asked, "Milk too?"

Mrs. Torras put two big glasses on the table and started filling them with milk. Her reply was, "Yes, milk too." As she watched the two girls gobble the biscuits and honey she couldn't help but wonder what their mother was doing to them. She also decided she was going to have to find another medicine glass so the girls could drink at the same time.

Things continued about the same for the next few years.

Bobby Ray's routine of going to work early at the plant, stopping at Moody's to pick up an appliance or two that needed repairing and being home no later than 6pm so he could have dinner with his children remained the same.

BJ still left for work very early and she still came home late while continuing to sneak out most nights. She also continued her little nightly talks with her older girls.

Mrs. Torras continued to find ways to do the best she could for the Turnbull children.

BJ still kept all of her paycheck. She didn't contribute to the household expenses at all and never bought much for the older girls. However, each week when she got paid, she would bring a little something home to Edna.

Bobby Ray had done some checking on the transport company where BJ worked and found out nothing good. He'd found the transport company did start work early, but he also found out the office people got off work at 2pm. BJ worked in the office, but never came home right after work. She sometimes went to her social club and other times she went to a pool hall over by the transport company and waited for the drivers to get off work. What Bobby Ray was told was she liked the pool hall better than the social club because she didn't have to worry about whether her old man would walk in on her.

He didn't like it but when his wife was working and partying she was easier to live with. He couldn't take the complaining and screaming. This way he didn't have to worry about what she was doing with the house money. Plus he was putting some money in the savings account every week when he cashed his check.

Bobby Ray still had hopes of saving enough money so he could buy a little house in the country for him and the girls. He thought someday BJ might get a wild hair and leave him and the girls. He hoped he'd have enough for a down payment on a house by the time she got tired of being with the family.

CHAPTER 7

Edna turned 5 and BJ threw a big birthday party for her. Leah and Misty were surprised when they heard their mother talking with a friend about a party for "her baby". She had never given them a party. They'd been lucky if she even remembered their birthdays and came home to have dinner with them. The other surprise was BJ invited Mrs. Torras and all her children.

BJ arranged for the party to be held in the yard in back of the apartment building. She had a cake from the bakery down the street, ice cream and lots of lemonade. Everyone was having a wonderful time when out of nowhere BJ said to Mrs. Torras, "Well, I guess you'll have to go find yourself another job now."

Mrs. Torras was startled and said to her, "What do you mean, Mrs. Turnbull? Are you quitting your job and staying home with the children?"

"Of course not, but since Edna will be in school this year, we won't be needin' your services anymore."

"Who's gonna get them ready for school?" asked Bobby Ray overhearing the conversation.

"They don't need no help. Leah and Misty can make sure that Edna is dressed and fed before they leave. They're big girls now, they don't need a baby sitter no more."

"Fine, BJ. But who's gonna clean the house, buy the groceries, wash and iron the clothes. You know, all the stuff you never done."

BJ was furious and started screaming, "I ain't gonna have you paying this Mexican one more dime when we have almost grown girls who can do that kinda work."

"Bobbie Jo! You can't expect them to go to school, get good grades and take care of the house too. They're just little girls. They need to have time to be children and have fun."

"There you go again' takin' up for them good for nothin' kids. They're stupid and ugly and they're old enough they need to be looking for a man to keep'um. I'm getting' tired of them being around the house all the time."

"Bobbie Jo,"

"Stop calling me that," she screamed.

"Okay! BJ! They're only 13 and 14. They have a long time before they need to be thinking about gettin' married."

"Who cares if they git married? I just want them gone!" With that said she threw her glass filled with lemonade at Bobby Ray. Then she walked over to the picnic table where the cake was, picked up what was left and threw it at Mrs. Torras.

"And I'm tired of her hangin' around all the time. She's tryin' to turn my kids into Mexicans and she's tryin' to take you away from me. Girls, look at her. She's fat. She's ugly. She ain't got no man so's she's trying to take mine. She can't, cause I keep any man I get and I can get any man I want!" After screaming all of that, she left the birthday party and walked out of sight.

Bobby Ray and Mrs. Torras just stood there totally embarrassed. After a couple of minutes, Mrs. Torras started cleaning up the mess BJ had made. With a few tears in her eyes she asked Leah and Misty, "Help me clean this up, will you?"

"Hell, no!" shouted Leah. "That's your job, not mine. You're the hired help so you do it."

Misty said, "Yeah. Hell, no! We got places to go. Don't we Leah?"

"Yeah, so let's go or we'll be late."

Misty and Leah were laughing as they followed the path their mother took to leave the party.

Once again Mrs. Torras was stunned. She bent to clean up the cake and Bobby Ray came over to help her.

"I think I now have three of them in the house. I've been trying to keep this from happening. I guess I failed."

"You can only do so much. Why does she have to be so mean and say such terrible things?"

"I don't know, Mrs. Torras. I just don't know."

"Mr. Turnbull, after all these years I think it would be all right to call each other by our first names. Especially since I won't be working for you anymore."

"You're right. My name is Bobby Ray. You will be working for me, but I'd still like you to call me that."

"What will your wife say?"

"How much more can she say than she's already said?"

"True."

"So what's your given name?" Bobby Ray asked his friend.

"Gloria."

"Fine, Gloria. After school starts we can figure out a schedule because I don't think those girls of mine are gonna be doing anything to help out. It will be less than before, so I'd understand if you need to get another job so you can get by. Let me know."

"Okay. We can talk about it after school starts."

The following weeks were tough on Bobby Ray. He was working overtime at the plant and he was still working for Moody doing the appliance repairs. He liked working with Moody. He was learning something new all the time and he was enjoying himself. Since the plant started working him overtime it was hard. Gloria always made sure he had dinner waiting so that wasn't a problem, but his wife and two oldest daughters were never home when he got there. When he'd ask Gloria where the girls were, she'd simply say they went out with their mother. He stopped asking about Edna, because the answer was always the same. BJ had fed her dinner and put her in bed before knocking on Gloria's door to tell her to listen out for any problems. He never understood how his wife could say so many nasty things about Gloria and then demand she listen out for her youngest child while she went out. BJ never even offered to pay Gloria for the babysitting.

Each night BJ would bring Leah and Misty, who were only 13 and 14, home about 10pm. She'd drop them off and then take off again. If Bobby Ray asked the girls where they'd been, they'd answer, "With mom". If he asked what they had been doing, they'd laugh and answer, "Doin' girl things" and that would be the end of the conversation.

BJ no longer got up early for work. In fact, he didn't know if she was even working. All he knew was Gloria would hear her leave sometime around noon. Getting the girls up for school fell to him. He'd quietly wake Edna who would get herself ready. Then he'd try to wake Leah and Misty. Sometimes he'd succeed and sometimes he wouldn't. Many weeks went by with him insisting the girls get up so they wouldn't be late for school. Most times he incurred BJ's wrath for making so much noise so early. After awhile his attempts to make sure they got up became half hearted. He felt BJ would get the call from the school and that would be enough for her to start taking some responsibility. When the girls wouldn't get up, he let them sleep. He rationalized it was very early and they could sleep in another hour. He was sure BJ would be able to get them up. He just didn't worry about it anymore.

Then one day in December he came home and Gloria was waiting for him.

"What a pleasant surprise", he said to his friend.

"Not so pleasant. I have to tell you what happened today", she replied to him.

Visibly upset he cried, "Did someone get hurt and they didn't let me know at work?"

"No, but the police were here today."

"What? The police? What did they want?"

"They were looking for you and your wife and the two girls."

Gloria didn't need to tell Bobby Ray what two she was talking about. Instead he asked, "What did they want for heavens sake?"

"The girls haven't been going to school."

"What? The girls aren't going to school? I had no idea. Well, maybe I did but I guess I didn't want to believe it. Where're they now?"

"Edna's in the bedroom and I don't know where the other's are. They all left about the time the buses came. I thought they went to work and school at the same time."

"They haven't come home yet?"

"No. She called me and told me to feed Edna tonight because she was going to be late. The police told me to tell you and the missus that you'd better call them the minute you get in. Here's the number they left."

"Thanks and sorry for the trouble. I just don't know what's going on." Right then both Bobby Ray and Gloria heard voices in the hallway.

Gloria said, "I'll be in trouble again with her".

Before Bobby Ray could answer her, the door to the apartment flew open and in walked his two oldest daughters, but no BJ.

"Where have you been?"

"What's she doing here?" cried Leah in an accusing voice.

"If it is any of your business, she was delivering a message from the police. Answer my question?"

"What're you in trouble with the police for?"

"I'm not. You two are. Now answer my question."

"We was just out having some fun", replied his youngest daughter, Misty. "How're we in trouble? We didn't do nothin'."

"Right. That's exactly right. You didn't do nothin'."

The girls started laughing. "See we can't be in trouble so we're goin' to bed."

"No you ain't. Sit down cause ya're in trouble."

The girls stared at him and decided to sit down. Gloria took that opportunity to slip out the still open front door. In her heart she wished her friend luck. She knew he would need her wishes and more to get through those two growing up.

Bobby Ray spent the next half hour talking to his two daughters. He finally stopped talking when he realized all of his lecturing on how important school was and how important it was to get an education was being wasted. This was the day that he gave up on them. As they were yawning and talking to each other instead of listening to him, he realized he'd lost them. Instead of saying anything to them about how disappointed he was in them, he just got up from the couch and walked away.

"Ya done?" asked Leah.

"Yeah. I'm done", answered Bobby Ray.

"Good, cause we're tired", Leah replied. With that, the two girls got up and walked into the bedroom all the women in the house shared.

Bobby Ray always slept on the couch now. It was easier on him. Everything would be even easier on him now. He decided he wouldn't try anymore to wake the girls up for school. BJ had won. Even though she had a good education, she didn't think it was worth anything for the girls to attend school. He didn't know how many times he'd heard her tell them that she would be the one to teach them what they needed to know about life. Bobby Ray had always been afraid to ask her what she meant. In his heart he knew. She was teaching the girls how to party like an adult. He didn't like it but there was nothing he could do about it. In the morning he'd call the school and tell them he was no longer to be contacted about the girls. He'd them what the girls were doing and how their mother encouraged it. He'd tell them everything.

Just after midnight, Bobby Ray heard BJ come in the apartment. "I've been waiting for you to come home."

"Well, I'm tired and I don't wanna listen to anything you have ta say."

"Yeah, well you're gonna listen cause the cops were here looking for the girls and you."

BJ was wide-awake now. "What do ya mean?"

"I thought what I said was plain enough. The girls haven't been going to school and the cops were sent out to the house this afternoon."

"What were you doing home in the afternoon? Cutting work so's ya can spend time with your girl friend? Don't ya think I know it's still goin' on?"

"I wasn't home. Mrs. Torras told me they were here."

"What business is it of hers?"

"The cops knocked on her door when they couldn't get ahold of anybody here. They said you had to call them in the morning. Here's the number."

BJ took the card from her husband and then said. "These ain't real cops. This heres a number at the school. They must'a been the truant cops. I ain't afraid of them."

"BJ, this isn't about being afraid of them. This is about the girls not going to school. Did you know they weren't going?"

"Yeah. So what? I'm taking them with me most days so's they can help me and so's they can learn what girls need to learn. School's a waste. Don't teach nothin' a body needs to know. I'm home schoolin' them, that's what I'm doing."

"Well then, you need to call them tomorrow so's they know you're home schoolin' them. If'n ya don't they'll be sending them cops out again."

"Fine. Fine. I'll call um if'n I get the chance. Get off my back. They're my children and they're gonna do what I think they should do - so butt out."

"You got it, BJ. I'm butting out. Just to let ya know, I'm calling the school tomorrow and telling them the girls belong to you and I don't got no say in what happens with them. Isn't that what ya're sayin'?"

"That's right!"

"Funny how things change. When ya were birthin' them ya never told anybody ya was pregnant and led people to believing that I had them babies with somebody else and was makin' you to take care of them. Now all of a sudden, them girls belong totally to you. Real funny!"

BJ didn't respond to her husband's remarks. She just shrugged her shoulders and walked into the shared bedroom.

As she shut the door, Leah said to her, "Ya sur' told him."

"Yeah, I sure did - now go to sleep. I'm tired."

"Momma. Is what I heard true?"

"What's that?"

"That we don't havta go ta school no more."

"I don't know. I gotta call the school tomorrow and see what I can work out. I don't wanna have ya wasting your time goin' there all the time. I'll let ya know what I work out."

"That'd sure be nice. What about Edna? Will she hafta go?"

"Yes. She hasta go."

"Why? If we don't hafta go, why does she?"

"Shut up! Just shut up," BJ screamed at her daughter. "She does cause I says she does. Now shut up and go to sleep before I give ya somethin' to make ya sleep forever!"

Leah knew she had pushed her mother too far so she turned over and pretended to go to sleep.

The next morning, Bobby Ray called the school and told them what BJ had said. They told him he'd have to come to the school to sign some papers in order to take him off the emergency call list. They went on to tell him that until he signed the papers, he was still responsible for the girls getting to school. Upon hearing that, he told them he would be in that day on his lunch hour. As he hung up the phone, he went to his supervisor and told him there was

something he had to take care of at his daughters' school and asked
if he could leave the plant on his lunch hour. The supervisor said it
was all right, but requested that Bobby Ray not take any longer than
necessary. Bobby Ray assured him he would eat his lunch in the car
and would be back to work as quickly as possible.

When his lunch hour came, Bobby Ray went to the school. The
paperwork was ready for him to sign so he was able to get back to
work very quickly. He didn't like doing what he'd just done, but
there was no way he was going to be held responsible for his
children when he had no say over what they were doing. He signed
the paperwork to protect himself. That night when he got home, the
apartment was empty as usual. Right after he walked in and started
thinking he needed to fix something for his dinner, there was a
knock at the door. His heart jumped a little. When he opened it, he
found Gloria standing there with a small casserole pot in her hands.

"I thought you might want to share some of what I cooked for
dinner. I always cook too much."

"Thanks. You wanna come in for a minute?"

"Sure, as long as it won't get your missus mad."

"She won't be home for hours. I wanted to tell you how sorry I
am for her yelling at you and saying we didn't need you anymore."

"I understand. Things change. Things have changed in my house
too. My two oldest children are out on their own, so now I only
have the one boy left with me. You helped me a lot by giving me a
job when I couldn't go out to work because of all the children being
at home. I really appreciate it."

"The bad part is we still need you, but I don't want you to
continue being a slave to my wife."

"I understand."

Bobby Ray went on to tell his friend what he had done that day
at the school and what his wife had said to him about the girls.

"She's sick in the head, Bobby. She's been sick in the head
forever. It's not your fault."

"I know, but somehow I can't help but think there was something I could have done. I keep thinking there's something I still
can do. This is a terrible life. I've been working two jobs so we
could buy a house someday. And do you know what I found out not
too long ago?"

"No. What?"

"I found out all the money I thought was in the bank being saved for the house, ain't there. All the money I thought she was depositing in the savings account was never put there. Plus I just found out that since I took over going to the bank with my own checks and I've been putting money for sure in the savings account, there still ain't no money there."

"What happened to it?"

"According to the bank records, I'd deposit the money on Friday after work and it would be withdrawn on the following Monday."

"How can that be?" asked Gloria.

"Me, like a fool, put my wife's name on the account all those years ago. Now I can't take it off without her permission or without closing the account. I don't wanna do that cause then she would know I knew what she's done. I'm saving that information.

Someday she's gonna file for divorce and will be wanting money. I want the proof that she already got it."

"Open another account."

"What?"

"I'd open another account, but maybe at another bank."

"Why?"

"Well, you want to save some money. Right?"

"Right."

"If you keep putting it in the same account, she'll keep taking it out. Right?"

"Right."

"And if you open another account at the same bank, the bank people might just tell her and then she'd be mad. Right?"

"Right."

"So if you stop cashing your check at that bank and stop putting money in that savings account she'll still be mad, but she can't say anything to you without you finding out what she's been doing. Right?"

"Right."

"So then you find another bank. You open an account there and you put the money in that account. She won't know. She'll be mad but what can she say without telling you what she's been doing?"

"I can do that. In fact, I always have to hurry to get to the bank before it closes on Friday because it's so far from work. I got it close to home to begin with so she could walk there. I could get a bank closer to work."

"Sure you could. She'd never have to know. She would suspect something was up, but she would never know. Or you could cash your check at the bank she knows about but not put anything in the account. That way if she asked if you had been in, the bank people would say yes and she would be even more confused."

"I'll have to think about what'd be best. Thanks for the information and thanks for dinner. Let me wash this dish for you and I'll bring it back."

"No, just hand it to me. I'll wash it with my other dishes. What do the children do for dinner?"

"Don't know."

"Where's Edna? I guess the older girls are with their mother, but Edna is usually home."

"Don't know that either, but I'm gonna try and find out. I had hoped that she at least would still be going to school."

Gloria just nodded. There wasn't much she could say to her friend. She knew that no one had left for school that morning. She knew that a man came by the house almost every day about 10am. She knew that her friend's wife was cheating on him with the girls in the apartment. She knew, but she couldn't tell him. He was a nice man. He didn't deserve as bad a wife as he had. He didn't deserve to have tramps for daughters. If he would ask her if she knew anything she'd tell him, but she would never tell him without his asking. She'd say a little prayer for him tonight. She used to say prayers for the girls, but now she only says them for him. The girls had chosen their way and her prayers were wasted on them. She liked Bobby. She wished he were Hispanic instead of white. She might be interested in him as more than a friend if he was.

The next Friday, Bobby Ray hurried to the bank just like usual. This time, however, he just cashed his check. The teller was surprised. "Don't you want to make your normal deposit in the savings account?" he asked.

"No. Not today", Bobby Ray replied. The teller looked at him a little strange, but said nothing more. Bobby Ray had wanted her to say something so he would have the opportunity to ask some questions. Because the teller remained quiet, so did Bobby Ray. When he walked out of the bank with the extra money in his pocket, he felt a little guilty. BJ had been taking money out of the savings every Monday for years. One side of his brain said she must have needed the money to buy necessities. The other side of his brain wondered if he was insane. BJ was working. He was paying all the bills and buying all the groceries. He provided all the necessities. Walking to his car Bobby Ray wondered what Monday would bring.

When he got home he walked over to Gloria's apartment. "Would you be able to do me a favor?" he asked his long time friend.

"Sure", she said without hesitation. "Could you keep this $20 for me? This is normally what I put in the savings account. I didn't do it today, but I don't want to be carrying it around either. I can't keep it in the house; cause BJ or one of the girls would find it. I know it'll be safe with you."

"Sure. I'll find a place to hide it for you. No problem."

"Thanks."

"Do you want to eat dinner with us? It's all ready."

"Sure. This way it'll save you from having to wash an extra dish."

This was the beginning of what would happen every Friday night from then on. In fact, Bobby Ray would eat dinner with Gloria and her son every night he got home by 6:30pm. After awhile Bobby started giving Gloria money for groceries and just about stopped buying groceries for the house, except for cereal, bread and lunch meat.

The Monday after Bobby Ray's first visit to the bank without making a deposit in their savings account, BJ went there to make her normal withdrawal. As usual she stopped at the podium in the center of the bank and made out the withdrawal slip. She then walked to the window of the teller she had made friends with and slid the slip of paper. She smiled at the teller and said, "This is a fine morning isn't it? I'll just have the usual amount, thank you."

BJ hadn't noticed, but the teller wasn't smiling. In fact, the moment she'd seen BJ walk in the door she'd franticly tried to get the head teller's attention to ask if she could leave her position for a few minutes. She had not been successful and was forced into facing BJ.

"I'm sorry, BJ, but I can't give you the money", she said.

"What", was BJ's reply.

Softly the teller once again said, "I'm sorry but I can't give you any money."

BJ had heard her correctly, but she still didn't understand. "Why not," she said a little too loudly. A couple of people in the bank turned to look her way to see why someone had spoken so loudly in the bank. Things were normally very quiet there.

The teller quietly motioned for BJ to come a little closer and then she said, "I can't give you any money today because there's none to give you."

"What", BJ shouted. "What do you mean, there's no money? This is a bank, of course there's money."

The teller was frantically trying to keep the whole situation quiet. She didn't want her supervisor coming over. She was always being told she was too friendly and got too close to the patrons of the bank. This would really make her supervisor mad. "BJ, you have to be a little quieter", she hissed.

"Quiet? I ain't gonna be quiet when you won't give me my money. I been takin' money outta here every Monday for years and I want my money just like usual. I ain't gonna be quiet until you give it ta me."

"BJ, I can't give you any money because your husband didn't put any in when he cashed his check."

This got BJ's attention and she became very quiet. Of course it was too late as everyone in the bank had their eyes riveted on her and the teller. BJ came very close to the window and hissed at the terrified teller, "What do you mean he didn't put any money in the account. He's been putting $20 to $40 in that account every Friday for years."

"You're right, except for this past Friday. He cashed his check and left."

"Why didn't you stop him?"

"I did remind him about his savings account, but I can't force someone to put money in the bank."

"What did he say when you asked him about it?"

"He just said, not today."

"I'll see about that tonight when he gets home. Well, how much can you give me?"

"There's only the $5 in there to keep the account open. I can't give that to you."

"Where's all the money gone that he's been putting in there."

"You take it out as fast as he puts it in."

"Look, I only take $10 or $20 at a time. I couldn't have taken it all."

"You have. I could show you if you like. When a withdrawal is made, a code is entered to show who took the money out. If it's the primary holder of the account, we have to enter in a 1. If it's the secondary holder of the account, we enter a 2. You're the secondary holder of the account so anything you take out is coded as a 2. Every withdrawal is coded as a 2."

"Damn. What is he doing with all the money he makes", BJ kind of muttered to herself. Leaning towards the teller she whispered, "You know he has lady friends on the side, don't you?"

When the teller didn't answer, BJ went on, "One of them is a Mexican who lives in the building where we do."

"That's none of my affair", responded the teller.

"Yeah, and the children are his ya know. He brought them home for me to raise. That's the kind of man he is. I don't know how I ever got mixed up with him." Then as quick as snapping your fingers, BJ's attitude totally changed, "Well, I'll see ya next Monday. Have a great day!" She then turned and walked out of the bank as if she had gotten the money she had requested.

Everyone in the bank, especially the teller, shook their heads and wondered if that woman had all her marbles. The head teller walked over to Belinda, the teller who had waited on BJ. "What was the problem with your last customer?"

Belinda gave her supervisor the short version of what had been going on for years and then what had transpired last Friday. She told the supervisor how crazy BJ had acted and what she had demanded. Belinda went on to tell the supervisor about the explanation of the withdrawal history and how BJ had responded. The supervisor had heard most of what had transpired and was looking to hear the teller's version. The teller had admitted to being a little too close to the situation and explained how she had tried on several occasions not to wait on BJ so that tie could be broken but with no success. After hearing the whole story the supervisor gave Belinda the authority to close her window and go to the back room whenever BJ came in the bank. She told Belinda, "If you see her come in again, find me so I can be sure someone else waits on her. You've done well handling the situation, but it's gotten out of hand. You did the right thing; however, someone else needs to take over from here on. We aren't supposed to do anything to lose customers, but I'm not worried about losing her as a customer. It appears if her husband is really our customer, so let's try to save his business. Next time you see him come in the bank, come and get me so I can talk to him."

Belinda was happy that she wouldn't have to deal with BJ any longer, but she knew it wouldn't be easy. She knew BJ's way of doing things. "Miss Nichols?"

"Yes?"

"If he comes in again, he won't be in again until Friday."

"Do you think he might not come in again?"

"I believe he's finally found out about what his wife's been doing and I think he'll probably start going to another bank."

"Do you know where he works?"

"The check he cashes is from the plant on the other side of town."

"Do we have a phone number for him?"

"Yes, it's on his account."

"I'll call him. If he works on the other side of town, it might be more convenient for him to bank at our branch office near the plant. I'll contact the head teller over there and explain the situation. Then I'll see if I can get hold of him."

Belinda sighed with relief. Maybe that would totally solve their problem and still keep him as a customer. It wouldn't keep BJ out of the bank, but if there was no money in the account then maybe she'd eventually stop coming in. Until then, Belinda intended to hide in the back room whenever she saw her.

All during the week Bobby thought about opening a savings account at a different bank, but never got around to doing anything about it. Before he knew it Friday had once again arrived and he was racing across town to cash his check.

Belinda was just finishing up with a customer when she spotted him walking in the door. She immediately walked over to her supervisor and told her Mr. Turnbull was in the bank.

"Who?"

"You remember last Monday? You remember the hassle with BJ? The lady who wanted to make the withdrawal from the savings account."

"Oh – right. I had forgotten. Ask Mr. Turnbull to come and see me, please."

"Right away, Miss Nichols", Belinda said and immediately walked over to her position. "I can help you over here Mr. Turnbull", she almost shouted.

Bobby Ray changed direction and headed towards the teller cage with the pretty brunette in it. "I didn't see you standing there."

"Well, I wasn't here a minute ago. I was talking with Miss Nichols, my supervisor."

"Oh, well at least I hadn't gone blind for a minute", replied Bobby Ray laughing a little.

"Mr. Turnbull, my supervisor would like to speak with you."

"What?"

"Miss Nichols would like to speak with you. We think we can do something to help you with the situation you're going through."

"What?"

Belinda leaned forward and whispered, "You know, the situation with the savings account."

Bobby Ray was startled. He didn't think anyone knew what BJ had been doing except him. He did want some help because he couldn't figure out what to do. "Where is she?"

"Come down to the end of the teller cages. There's a door there. I'll open it and show you where she is."

Bobby Ray just nodded and started walking to the end of the teller counter. As he got to the door he'd never noticed before, he heard a click and it opened. On the other side stood Belinda, now holding it open for him. As Bobby Ray walked in, she shut the door and he heard another loud click.

"Follow me."

Bobby Ray did as he was told and followed the brunette teller down a hall. She stopped in front of another door and knocked. From inside a woman's voice said to come in. The teller opened the door and said, "Miss Nichols this is Mr. Turnbull."

"Mr. Turnbull, please come in …and shut the door behind you if you would please."

Bobby Ray did as he was told and then said, "That teller lady said you might be able to help me with a situation I'm going through."

"Yes. Last Monday, Belinda, the teller who helped you today, had a customer who was giving her a hard time."

"Musta been my wife."

"Ah, yes it was. After Mrs. Turnbull left, Belinda explained the situation. She told me that for several years you've been coming in on Friday, cashing your check and depositing some of it in your savings account."

"That's right. I've been trying to save up for a down payment on a little house for me and my family."

"She also told me that for quite some time now your wife has been coming in on Monday and withdrawing money."

"Yep. I just found out about that not too long ago. BJ's been working, at least I'm told she's been working, and I thought she was spending her money not our savings."

"I'm so sorry. Now Belinda says she thinks you work on the other side of town. Is that true?"

"Yes. I work over at the plant."

"She thought she remembered that from your payroll checks."

"She's got a good memory."

"Yes she does and she cares about her customers. She's felt terrible about what's been happening each week, but there's been nothing she could do about it. That is not until this past week."

"What changed?"

"You didn't make a savings deposit and since there was nothing left in that account except the minimum to keep it open, your wife couldn't withdraw anything."

"How does that change anything?"

"You see your wife caused a scene."

"I'm so sorry. She does that a lot. Nuthin' I can do about it. I've tried."

"Not your fault so please don't feel you have to apologize."

Bobby Ray just nodded.

"Your wife making the scene brought the situation to my attention. That's when Belinda told me what's been happening. She also told me she felt you'd think your only option would be to close your account."

"She was right. I just never had time to get to another bank. I've banked here for so long, I didn't know where else to go."

"I'm glad, because you don't have to go anywhere."

"If'n I don't, I'll never be able to save anything."

"Yes, you will. We have a branch right around the corner from the main entrance to the plant. We opened it there just a few months ago."

"How does that help me? I don't know anybody there and if I don't have money in an account I won't be able to cash my checks. You people been nice cashing them when you knowed what was happenin'."

"We simply open you another savings account in just your name. We leave the joint account here and we transfer the other account to the branch office. I'm in charge of doing that so I would simply talk to the head teller there."

"How would that help?"

"You leave the joint account here, but you cash your check at the other location. Then you can put money in your savings account and she can't touch it."

"She'd find some way to get her hands on it."

"She can't. This isn't a community property state. This would be totally in your name. I checked our records and the joint account used to be just in your name. Isn't this correct?"

"Yep. It was mine before I was married."

"Okay then. I make a note on the account that the new account was a transfer from that original account. Besides, if she doesn't know about it, she can't touch it."

"It might work and then I wouldn't have to worry about getting a speeding ticket trying to get here before you close. Why're you doing this for me?"

"To be honest, Mr. Turnbull, this will help us as well."

"How?"

"You won't be cashing your check in this office and you won't be putting money in the joint savings account. Only Belinda, you and I will know there is another account in the other branch and we definitely aren't going to tell your wife about it."

"So?"

"So, for a couple of weeks your wife will still come in to see if there's money in the savings account. When there isn't, she's either going to stop coming in or she's going to ask if you came in to cash your check. Last Monday she asked Belinda if you had been in. Belinda will honestly be able to say you haven't been in and she'll eventually stop coming in. Then we'll have gotten rid of a problem."

"What if she goes to another teller?"

"Most of the tellers are aware of your wife, but if not they will simply tell her what they know and that is that there was no deposit made into the savings account."

"She'll be mad."

"Yes and she'll cause one last big scene and then it'll be over. Except, I'm sure you'll hear about it."

"No. I don't think so. Ya see, she doesn't think I'm smart enough to catch on to what she's been doin'. I didn't catch on for so long. I trusted her."

"That's what you're supposed to be able to do."

"Ok, I think this might work. I know it's past closing time now, so when can we set this other account up?"

"If you had the account open today, would you make a deposit?"

"Yes."

"Fine, then let's open that account. That way, I can immediately transfer it over to the other branch."

"It's Friday."

"I work late on Friday and we have a late courier over to the other branch. If we hurry, we can have this all taken care of and in place for you by Monday morning."

Bobby Ray was the last customer out of the bank. He was so late, the doors had already been locked and the guard had to get the key to let him out. Bobby had no idea that all the bank employees stayed after the bank closed. He thought they just went home. When the guard unlocked the door to let him out, Bobby Ray thanked him for his trouble.

"No trouble, Mr. Turnbull. No trouble at all. You have a nice weekend."

Bobby Ray hadn't been called Mr. Turnbull in a long time. The girl's teachers used to call him that, but no one else ever did. It was always Bobby Ray this and Bobby Ray that. He liked being called Mr. Turnbull once in awhile. Then he realized his supervisor didn't call him Bobby Ray anymore, he called him Bobby. Finally he realized he had started to think of himself as Bobby and not as Bobby Ray.

Sitting in his car he said out loud, "Bobby. My name is Bobby Turnbull. Mr. Bobby Turnbull." It sounded good to him. From now on, he decided, he'd introduce himself as Bobby. Bobby started his car and drove the short distance to his apartment. He was late, but he knew no one would be home. He'd have to apologize to Gloria for being late and explain to her what had happened at the bank. He talked over just about everything with her. Then he thought about dinner and he hoped she hadn't held dinner just for him. He didn't want it to be ruined for her.

Just as he expected, his apartment was quiet when he walked in. As he was cleaning his lunch box, the door opened and Edna walked in.

"Hurry up Daddy. We've been waiting for you and we're all hungry. Where've you been?"

"Sorry, honey. I got tied up. Let me wash up and I'll be over in just a minute."

"Ok, but just one minute and then we start without you", Edna said laughingly.

Bobby looked after her as she left and thought, "Perhaps she's learning from Gloria how to be a nice person. The other girls are lost to BJ and there's nothing I can do about it." He finished drying the lunch box, his hands, put the towel on it's hook and walked to the door to go have dinner with Gloria, Edna and Gloria's son. He knew the evening would be a pleasant one until his wife and older girls showed up.

After dinner Bobby said, "Well Edna, do you have any homework to do?"

"I already did it. Señora Torras helped me."

"Did you thank her?"

"Of course, I did. Then she let me help her make dinner. I made the tortillas all by myself."

"You did?"

"Yep!"

Bobby looked over at Gloria who had turned her head when the child started talking. She caught his eye and nodded yes every so slightly. "I'm really impressed. They were great! I guess we know who's gonna be cooking dinner at our house."

"Daddy. That's all I know how to make."

Just as Bobby was starting to answer his daughter, there was a terrible pounding on the door and it came flying open. Standing there was BJ and the two oldest girls.

"See there. I told ya he'd be here with his Mexican girl friend." BJ rushed over to Edna and slapped her hard on the face. "Didn't I tell you never to come over here? Didn't I?"

"Yes, but...."

BJ slapped Edna again before the child could finish her sentence. "Don't talk back to me", BJ screamed. "Get back to our place and don't never come here again. Do you understand me? Do you?", BJ howled.

Bobby hadn't had a chance to stop BJ from hitting Edna, but now he was standing next to his wife. "BJ, don't ever touch her again. The child hasn't done anything except be a good girl."

"That's what she is all right, just a good girl. She ain't gonna get nuthin' outta nobody by being a good girl. If'n I hav'ta slap her silly, she'll learn what she needs to learn. All she does is go to school and read books. I can't get her to listen to me at all."

"I think that's wonderful and I don't want you hitting her again."

"She belongs to me and I'll slap her whenever and wherever I please and you can't stop me. I'll just wait until you're gone and do what I want to the child. She's mine!"

"No, she's our child and I'll call the police on you."

"I have friends. They won't do nuthin' to me so go ahead and try."

"Don't push your luck, BJ. You've ruined two girls. I'd like the third to turn out normal."

BJ didn't respond to her husband. Instead she grabbed her youngest daughter by her hair and pulled her along as she walked out of the apartment.

Once again Bobby found himself saying he was sorry to Gloria. "Now I've brought that evil woman and her foul temper into your home. I'm so sorry."

Gloria just nodded. When BJ had burst into the room she had automatically moved to a position next to her son. She couldn't do anything to protect Edna but she could and would do everything in her power to protect her son.

"Thanks for the dinner. It was wonderful, as usual", said Bobby as he walked out the door and quietly shut it behind him. He was so angry with BJ. Gloria was right, the woman is sick in the head. He took the couple of steps to the door of his apartment, opened it and walked in. BJ was waiting for him.

"I don't want my baby with her ever again."

"Are you going to be home to cook her dinner and help her with her homework?"

"Maybe."

"If I come home and find you're not here with dinner started and she (waving his arm generally in the direction of Gloria's apartment) offers us a hot meal with good conversation, I'm taking her up on it."

"Even if'n I was home, there's no food in the house so I couldn't cook."

"Whose fault is that?"

"Yours."

"I figured you'd say that. Why is it my fault?"

"You don't give me any money to buy them with."

"That's true and you know why. You don't drive and you don't know how to shop. When I did give you grocery money we still didn't have food in the house because you spent it on other things. If you want this marriage to work, you're going to have to change a few things."

"Like what?"

"Like no more going out to party every night. Like getting the girls up for school and making sure they get there. Like making sure a hot meal is on the table for the family at night. Like cleaning the house."

"I ain't nobody's nigger."

"No you aren't. You're supposed to be a wife and a mother. Those jobs are part of it."

"What about my job?"

"Are you still working?"

"Yes."

"At the same place?"

"No. I had to be there too early and the bus always made me late so I quit."

"Okay. Where're you working now?"

"I just started a new job just around the corner."

"Okay. Where around the corner?"

"At the social club."

"What? What do you do there?"

"I'm learning how to be a waitress."

Bobby was skeptical as that's where his wife's party ways started.

"What hours do you work?"

"I just work the lunch time for now. That's just from 11am to about 2:30pm."

"How much are you paid?"

"As a trainee I get $.50 an hour plus tips. Once I larn what to do and do it good, it goes up to $.75. Tips is what waitresses make the most. Tips is good money."

"BJ, what made you start talking like you do?" Bobby just realized when he first met Bobbie Jo, she spoke so well and now she talked like an uneducated tramp. He also realized she used to dress nicely and now she dressed like she spoke. He wondered what happened to make her change.

"Whacha mean?"

"Just that. You run all your words together. You didn't used to do that. You have a fine education. Why don't you use it? You could be a bookkeeper trainee, not a waitress. Why don't you try for something better?"

"Do you really want to know why", asked BJ.

"Yes, I think I do", replied Bobby all the while hoping he could handle the answer.

"It scares men off."

The reply was just about what Bobby had expected. "You're married, BJ. Do you remember that? It shouldn't matter if you speak and dress nicely and scare men off. You already have a man – me."

"Bobby Ray. I'm staying with you only until the two oldest girls are gone. Once that happens I intend to find someone who'll take care of me proper like. So you might as well get used to the new me, because the old me only attracts men like you."

"Fine, but that's four or more years from now so let's stop with the act. We'll share the same apartment. You can go out and party when you want as long as the girls are in school and there's no trouble. We will eat as a family when your work allows. When you don't come home for dinner, the girls and I are free to eat dinner with the Torras family, if we're ever invited again. Since you don't have to be to work until 11am and it's right around the corner, you'll have plenty of time to clean the house and do the laundry."

"Are ya tryin' to work me ta death?"

"No, I'm just asking you to do something around the house. I'm working at the plant and with Moody so I don't have time to do much of anything else. A clean house, clean clothes and a meal on the table once in awhile is not much to ask. I pay all the bills and, believe it or not, buy all the food for the house. You don't contribute anything to this house except pain and misery."

"Oh yeah, well where's all the money goin'? There ain't nothin' in the bank and we don't have a house yet. If'n you got me a house I could be proud of it would be different around here."

"Yes, I know there's nothing in the bank. I found that out awhile back. You never put the money in the savings account like you were supposed to be doing when you were paying the bills. Plus when I started putting money in the account, you started taking it out faster than I could put it in."

BJ was silent as Bobby continued. "Do you want to know how I found out?" When he got no response Bobby said, "I figured there should be enough in bank to make a big down payment on a house for us. Lucky for me I checked before I started talking to the real estate man."

BJ replied, "There wasn't no sense in putting just $5 or $10 in the bank. It takes more money than that to buy a house like I want."

Bobby just shook his head. "If you would have left it there we would have at least $3000 by now."

BJ screamed at him, "No way! Ya're a liar."

"Do the math BJ. Do the math." Bobby then said, "I'm done talking. I'm taking a shower and going to bed. I expect the girls to be back in school on Monday. We'll stay together until they're grown, for their sake, but with my rules not yours." With that he walked into the bedroom, picked through the towels to find a relatively clean one and went into the bathroom to shower.

While he was showering, the two oldest girls and BJ sat down at the kitchen table to talk. They didn't want to go back to school and BJ didn't want to become a housewife. Together they had to work out a plan to keep Bobby Ray off their backs. Edna sat on the couch reading a book. She just wanted to stay out of everyone's way. She would really rather have been over with Mrs. Torras. Her house was always so happy and safe feeling.

Life went on for the Turnbull family. BJ was home once in awhile to fix a dinner. The older girls went to a continuation school that only lasted a couple of hours a day. Bobby cashed his check in the bank by the plant and made his little savings deposit each week in his own account. BJ would go out and party almost every night, but she no longer took the older girls with her. Bobby and Edna ate dinner with Mrs. Torras and her son a couple of nights a week. BJ and Bobby hardly ever spoke anymore. It was like everyone was in a jail of sorts, just waiting for time to pass so they could get on with their lives.

CHAPTER 8

It's 1976 ......

It's the first workday of the New Year Bobby was driving to the plant. He was somewhat sad. He and BJ had been married 17 years in December. She didn't remember or didn't care. He was feeling as if his life had been a total waste. Then he thought of his three beautiful girls.

Bobby still had hopes that the two older girls would finish continuation school and get their high school diplomas. They were going to school. He didn't know how they were doing because no one ever mentioned anything about grades. But they did talk about people at the school. However, he knew BJ didn't feel any responsibility in her children's education. She felt anything that went wrong was the school's fault. He never heard from the continuation school like he did the old school, but he figured it was because of the documents he had signed all those years ago so he wouldn't be put in jail if they ditched anymore. What he didn't know is BJ had listed herself as divorced when she enrolled Leah and Misty.

He was daydreaming about his girls and the hopes he had for them. All of a sudden, he snapped wide-awake as he saw his two teenaged girls laughing and staggering down the street towards the apartment. He quickly pulled to the curb and jumped out of the car to confront them.

As he walked towards them, Leah said to her sister, "Hey! Look who's here? Hey, are you just comin' home too?" Both girls laughed in a drunken laugh.

"What are you doing out here at this time in the morning," he shouted?

"Goin' home, of course. We're tired and need some sleep."

"What do you mean?"

Both girls laughed hysterically at their father, in unison said, "What part of them words don't ya understand?"

"Get in the car", Bobby hollered.

"Don't think so. Our mama said never to get in a car with a stranger and boy do you look strange", said Misty.

"Get in the car or I'm calling the police."

"Oh yeah? Just how ya gonna do that? Ya ain't got no phone in y'ar pocket", said Leah. Both girls laughed even harder and started staggering down the street towards the apartment.

Bobby was left standing on the sidewalk not knowing what to do about his daughters. Slowly he turned away from the sad sight, got back in his car and continued on his way to work. He was trying to think what to do. If he turned around and waited for the girls to get home, he'd be late for work and he might lose his job. He couldn't afford for that to happen. By the time he got to work, the girls would already be home and probably asleep so he couldn't talk to them. If he talked to BJ she'd tell him it was none of his business. If he called the police, they would question why he didn't know they were out all night. There was nothing he could do. The girls knew that. BJ had taught them well.

Bobby silently and sadly decided that continuing to stay with BJ was not working. He'd hoped that by staying together and living by his rules, the girls would turn out okay. He had thought his rules were working. Today he discovered the rules meant nothing. He didn't care if they meant nothing to BJ. He cared that his daughters didn't respect them. They were only 15 and 16. What was going to happen to them when they grew up? Then Bobby stopped thinking and said, "What am I talking about? When they grow up? They are grown up. They've grown up early and just like their mother. What in the world am I going to do?"

Just about then he pulled into the plant parking lot. He sighed a big sigh, got out of the car and shuffled into the plant to put his lunch in the break room cooler. As he was walking towards the time clock to punch in, a girl who looked somewhat familiar spoke to him, "Mr. Turnbull! I haven't seen you in a very long time. How are you?"

"Oh, I'm fine."

"You look like you just lost your best friend. Are you sure you're all right."

"Yeah, I'm sure," said Bobby as he walked on to his work area.

The girl looked after him and thought, *"He sure looked awful. I bet he doesn't remember me from the bank. I'll have to find out what area he works in so I can look him up. He needs someone to cheer him up."* She tried to see where he went but had no luck. The plant was very large and she'd only been there a couple of days before the holiday at the end of the year. She still wasn't sure she'd done the right thing, leaving the bank and all. But she had to think of her future and the bank didn't offer a good medical plan and no retirement. She knew they'd take her back if she found she didn't like the work, but she had to try this out for a while. She was on a 90-day probation. By that time, she'd know.

When she arrived at her work station, she said hello to all the people already gathered in the area. Then she walked over to her work partner, Sandy.

"How was your holiday, Sandy?"

"All right, I guess. We didn't do anything, but sit home and watch the tube. We stayed up late and watched that big ball drop in Times Square. All those people, boy, I wouldn't want to be in that crowd."

"I know what you mean. I'd be so afraid of being trampled to death. Changing the subject, "Do you know a Bobby Turnbull?"

"Sure. He works over in area 74. He's worked here a long time. How do you know him?"

"From my last job. He seems like a nice guy."

"Yeah. He works here full time and on the side he's learned how to repair small appliances. He works for Moody at night and on the weekends."

"Why does he do that? I would think he gets paid pretty good here."

"I'm sure he does, but he has 3 girls and two of them are teenagers. Everybody knows how expensive it can be raising girls."

"That's for sure. No wife?"

"Oh yeah. He has a wife." With that Sandy took a step closer to Belinda and whispered, "From what I hear she runs around on him."

"Really! He's a nice looking man and he works two jobs. What's wrong with her?"

Sandy replied, "Personally, I think she must be crazy in the head. I remember when she was pregnant with the last baby. He was out of here like a shot everyday so he could run home and make dinner. I guess she must of had a hard time of it cause after the baby was born she wound up in the hospital. She stayed there 'til the insurance ran out."

"Who took care of the children?"

"He has a neighbor lady, a widow I think, who took care of them."

Belinda nodded her head. "Boy, was he lucky. I've had a hard time finding a sitter for my son."

"Maybe you should talk to him. He seems to be the one always caring for the kids. He might have an idea who you could get."

Belinda thought a bit, and then said, "I just might do that. That is, if I ever see him again. This place is huge."

"You probably will. Area 74 takes breaks the same time we do."

"They do? How come I didn't see him before the holiday?"

"He was probably off. He has a lot of seniority so he can probably take time off whenever he wants to."

Belinda thought back to when he was coming to her bank. It didn't seem like he ever took time off. She made a mental note to look for him during the morning break. Just then the start work whistle went off and the machines started up.

A couple hours later, the area supervisor came up to Belinda and Sandy's station. "Sandy, can you run the station by yourself for an hour or so?"

"Sure," replied Sandy. Sandy knew it wouldn't do any good to say no and she knew the supervisor was aware being down a person would slow production. It was easier to say okay than to cause a scene.

Then the supervisor said, "Belinda, come with me to the office."

Belinda was startled, but took off her gloves and followed him.

Once they were in the cubicle he used as an office, the supervisor said to Belinda, "We've noticed that you worked for a bank for a long time."

"That's true."

"Well, we were wondering why you would want to work on the line instead of staying at the bank."

"Money and benefits."

"What?"

"The line pays more than the bank and if I make it through probation I'll have a medical plan and the start of a retirement plan."

"Makes sense, but why the line and not the office."

"No openings in the office."

"Well, not officially, but Mr. Carlson wants to talk to you about a position that might be coming up."

"Who's Mr. Carlson?"

"He's over Accounting."

Belinda's heart jumped. "Really?"

"It's a lot different in accounting than it is on the line."

"I can imagine."

"Well, do you want to talk to him?"

"Sure, but I'm not dressed to go to an interview."

"Yes, you are. You're dressed just fine. He knows you just started on the line and he wouldn't expect you to be dressed any different. He isn't looking to see how you're dressed. He's looking to see what you know."

With that Belinda nodded and got the directions to Mr. Carlson's office. She totally forgot about Bobby Ray Turnbull and how sad he looked.

Sandy wondered what was going on but didn't dare ask. She thought her new partner was doing okay, better than most even if she'd never done this type of work before. She worked hard and pulled her weight. And she wasn't afraid to tell you when she was having a problem. She'd hate losing her.

While Sandy was wondering what was going on, Belinda was trying to find Mr. Carlson's office. After a couple of wrong turns and asking directions a couple of times, she finally arrived. The door was closed and no one was sitting at the secretary's desk. Belinda wasn't sure what to do. After standing there a minute, she decided to knock on his door.

"Come in," came booming from behind the door in response to her quiet knock.

Timidly she opened the door just a crack large enough to get her head in. "Mr. Carlson", she asked quietly?

Once again, the booming voice exploded on her ears, "Come on in, I said."

"Yes sir," replied Belinda as she walked in.

"You the bank girl?"

"Yes sir."

"You like working on the line?"

"I like the money."

Mr. Carlson laughed. "Come and sit down so we can talk. I like a person who tells the truth. You always tell the truth?"

"No, but I surely try."

Mr. Carlson laughed again. "Young lady, I think we're going to get along fine."

Just before it was time to break for lunch Sandy's supervisor once again walked over to her area.

"I know I'm behind," she said to him before he had to chance to yell at her. "It doesn't move as fast with only one person."

"I know that Sandy. I'm sorry you've been left alone all morning, but I had to wait until I found out for sure before I replaced your partner. I'll have a new trainee for you right after lunch."

"New trainee? Did Belinda get canned? She was just starting to catch on."

"She'll still be working for the company, just not on the line."

"I thought she belonged somewheres else. Her hands were too soft."

"Well, you were right. Carlson grabbed her for his department."

"She'll be back to get her stuff in a bit, then I guess we won't see her again. Hang in there until I can get someone over here. Okay?"

"Okay," she replied. However, she thought, *"What am I supposed to say? No, it isn't all right. Or how about, I'm tired of breaking in new people and then you moving them on to someone else after they're trained. Boy, I wish I could say something other than okay."*

Just as the lunch whistle blew and the machines were grinding to a stop, Belinda appeared at her old station. "Sandy, I came to say goodbye."

"Yeah, I heard you're moving on."

"Mr. Carlson wants me to start over in accounting right away. I just came to get my stuff and eat lunch with you one last time."

"You mean you're starting this afternoon?"

"Yes and I'm so embarrassed."

"About what?"

"The way I'm dressed, of course. I'll be the only one in the department who's in jeans and a cotton shirt. He said I should come get my stuff, eat my lunch and be back in 45 minutes. I told him I wouldn't have time to go home and change. He didn't care, so everyone's going to be looking at me wondering what I'm doing there dressed like this."

"Don't matter what they all think about you and the way you're dressed. You ain't there to impress them; you're there to do a job for Mr. Carlson. He's the only one you hav'ta impress."

"I guess you're right. Let's go eat. I'm starved". With that the two women started walking to the lunchroom. Belinda had totally forgotten about Bobby Ray.

Bobby was having a terrible day. When the lunch whistle blew, he almost ran to the lunchroom cooler to get his sack so he could get out to his car and think. He needed to figure out what he was going to do about his girls so he could get his mind on his work. Twice his supervisor had come over to him to ask him what was wrong. He just kept messing up. It had to stop or he'd be pulled off the line and talked to.

While eating his bologna sandwich and his small bag of chips, Bobby finally decided he'd talk to BJ about getting a divorce. He couldn't take watching his daughters turn into tramps any longer. He' d tell her he wanted Edna and she could keep the other two. It had been so hard making that decision, but once he made up his mind he felt better. An hour goes by quickly when you're wrestling with a hard decision and Bobby just made it back to his station when the whistle blew to start the machines. Out of the corner of his eye he saw his super watching him. He knew he was on thin ice, but the afternoon went a whole lot better and before Bobby knew it the day was ending. Just as he was pulling his gloves off, his super appeared at his side.

"You had a good afternoon, Bobby. Don't know what was wrong this morning, but you mor'n made up for it this afternoon. Watch out for them slumps. They can ruin a man."

"I'll try boss," said Bobby. "I'll try." Bobby just walked away.

He had to figure out a way to talk to BJ without her screaming too much. He wasn't looking forward to what he had to do, but it had to be done. He couldn't keep living the way he was. When he got to the little apartment that had been his home for so long a fear of dread filled him. As he turned his key in the door he took a deep breath. He turned the knob and walked in - to a totally dark room.

"Hello? Anybody home?" No response. He continued walking and asking if anyone was home. No response. The apartment was empty. Next he walked over to Gloria's door and knocked. When she opened the door and said hi, he couldn't help himself, he had to smile. She was always so pleasant and the opening of the door released a wonderful smell into the hallway.

As he was thinking, *"Her place is always so bright and cheerful",* he said, "Any of my kids here?"

"Just Edna. The others left a short time ago in a taxi."

"A taxi? Where'd they go?"

"Your wife didn't tell me. She just banged on the door and shoved Edna at me."

"They went to the doctor," offered Edna.

"The doctor? What for?"

"I don't know, but mother was mad."

"About what?"

"Don't know. She just kept yelling that she thought she taught them better."

"Taught them better?"

"That's what she said," replied his youngest child.

Gloria looked visibly shaken.

"Gloria, what's wrong? Do you know what she meant?"

"I have an idea, Bobby. Come into the kitchen with me so we can talk."

Once in the kitchen, Gloria whispered to Bobby, "I think it might mean that the girls are pregnant."

Bobby felt like he had just taken a knife in his heart. He breathed a deep breath and then said, "They're just babies themselves."

"Yes, but look at the way they dress. Look at how they act."

Bobby just nodded his head. He had witnessed all of that and more. He became weak at the thought and then realized he wouldn't be able to divorce BJ if the girls were really pregnant. "Let's go back now. I wouldn't want Edna to think something was going on. She's afraid of her mother and tells her everything."

Together they walked back to the living room. "Edna, let's go home now."

"Can't we eat with Señora Torras tonight? Mother isn't home."

"Not tonight. I think your mother and sisters will be home soon. I want to be in our place when they get there. I need to talk to your mother.

About an hour later Bobby heard a car pull up in front of the apartment building. He didn't bother to look out as he could hear the voices of his children through the open windows of the apartment. A few minutes later the front door burst open and BJ, Leah and Misty came in. They all acted as if they'd been drinking.

BJ said, "Well, look who's here. How come ya ain't over with ya're Mexican lady friend?"

Bobby didn't respond, he just quietly said to the girls, "Will all of you go into the bedroom, I need to talk to your mother.

Normally the two oldest girls would have sassed back, but this time BJ looked at them and nodded. They didn't even talk as they walked into the bedroom.

"You too, Edna," said Bobby.

The little girl looked at her father and mother and then followed her sisters to the communal bedroom.

"Where did you and the girls go in a taxi?"

"Ya're Mexican friend tell ya?"

"Yes, but that doesn't change the question. Where'd you have to go that you couldn't wait until I got home?"

"I was gonna tell ya anyways. We went to the doctor."

"I didn't know about any appointments."

"I didn't make an appointment. I took 'um to one of them clinics."

"Clinics? What kind of clinic?"

"Them kind that take care of pregnant people."

"Who's pregnant?"

"No one."

"Okay, who did you think was pregnant?"

"Both girls."

Bobby just nodded his head and silently thanked Gloria for giving him a heads up. "Aren't they a little young to be thinking they're pregnant?"

"Hell, no! They've been doin' it for a long time now. They're supposed to be taken them pills and they ain't been. I just found out and hadda take them to be checked out."

Bobby just shook his head. He couldn't believe the words coming from his wife's mouth.

"They know better now. I had that doctor talk hard to them. Then I talked to them on the ride home."

"About what?"

"About how they have to be sure that they can trap the right man before they go and get pregnant."

"Was that all you talked about?"

"Sure. What else is there ta talk about?"

Bobby could think of a lot of things she should have told them, but decided it was a waste of his breath. "Nothing, I guess." Bobby started to walk away when BJ stopped him.

"There's somethin' else I want ta talk to ya about."

Bobby turned towards his wife wondering what she was going to lay on him. As if she hadn't done enough to him already today.

"I want a divorce."

"Excuse me," said Bobby.

Instead of her usual remark, BJ said, "I want a divorce."

Bobby's heart jumped. He almost smiled. "What brought this on?"

"This arrangement we have ain't workin'."

Bobby couldn't believe his ears.

"And I'm takin' the girls and moving from this dump."

"Okay."

"I don't want my girls around that fat Mexican friend of yours any more."

"Okay."

"Is that all you can say," BJ shouted.

"No. There is a lot more I could say, but I think you've said all that needs to be said."

"I got me a lawyer."

"Okay." Bobby wondered how long she had been planning this.

"You need to get one too."

"Why? Can't he handle both sides? I've heard that lawyers do that when there's no question about the divorce."

"We have a lot to divide up and I want to be sure I get my fair share."

"Fair share? You haven't contributed a thing to this house or anything in it. Besides, what's there to divide? You can have all the furniture, such as it is, but there's nothing else."

"Yeah, well when I told my lawyer how much ya made and how's ya put money in the savings every week to buy a house and how's we don't have that house, he told me I could get that money so's I could get me a house."

"Didn't you bother to tell him you've been taking it out as fast as I've been putting it in?"

"Ain't true."

"I can prove it."

"All lies. Then I told him how ya been carrying on with that Mexican all these years, he said I could get all of it."

"She watched the children and cleaned the house. Besides being a friend to everyone in this family, that's it. Have you lost your mind?"

"I got my side and you got yours. And my lawyer says you gotta pay his fee for me."

"Why's that?"

"Cause ya're working and I'm not."

"You're working too."

"Not no more. I quit."

"What? When did this happen?"

"A few weeks ago. The work was too hard."

Bobby was flabbergasted. Again he found himself shaking his head in wonderment. He thought he'd heard it all from her and yet, over and over she continues to amaze him. He wonders why he ever married her. To BJ he says, "You might be right in one thing."

BJ smiled, "Yeah, what's that?"

"We should be divorced and we do have something to divide."

Again, BJ smiled. "I know'd I was right. Ya been hiding money and I aim to get it."

It was Bobby's turn to smile. BJ had no idea he was talking about the children.

The next day Bobby called a lawyer and made an appointment. At the appointment the lawyer told him he'd have to pay child support and probably alimony. Bobby said alimony was out of the question. He explained BJ had a better education than he did and that she chose not to work. The lawyer also told him he had no chance of getting custody of the youngest child. When Bobby asked why, he was told the judges in the area didn't feel that fathers were fit to raise girls. The lawyer went on to say that if the youngest had been a son, there would be a slight possibility. Bobby was upset, but accepted the information. The lawyer then said Bobby would be given liberal visitation rights. Bobby didn't like what he'd heard but accepted it. Finally he just requested the divorce be finalized quickly to keep the costs down.

In May 1976, the divorce of Bobby Ray Turnbull and Bobbie Jo Milhouse Turnbull was finalized. It turned out just as his attorney said it would. Bobby didn't get custody of Edna and BJ didn't get any money, because the "big" savings account issue had been settled with a document from the newly promoted bank manager, Miss Nicoles. He was ordered to pay child support and she was told to get a job and keep it.

A very small article was posted in the legal section of the Covington Gazette. Sally was much older, but still worked for the Turnbull's. She still read the newspaper and still kept up the family bible. Just as when the children were born, she said nothing to her employers about what she read. She just made a note in the bible.

The day the divorce was final, Bobby asked for a little extra time on his morning break so he could go to personnel to make some changes. So when the whistle blew and the machines were shutting down, Bobby pulled off his gloves and quickly walked to personnel. When he arrived the door was closed and locked. He didn't know what to do, as he didn't have too much time to wait around. Looking around he saw the door to accounting was open so he went in.

There was a brunette lady sitting with her back to the door, so Bobby said, "Excuse me."

"Oh, I'm sorry. I didn't hear you come in."

"That's all right. I was really looking for personnel and the door's locked."

"She's off sick today. I don't know when she'll be back, Mr. Turnbull."

"How do you know my name?"

"I guess you don't remember me. I'm Belinda. I used to work where you used to bank - on the other side of town. I was the teller that took you to talk to Miss Nichols."

"Am I ever embarrassed? I'm so sorry. You saved me so much trouble and then I don't even remember your face. Wait! I ran into you a couple of months ago, didn't I?"

Belinda laughed, "Yes. You were coming out of the lunchroom just as I was heading in. You looked so sad that day. I meant to talk to you later during break, but I got called to the office. That's how I was pulled off the line and given this opportunity."

"I do remember that day. It was a major bad day."

"I'm so sorry I didn't take the time to look you up."

"Probably best. I was really in a foul mood."

"Hope things worked out."

"They did, in a fashion. I'm divorced now."

Belinda didn't know what to say.

"That's why I needed to see someone in personnel. I need to change all the paperwork."

"I can help you with that. She has all the packages set up, so all I have to do is pull one out of the file and hand it to you. You can take it home, fill them out and then bring the package back. Just don't sign any of them. That has to be done in front of a witness from the company. Wait here a second and I'll get a package for you." Belinda, who had moved from her desk to the counter where Bobby was, turned and walked to the back of her office. He couldn't see where she went but in a very short time she reappeared. In her hand she had a manila folder. "Here you are. If you have any questions I should be able to answer them if she isn't here."

Bobby looked at his watch; break time was just about over. "Thanks. I'd better run so I don't miss the whistle. I hope I see you again."

"Me too. Take care," Belinda shouted after him. She thought, *"Probably best he's free of that woman. She was such a witch!"*

Time passed and Bobby's life was pretty quiet, except when BJ would call to say she needed money to buy something for Edna. She always said it was for Edna because if it was for anyone else she knew her chances of getting it were slim. He was supposed to have liberal visitation rights. He had the rights; he just didn't have the visits. He would arrange to see the girls and when he' go to the house where they were living, no one would be home. Many times he thought he heard voices from inside, but no one would answer the door. Bobby was always disappointed, but he kept trying. He still lived in the same apartment only now it didn't have much furniture - BJ took almost everything. He'd done some garage sale hopping and picked up a sofa and a bed. The kitchen still had the small table that was there when they first moved in. BJ had tried to take it too, until Bobby stopped her saying it belonged with the apartment. She argued and lost. Most nights he ate at home alone. Gloria always asked if he wanted to eat with her and her son but he usually said no. It was a quiet and lonely life, but it was better than when he and BJ were together.

October came and the different areas of the plant were starting to put up posters for the upcoming holiday parties. Most of the areas invited the workers from the adjoining areas. If someone was so inclined, they could be attending parties every weekend from the beginning of November until New Year's Eve. That's when the plant put on the holiday party for all their workers. Bobby never attended any of the parties when he was married to BJ but he was seriously thinking about going to a lot of them this year. He'd heard you get to meet a lot of people and maybe make a lot of friends. He thought, *"It wouldn't hurt to make some friends plus I might pick up some appliance repair business."*

Finally Bobby stopped at the bulletin board to add his name to the growing list of attendees for the first of many holiday parties. Looking at the paper he saw that after each name was written a food dish. He was puzzled.

Just then a female voice behind him said, "Are you coming to our party?"

He turned to see Belinda standing behind him. "I was thinking about it, but I didn't realize you had to bring your own food."

Belinda laughed, "Haven't you ever heard of pot luck."

Puzzled, Bobby said, "No. What is it?"

"You've really never heard of pot luck."

"No", Bobby said emphatically.

"That's where everyone who attends brings a dish to share. In this case, we ask everyone who signs up to bring a dish that's enough for 4 people. It's all put on a huge buffet table and people fill their plates with a little of this and a little of that. It's usually wonderful."

"But I don't cook and I don't think people would like to eat a bologna or peanut butter sandwich."

"Okay, but you can buy bread or rolls can't you?"

"Sure, but that isn't a dish."

"Same thing silly. Here look at the list of things needed. See, here are bread and rolls and butter. Or you could bring some disposable knives and forks."

Bobby hung his head a little and said, "I guess you can tell I ain't ever done this before."

"No problem. You'll be very proficient by the time the holidays are over. See you there," said Belinda as she walked off.

Bobby made his choice from the list, made his mark next to rolls and butter, and then signed his name to the front of the list. His step was a little lighter thinking he was going to a party and maybe he'd see Belinda there. Each time a new sheet would go up on the board, Bobby would sign up to bring rolls and butter. By the time Thanksgiving arrived, he had been to four parties and was getting very good at finding fresh rolls to bring.

He planned to eat Thanksgiving dinner with Gloria. Just like for the parties he told her he would bring the rolls. He knew Gloria baked bread, but he wanted to bring something to contribute. The day before Thanksgiving he stopped on the way home from work and bought the rolls. On a whim, he also stopped at a flower stand and got a little table decoration that had a pilgrim couple in it and a few flowers. He thought she might like it. As he was walking in his apartment with his purchases, the phone started ringing.

As he picked the receiver up he heard, "It's about time you got home. I been callin' for hours and hours!" It was BJ and she sounded mad - as usual.

"What do you want?"

"Ta talk to ya."

"Well, talk. I've got things to do."

"Ya're Mexican lady is probably waiting. Ha! Ya still like them fat ones? What a pig!"

"Did you want to tell me something or not?"

"Oh yeah, I almost forgot. Leah's pregnant. So what'cha gonna do?"

"Excuse me?"

"Hav'ya gone deef. I said Leah's pregnant," BJ shouted.

"I heard you the first time. I just couldn't believe my ears."

"Yeah, well believe it. So what'cha gonna do?"

"I'm not doing anything. You have sole custody of the children. She's your responsibility. Remember you're the one who said school didn't teach them anything and that you were teaching what they needed to know. And remember you told the judge they were your children and convinced them I was the one who was the problem."

"I could'a figgered you'd throw'd that up ta me. Ya never was there when I needed ya."

Bobby didn't respond to her comments. He just quietly answered her first question, "I'm not going to do anything. You handle it." Then, without waiting for a response, he put the receiver back in its cradle.

When BJ realized that her ex wasn't on the line any longer, she too hung up. "I sure told him," she said to the girls. "We're on our own now. Ya know how I told ya money was tight cause he never paid alimony to me, well now he's refusing to help us out with this little problem. Just like always, I have to take care of things by myself".

About two hours after Bobby hung up on BJ, he heard a soft knock at his door. Upon opening the door, he saw Gloria standing there with a small covered dish in her hands. "You didn't come over to dinner, so I figured something bad happened."

Bobby had totally forgotten he had said he'd eat dinner with her. "I'm so sorry. Something bad did happen, but that's no excuse for me forgetting about you and dinner. Forgive me?"

"Sure. But you do need to eat, so I brought this over for you."

Bobby replied, "After I was so rude to you, how can you still be nice to me?"

"Because I know you didn't do it on purpose. May I ask what happened?"

"Sure you can. Come on in and have a cup of coffee with me while I eat and tell you all about it." Gloria walked into the almost empty apartment and followed Bobby to the little kitchen table. She sat down while Bobby made coffee for both of them, and then watched him eat while he told her all about the phone call. She wasn't surprised.

She had seen and heard so many things and if he asked she would tell him. He never asked, so she didn't tell him. He was hurting enough without knowing the whole truth.

One Saturday, just before Christmas, Bobby was sitting in Gloria kitchen reading the evening paper. In the family news section he saw the two simple lines.

Leah Turnbull and Chad Ramsey were married December 16th. Judge Hurschell officiated.

Bobby put the paper down and signed. Gloria turned towards him and asked, "What's wrong?" Bobby picked the paper back up and read the wedding announcement to her.

Neither one said anything but Bobby wondered if BJ ever thought about telling the girls the family secret - probably not. Once again, he found himself praying. This time praying for the children of his children – that they would be normal.

Back in Florence, the Milhouse family was also having a sad holiday. Sally had been ill for some time and had finally given life up. Robert and Josephine Milhouse were just starting to realize how much they were going to miss her.

Sally was the only one who cared enough to record the major changes in the lives of the family she worked for. The Turnbulls never knew what Sally had done for them, without being asked. They didn't know she'd kept up their family bible in addition to her own. They didn't know the link to family had been severed with Sally's death. They probably didn't care. They were just concerned about their daily needs and who would take care of the things Sally had always taken care of and that they had come to take for granted.

On Christmas Eve Bobby was allowed to take Edna for the day so he could buy her some presents. While shopping Edna told her father that Leah moved in with Chad and his family and that Chad's parents insisted he stay in school until he graduated. He also found out that sometimes Edna stayed with them too. As Edna said, "But only when mother is too busy working."

"How often is that, honey", asked Bobby?

"Not real often. Just a couple of times a week and sometimes on Saturday."

Bobby wondered what his ex was doing that she had to leave her youngest child so often, but he knew it would do no good to ask his daughter. If he asked BJ, it would get Edna in trouble and he'd never get to see her again.

CHAPTER 9

It's 1977 ......

The New Year started off quietly for Bobby. Now that the holidays were over, he fell into a routine of getting up early, working on some small appliance or other, going to work at the plant, stopping at Moody's to drop off or pick up more appliances to be fixed then heading home to read the paper and have a quiet dinner with Gloria before going to bed.

Once in a great while he was allowed to take Edna but when he did BJ always had a list of things he was allowed to do during the day. Edna didn't seem to care whether she visited with her father or not. Most of the time she was very withdrawn and sleepy when she was with him. One day, in February, however, she was very talkative. In fact she acted like her old self. Finally Bobby couldn't resist and asked her, "Edna?"

"Yes, Daddy?"

"Usually you're so quiet and sleepy when you come with me, but today you're happy and full of life. I was wondering what was so different about what we're doing today to make you so happy. I like it when you're happy and want to be sure and do whatever we're doing every time I see you."

Edna laughed and jumped up in the air. "I don't know," she exclaimed jumping and running around her father.

"You're so full of energy today. Just like you used to be. There has to be something different? Did you eat your Wheaties this morning?"

Edna stopped laughing and stood still. She screwed up her face, deep in thought, and then said, "Well, the only thing different that I can think of is that Mommy hasn't been giving me any medicine for awhile. She said she ran out and can't afford to buy anymore."

"Medicine? Are you sick?"

"I don't think so. I feel good. Maybe I'm all better now and that's why I feel good. No, that can't be it, cause Mommy said she couldn't afford to buy the medicine for awhile since she has to buy things for the new baby."

"Oh, that's right. Leah's baby will be coming along soon now."

"Not Leah's baby, Misty's."

When Bobby heard that, he stopped walking and looked at Edna. When he spoke, his voice was quivering. "Honey, did I hear you right? Did you say Misty is having a baby too?"

"Oh yes and Mommy said it's about time she did cause she's almost 16."

Bobby was so stunned he didn't respond to his youngest daughter. Edna didn't notice the look on her father's face and kept talking.

"Mommy says we're going to have to get me another new dress cause of Misty getting married to Sam. That's why she can't buy my medicine cause of the baby needing stuff and my needing a dress for the wedding. But don't worry Daddy, she promises she'll get me the medicine after the wedding is over and she gets some more money."

It took all of Bobby's strength to keep calm. To his daughter he said, "Okay honey." He couldn't say anymore. Edna went back to running, jumping and laughing. Bobby's mood was much more somber. He couldn't wait to finish the day so he could talk to BJ about Misty.

Usually Bobby just stopped in front of the house where his ex and children were living and let Edna go into the house by herself. This time he said, "I'll help you carry your packages in."

"Oh Daddy, I don't think Mommy would like that."

"Why not?"

"She might have company and not be dressed. She wouldn't like you just coming in on her. She gets mad if you do that to her. I don't want to make her mad."

"Okay, but how about we go to the door and knock on it. That way she'd have time to get dressed."

"Oh Daddy, you're so smart. Mommy says you're dumb, but she's wrong. Come on; let's go knock on the door. She'll be so surprised when she opens the door to find out it's just me and not a visitor." She grabbed her father's hand and pulled him to the front door. Then she whispered to him, "Knock three little knocks."

"What?"

"Knock three little knocks. That's what all her men friends do. When she hears those knocks, if she already has a visitor, she yells to come back later. If she doesn't have a visitor, she tells me to pick up the room, go into my bedroom and shut the door. I do, but then I lay on the floor and put my ear next to the crack so I can listen. Don't tell her. Okay?"

Bobby was once again stunned into being quiet. "Okay, honey," he replied and then knocked three times on the door. After he knocked, he heard some scurrying sounds coming from inside.

Edna heard them too and giggled. "She's having to empty her own ashtray and put her tea glass in the kitchen." Edna covered her mouth and giggled softly some more.

They both heard footsteps coming towards the door. Then Bobby heard this soft feminine voice saying, "I wasn't expecting company this early, but I guess it's ….", as the door opened. When BJ saw her ex husband and youngest daughter standing there, she screamed, "What the fuck do you think you're doing?" She grabbed Edna by the arm and pulled her into the house, giving her a smack along the side of her head. "I don't like tricks, you little bitch." To Bobby she said, "Well, whadda ya want?"

"I just wanted to talk to you and I didn't think it was right to just walk in so I made Edna wait until I knocked." It wasn't the truth, but he couldn't stand seeing his little girl beat up.

BJ turned to Edna and said, "That right? And don't ya lie to me if'n ya know what's good fer ya."

Little Edna just nodded her head.

"All right then. Go to ya're room. Then she turned and once again said to Bobby, "Well, whadda ya want?"

"I heard that Misty's pregnant."

"Yeah, so what?"

"Well, isn't she a little young?"

"No. It's about time she got a man of her own and out of my house. I'm tired of taking care of all these youngins."

"Is she getting married?"

"Yeah."

"BJ, couldn't you just tell me the whole story without me having to ask a million questions to get it?"

"Suppose so. Misty's pregnant. She's gonna marry the father, Sam Hicks. You're not invited to the wedding. Sam's seventeen and old enough to support her and the kid so I don't have to worry about her anymore. Anything else you wanna know?"

"I guess that does it."

"Fine, now get the fuck outta here," and she slammed the door.

Bobby was shocked. His two oldest children were both pregnant. Neither one finished school, both were getting married and both were still under age. Slowly he walked back to his car. On the drive home, he started wondering where he went wrong. Then he realized he went wrong when he married Bobbie Jo. He should have listened to old man Milhouse. The old man was right. Then he thought about Gloria and how she was never going to believe the latest.

As Gloria was putting dinner on the table, Bobby started telling her what he had discovered while visiting with Edna. Gloria didn't seem surprised. "Why aren't you surprised about all of this?"

"I heard about it over at the market."

"What? At the market?"

"Yes, Bobby, I always hear about her and the girls at the market. They still go there to shop, sometimes, and they talk loud. I think they do it on purpose so people will hear them."

"Really? What else have you heard?"

"Well, Sam Hicks' family has disowned him and are refusing to help him out so he's having to quit school so he can support Misty and the baby."

"Really. Well, that shows me something."

"He's found a job over at the truck farm and is saving up money so he can rent a place for he and Misty."

"Anything else?"

Gloria thought, *"Too bad you didn't ask about things a long time ago."* However out loud she said, "Not right now, but I'm sure I'll hear more. BJ likes to tell people what she's doing and who she's running with."

"When you hear, will you tell me?"

"Sure."

"Have you heard things before?"

"Yes."

"I never asked, so you didn't tell me. Right?"

"Right."

"Consider me asking whenever you hear something. Okay?"

"Okay."

Bobby's Saturday routine was to do his laundry, straighten up his apartment and write checks to pay his child support and any bills that had come in during the week. When all of that was done he'd work on the toasters, mixers and radios he'd brought home from Moody's. In the evening he'd go over to Gloria's apartment to have dinner. While there he'd read the weekend paper.

The first Saturday in March was no different. As he was reading the paper his eyes fell on the legal notice that announced his little girl, Misty, had married Sam Hicks. He couldn't help heaving a big sigh and feeling empty inside.

Gloria looked over at him but said nothing. She'd heard about the marriage and knew what he must have seen.

"Well," Bobby said, "I guess I can tear up the child support check I wrote and write a new one. BJ won't be happy but I have proof that two of my three children are no longer my responsibility. Gloria didn't respond. She knew he wasn't really talking to her.

Weeks passed by with Bobby hearing nothing from BJ so he was never able to see Edna. He had no idea what her life was like or how she was being treated. He was concerned, but there was nothing he could do about it.

Then on June 24th, his phone rang just as he was walking in the door. When he answered, BJ's voice responded, "Where the fuck ya been? I've been trying ta call ya for hours. Been with ya're fat Mexican friend, I bet."

"Why does she always start off her calls the same way?" he thought. But to her he asked, "What do you want, BJ?"

"Ta tells ya that Leah had her baby."

Bobby just sighed.

"Ain't ya gonna say nothing?"

"No."

"Why not?"

"BJ, there's nothing to say. It's a sad and worrisome event."

"I told her ya didn't care. I told her just that. Just like when ya cut our money off. Ya did it cause ya didn't care."

"Not true. The girls got married. They no longer lived with you. I only have one child left to support. That's why I give you less money."

"Well, ya don't send enough."

"I send what the court told me to send. Besides I thought this call was about the new baby."

"Oh yeah. I almost forgot. It's a boy. We named him Billy Ray. Billy Ray Ramsey is his name. Leah had a terrible time of it. All that pain and them doctors wouldn't do nothin' for her." Bobby didn't respond so BJ said, "If'n ya're interested, ya can see him in the nursery today or tomorrow." Then she hung up.

It was his first grandchild. One part of him was happy and wanted to see the baby and another part of him was scared and sad. He decided not to go to the hospital.

By August the gossip had started reaching Gloria who now always passed it on to Bobby. The rumor was that once Leah recovered from the pregnancy and could fit into her clothes again, she wanted to go back to her old ways of partying every night. Apparently Chad's parents, who had been supporting her, Chad and now the baby, put their foot down and told her she had to stay home and take care of the child or return to school. The story being told was that Leah threw a fit, grabbed the baby and told them they would never see the child again.

"It sure sounds like something Leah would do. I wonder how long it will be before I get a call from BJ?"

"Why would she call you", asked Gloria? "Leah's married and not your responsibility any more."

"You're right, of course, but if she moved back in with BJ, they'll try to find a way for me or someone to support them. BJ came from a wealthy family. She really believes she shouldn't have to work to support herself. She's brought the girls up to think the same way."

"Why doesn't she call her parents? If they have money, they should be happy to help."

It's a very long story. Let's just say that they disowned her a very long time ago."

Gloria didn't ask why. She just nodded her head and continued fixing dinner.

Bobby didn't have long to wait. The following Friday he heard his phone ringing as he walked the short hall to his apartment. He didn't rush to answer it. He knew who it was. He thought she'd hang up and try again later but the phone kept ringing. He didn't rush opening the door and took the time to put his lunch box down on the kitchen table. Finally he walked to the phone and answered it. Of course, it was BJ and she was furious.

"What's wrong with you? Why didn't you answer sooner?"

"Hello to you too, BJ."

"Don't be a smart ass."

"It's amazing. When you get mad you lose all the uneducated country talk. Did you know that?"

BJ ignored his comment and said; "Leah and Billy Ray are living with me now so you have to pay me more child support."

"No."

"What?"

"I said no. Leah's married. Chad's the baby's father, not me. I don't have to support them."

"I can't believe what you said. Here your daughter is running for her life with a brand new baby and you won't help."

"Tell Leah to go get a job," said Bobby. Then he hung the phone up. He waited a minute and then picked up the received to listen. When he heard dial tone, he laid the received on the table. He knew he'd eventually have to put it back on but he wanted a little peace and quiet.

"Well," BJ said to Leah. "he said he wasn't gonna give me any more money and that you should get a job."

"What? I have a baby, I can't work!"

"Yeah, well we'd better figure something out fast cause the rent's past due and I ain't got no money."

"Me neither," replied Leah. Then she asked her mother, "You goin' out tonight?"

BJ replied, "No. Somebody might come over so I don't plan to go out."

"Good, cause I got me a date."

"Oh yeah, who with?"

"Oh, just this guy I met at the social club."

"What guy? What's his name?"

"Harry."

"Harry?"

"Yep."

"Is he?" asked BJ laughing.

"Is he what?" asked Leah.

"Is he hairy?"

"Oh, I get it. I don't know, but I'm gonna find out."

"Family have money?"

"Dunno"

"Don't make that mistake again."

"Yeah, I know. I thought the Ramsey's were rich. Hell, they're just working people."

"Yeah, but I bet you can get support from them. For the kid, of course", said BJ laughing again.

"Right – for the kid. I'll work on that next week. This weekend, I'll work on Harry." Leah and BJ laughed some more.

Leah put on her tightest jeans and pulled her cleanest t-shirt over her head. She stood at the one mirror in the house admiring herself. *"No one would believe I had a kid a couple of months ago."*

BJ saw her standing in front of the mirror and said, "Ya gonna wear that?"

"Sure. What's wrong with these jeans."

"They're aright, it's that shirt."

"What's wrong? Is it too dirty?"

"No, it's too loose on ya. Don't ya have a smaller one?"

"No, I don't. This fits fine."

"No it don't. Take my word for it. If there's one thing I know how to do is attract men. Let's check in Edna's room. I think she has a pretty little thing that would be fine."

BJ went into Edna's room. Edna was lying on her bed, on her stomach, watching television. "When's dinner?" she asked her mother.

"Ain't no dinner tonight. Ya're father didn't send no money so we have ta cut back. I'll get some medicine for ya in a little bit. I need to find that new t-shirt I got ya to wear to school."

"I wore it yesterday, so it's probably over in that pile of dirty clothes."

"Did ya get it dirty?"

"No, I just wore it all day and it smells."

"Leah needs it so's she can go out."

"Mom, it smells."

"I got some strong perfume that'll take care of that. Besides, didn't I tell ya to start wearing some deodorant?"

"Yeah, but I forgot."

"If'n ya wear that stuff it'll take care of any body smells ya get when ya don't take a bath. We can't have ya wastin' water taking baths. Water costs too much. So don't make me tell ya again to use it."

Edna nodded her head and went back to watch the television.

"Here," BJ said to Leah, "this should be about right."

"That's too small."

BJ laughed, "As I said, I know how to attract men."

Leah put on the little t-shirt.

CHAPTER 10

It's February 1978 ......

After several months of dating, Leah moved out of her mother's apartment and in with Harry. He's 21 and she just turned 18.

BJ had been right. Chad's parents continued sending money for the support of their only grandchild, all in the hopes they'd be able to see the baby. This, of course, rarely happened. Leah called them to give them her new address, so she would continue to receive money from them, but she's left Billy Ray with her mother.

"Leah," BJ asked her oldest daughter one day, "you need to call the Ramsey's. They've stopped sending the child support."

"No they haven't," Leah remarked quietly. She knew her mother was going to have a fit.

"Sure they have. I ain't got a check this month. They ain't ever been late before."

"I got it."

"What? When you been here to get it?"

"Wasn't."

"Wasn't what?"

"Wasn't here."

"Then how'd ya get the check?"

"I called the Ramsey's and gave um my new address."

"What? You can't do that?"

"Sure I can and I did."

"But, I'm takin' care of the kid."

"Sure, but you have ta."

"Why?"

"Because ya're the brats grandma."

"So that means I have to support it and take care of it?"

"Yep. You and them Ramsey's."

"How do ya figure that?"

"Well, I been thinking. If you and them had raised us right, we wouldn't a been doin' what we did and we wouldn't a had a kid."

"So it's our fault that you got pregnant."

"Yep."

"You're crazy."

"Maybe, but you've got the kid to raise and I get the money from the Ramsey's and that's the way it is. And if you call them, I'm gonna tell them you took the baby from me. They don't care for me, but they really don't like you. They'll take ya ta court and get the kid from ya."

"So what. They can have him. I wanna life and he's in the way."

"May be, but ya ain't thinkin' right."

"How so?"

"The Ramsey's are giving me money, right?"

"Yeah?"

"So I have my own money I don't have to tell Harry about."

"Okay."

"You have the kid, cause I can't take care of it, right?"

"Yeah?"

"You can get welfare and food stamps from the county and the state. Plus, I think ya can get free medical for him."

"Really?"

"Think so. At least that's what I heard over at the social club a couple a weeks ago. I can ask about it when I see them women over there again."

"You have money to go to the club at night?"

"At night, I go with Harry and he pays. During the day I go, have lunch once in awhile, play a little pool, have a drink or two and listen to the people who come in to eat. Ya can learn a lot of things by listening to other people talk."

"What people?"

"Lots of women who work in different offices come in. They always talk about things happening in the places where they work. A person can get a whole edecation just listening."

"That's education, not edecation."

"Whatever. I just have to dress a little different and join them one day for lunch. I'll let ya know what I find out."

"Make it soon. I need to pay the rent."

It wasn't too many days before Leah had all the information for her mother on how to fill out the paperwork so she could start drawing all the different welfare benefits available for a poor, single grandmother trying to raise her unwanted grandchild.

When Misty had her second child the following month, BJ was pleased to pass on her learning experience to her second daughter. Misty went to the welfare office, with both children with her, said she was a single mother with no means of support and obtained enough money each month so she now had a feeling of independence. She started going to the social club for lunch a few times each week to obtain her "education". Before long, she filed for a divorce from Sam. It caught him totally by surprise. Misty convinced him that one lawyer would be cheaper. In the short run it was, but in the long run it cost Sam a lot. In February 1979, Misty's divorce is final and she's awarded child support until the children can support themselves and alimony for life, as long as she doesn't remarry.

With the newly found money, Misty and BJ moved into a little house in Covington on East 18th Street. They liked the house because it was still within walking distance of the social club. But the best feature of the house was it had two addresses. At some time a previous owner had put up a wall and rented out a few rooms. The wall had been taken down years ago, but the separate outside door, mailbox and address remained. It appeared as if mother and daughter were living next door to each other, when they actually were living in the same house. This arrangement worked out well and the social workers never caught on.

By the time April 1979 arrives, BJ is fed up and calls Leah to come get her child.

"I can't take him, Mama."

"Why?"

"I ain't never told Harry about him."

"How could he not know? Ya get money every month from them Ramsey's."

"He don't know that."

"Well ya better find out a way to tell him, or I'm giving the brat to the social worker next time she stops by. I can't take it any more. He's driving me crazy!"

"Okay, mama. I'll find a way ta tell him. Give me a couple a weeks."

"No. Ya got a couple a days, no more."

Leah just looked at the receiver after her mother had hung up. She couldn't believe her mother expected her to take care of the kid. She had no idea what she was going to tell Harry. He wanted kids, but she'd told him she couldn't have any. It wasn't a lie. She couldn't, not as long as she remembered to take the pills she got from the clinic.

BJ continued calling Leah telling her she had to come and get her child. Leah keeps telling her mother she's waiting for the right time to tell Harry. Finally, Leah contacted her mother.

"Well, I done it," Leah announced to her mother.

"Done what?" her mother asked.

"Done what? Are you crazy? I done what ya been hounding me ta do. I told Harry about the kid."

"You did?"

"Yep, and ya know what?"

"What?"

"He's excited to meet the brat."

"No way."

"Yep. I think he's crazy as a bedbug. He said somethin' like, "Now we're a real family."

"Your right, he is crazy."

"Well, anyway he's fixin' up the back room so the kid'll have a place to sleep."

"Why? He's been sleeping on the floor here and been doin' fine."

"Harry says a kid needs a room of his own."

"In the back?"

"Yep. I hope it's far enough away so's I won't hear the brat cryin'. That cryin' drives me crazy."

"When ya fixin' to pick him up?"

"Saturday."

"That should work out all right. That's near the beginning of the month."

"So what?"

"My food stamps and check comes in on the first. This way I'll get some extra money before it all stops."

"Why should it stop?"

"Cause I ain't gonna have the kid with me anymore. Ya dumb or somethin'?"

"How da they know?"

"Cause I hav'ta tell them."

"No ya don't."

"What if the kid ain't here when they come by?"

"Do they know he's sleeping on the floor?"

"Hell, no! I keep a little bed made up so's they think it's his."

"Well, if'n they come by, ya know, like a surprise, you tell'um that I took him for a little visit and ya call me."

"What if'n ya ain't home."

"Musta gone ta the park. Ya know I like to take him ta the park."

"No you don't. But that's a good answer."

"Sometimes they call first to be sure I'm gonna be home."

"Then ya call me and I bring the brat back. Just keep that little bed and some clothes and some of the baby things."

"He doesn't have much here as it is. I haven't bought him much cause there just ain't enough money to buy food, pay my expenses and get him stuff too."

"He's only a little kid. He don't need nothin'. Besides, if'n he needs somethin', Harry can buy it."

Leah and BJ work out all the details of their plan and when Saturday came, the child exchange took place. Leah and Harry both were acting so happy about taking Billy Ray and BJ managed to shed a few tears when they were leaving. Later on Leah called her mother to talk.

"That kid is on my last nerve already. How'd ya put up with him so long?"

"The way ya acted this afternoon, I thought ya really wanted him."

"Ha! It was just what ya just said, an act. I can't stand him, but Harry wants kids and he makes good money so I hadda do something to keep him."

"You're sure a good actress."

"Yep, I think so. I been practicing a lot."

"Ya gonna try out for some a them movies."

"Nah, too much work. Besides, that's what I do everyday – act. But ya didn't answer my question."

"What was that?"

"How did ya keep the kid quiet so's ya could think? All his does is holler."

"Did ya feed him?"

"Didn't ya feed him before we picked him up?"

"Sure, but ya hav'ta feed him more'n once a day."

"Yeah, yeah. I will, but how do ya keep him quiet in between."

"Well, when he got a little too active, I gave him a couple a drops of Vodka."

"Vodka? That stuff tastes terrible."

"I like it."

"Not me. Is that what ya drink at the club?"

"Yeah, cause it doesn't smell so strong on my breath."

"Whatever. I don't like it."

"Well, what do you drink?"

"They have something called Schnapps."

"Is that the thick stuff I see them pour in them small glasses?"

"Probably."

"I like a big drink, not that sissy stuff."

"Well, I like it cause it's strong and one drink goes a long way. Besides, it comes in a lot of flavors – peppermint, grape and some others."

"So buy a bottle of it and give some to the kid if he acts too bad. Ya wouldn't need a lot of it for him, so ya could probably buy one of them little bottles I see in the package store."

"I ain't ever been to a package store. Let's go there next week – when Harry's at work. That is, if I can make it that long. This kid is drivin' me crazy."

After the baby had been in the house for a couple of days Harry began to think he really didn't want any children. The continual crying was terrible. He didn't know if all babies were like that or if Leah didn't know how to take care of her own child. Either way he was trying to find a way to get rid of them both. But then, one day he realized the baby was quiet and Leah was back to the person he liked so he figured it just had taken them both a couple of days to work out a couple of issues. He never suspected that Leah was giving the baby liquor to keep him quiet. He did think the baby slept a lot, but when he talked to his mother about it she told him it was natural and that all babies cried. Harry never told his mother that he never saw the child awake anymore. He also never told his mother that he never saw Leah feeding the child. He just told his mother how much he cared for Leah and the baby and couldn't wait for Leah to get pregnant with his child. The baby was okay, but it wasn't of his blood. He wanted his own child.

Leah, on the other hand, kept telling her mother that the "kid" was driving her crazy with all his crying and that she didn't know what to do now that she was pregnant again.

"Again!" BJ shouted at her daughter. "How could you be? Ain't ya taken them pills every day?"

"Well, I try, but sometimes they make me sick to the stomach so if I don't want to be sick or if the baby is acting up some and I don't have time to be sick, I don't."

"Ya have ta take them everyday or else they don't work."

"Well, they should. It ain't my fault. It's them doctors. If'n they made the pills right this wouldn'ta happened."

"Lordy, Lordy. When ya do?"

"First a next year."

"Ya stopped takin' them pills when ya took the baby in, didn't ya?"

"No. Why'dia say that? You're always making things about to be my fault – and it ain't'."

"Your getting pregnant is all your fault. Whose gonna take care of all these kids? Not me cause I'm done takin' care of other peoples children."

Leah just took a big puff of her cigarette and blew the smoke to the ceiling. She was tired of hearing her mother rant and rave. Leah felt she was the one who always had to cook dinner for her sisters, not her mother. She was the one who had to wash clothes once in awhile, not BJ. If her mother only knew that Misty was going to drop another baby in December, she'd really have a fit. Leah didn't say any of what she was thinking, instead she said, "Well, I gotta go now. Harry will be home soon and if he sees me on the phone again, he'll have a fit. Besides, I should start to think about something for dinner. I'll talk to ya tomorrow."

After BJ hung the phone up, she was tempted to call her daughter back to tell her she should stop her smoking. It wasn't good for the baby she was carrying. She picked up the phone and then decided not to make the call. Leah didn't care about the child she was carrying. She just wanted the kid to keep Harry happy.

A month went by and Leah started, in spite of all her efforts, putting on a little weight. She didn't fit into her short shorts anymore and her less than ample chest had started to increase to the point she had to buy a bra. One day Harry noticed the changed and made the mistake of saying, "I guess you're not getting enough exercise."

"Whadda ya mean by that?"

"Just that you've put on a few pounds. I thought having the baby in the house would keep you active."

"Whadda ya mean by that?"

"Just that you've been chowing down a lot lately. Not that I mind cause you've been a little too skinny and I like the change. You have more of a girl's figure instead of a teenaged boy."

"Ya sure don't complain when we're in bed."

"No and I'm not complaining now. I'm just stating the fact that you don't look half bad."

"Well if ya must know, its all your fault."

Now Harry started laughing. "How's your chowing down and gaining weight my fault?"

"Ya up an' got me pregnant!"

Harry stopped laughing and looked at his girlfriend. "Really?"

"Really," Leah said trying to sound happy.

"When did you find out?"

"Just today, for sure," she said lying to Harry. She had known for six weeks but didn't tell him because she was trying to decide if she should have an abortion.

"Wow!" exclaimed Harry. "I don't know what to say. I have to call my mom. She'll be so happy."

Leah smiled at him, but was thinking how he was such a momma's boy, always calling to talk to her. Leah didn't know if she could go through with this. She really liked Harry. He worked hard, turned his paycheck over to her to pay the bills and never asked if there was anything left over. He never asked anything for himself and never questioned what she spent on herself or the baby. He even liked her cooking. But he said she was chowing down; she'd have to watch what she ate from now on. She sure didn't want to get fat, even if she was pregnant.

As time went by, BJ found out about Misty being pregnant with her third child. Misty's just 18 and this time she doesn't know who the father is. When the child's born in December (1979), Misty immediately goes to the welfare department so they know she about the new baby and will increase her monthly payment. Her next stop is to her mother to drop the child off. She has no intention of keeping the child; she only wants the extra money. She tells her mother she'll give her the difference in her monthly check, once she starts receiving it. BJ knows she'll never see the money, but won't let the child go without either.

Leah has her baby, a son, on January 9th, 1980. Harry tells Leah he wants the baby to be named Andy. Leah hates the name, but smiles and agrees. In reality, she really doesn't care what the child is called. She'll always refer to him as kid, just as she does his half-brother.

Harry's overjoyed at having a boy child. He's been working on a nearby farm to support himself, Leah and her first child. Now he picks up a job working nights at a factory on the other side of town so he can start saving for a farm of his own. He hardly ever sees Leah and the children as he's gone by 5am to the first job and goes directly to the second from the farm. He gets home about midnight every day. Many times Leah is waiting for him when he comes in. He's pleased to see her, but exhausted so he grabs a sandwich, if there's anything in the fridge, showers and goes to bed. Leah, however, is furious. The babies are asleep, with a little help from some alcohol, and she's ready to party. Many times after Harry goes to bed, she slips out to the club in the neighborhood and gets home just before he gets up to start his routine over again. She's determined to continue her life with or without Harry. She just needs him to fund it so she starts making plans on how to make it happen.

It's taken Leah 18 months, but she's finished building her stories about Harry and has started drawing welfare for herself and the children. Over the past year and a half, she's told everyone how she's a battered wife and how crazy Harry is. She's told all kinds of stories about how he neglects and abuses them all. She's fabricated how she has to step between him and the children so he won't hit them. She shows everyone who will look, the bruises he's given her. In reality, she's gotten quite good at applying makeup to look like bruises and wears clothes that will show her artistry off. She tells how she has to hide her children in a safe house, so Harry won't kill them.

While telling the stories, she tears up and finally cries her heart out. Everyone believes her. They never once think of checking her story out. They just assume the boyfriend is a bad guy. Little do they know the "safe house" is with her younger sister who is about to give birth to her fourth child. Plus they have no idea the welfare and the money she receives from the Ramsey's is spent is bars. If anyone took the time to verify, they would see all the checks are all cashed at the neighborhood social club. They'd also find that Leah's mother and sister are the ones who've been feeding and clothing her children. You see Leah has lied to her sister and mother as well. She's told them the Ramsey's stopped sending support for Billy Ray, Harry has refused to pay child support and she hasn't been able to collect welfare yet.

In November 1981, Misty has her fourth child. She doesn't know who the father is and, in what has become her pattern, makes the first stop out of the hospital to the welfare office. She files for additional support for the latest child. The social worker advises Misty she needs to get on birth control pills. When Misty says she can't afford them, the social worker tells her to learn to control her sexual drive. Misty is furious. Arriving back at her mother's house, the old duplex, she tells her mother what the social worker said to her.

"Well, Misty, you do have four children now and you ain't 19 yet. Don't ya think it might be time to fix this problem–permanently?"

"I ain't gonna do nothin' unnatural to my body. If God wants me to have 50 children, then that's what I'll have."

"God? Since when do ya believe in God? God ain't got nothin' to do with you having sex and having babies."

"You got a filthy mind. It ain't my fault if God wants me to have a bunch of babies. It just ain't my fault."

CHAPTER 11

It's September 1982 ……

BJ's life hasn't changed much. She works only when she has to. She pretty much ignores her youngest child, Edna, as she won't party with her mother and sisters. Edna, only turning 13, tries to spend as much time away from them as she can.

All of the grandchildren are young and, therefore, pose a problem for the three Turnbull women. Someone has to watch them. They can't be left alone. So it becomes a game of who gets a date each night and who doesn't. The last one without a date has to watch all the children while the other two go out and party. More times than not, BJ's the one watching the children as she's the only one making an attempt at working.

During the day, the children make the rounds of social agencies, welfare offices and food kitchens with their mothers. The girls are well known in the area so they no longer see the need to go separately. Everyone working in the respective places shudder when they see the two young girls and their six always-dirty charges rush through their door. It's never a pleasant scene and even though assistance is only supposed to be monthly, the rule is broken just to get them to leave.

Mrs. Whitby, at the food stamp office, learned early on not to give either Misty or Leah their full allotment of stamps when they come in. She did the first time they applied and when the girls showed up a week later demanding more help, she caved in. Now she only gives them a portion of their allotment as she knows no matter how much she gives them, they'll be back in a week. It's more work for her, but she does it and doesn't broadcast that it can be done so all of her clients don't ask for the same treatment. She's been clever about it, however. She separates the total amount of food stamps into four envelopes at the beginning of the month. She keeps the envelopes at the front counter, so when the Turnbulls come in, she just opens the drawer and hands them the envelope.

This way, the loud group is in and out of the office in very short order. This quick turn around also gives the impression that they didn't receive anything.

After one such episode, Leah said to her sister, "Ya know what?"

"Yeah, I know I got money to go party with tonight," replied Misty.

"That too, but what I meant was how smart we are and how we got that Miss Whitby beat."

"How ya figure?"

"We don't gotta go in that awful place the same days other people. Right?"

"Right."

"We don't gotta wait in a long line like them other people. Right?"

"Right."

"We get stamps every week not once a month like them others. Right?"

"Right."

"We got her beat. Damn we're good," laughed Leah.

"Right!"

"We got a bunch of kids that keep us in money and we got a mother who'll watch 'em when we go out cause she hardly never has a date herself."

"Right."

"We got it made."

"Sure are right. Speaking of goin' out, where we goin' tonight?"

"Have to think about that. Who hasn't cashed our food stamps in awhile?"

"Dunno. Have to think on it a bit."

On the same day Leah determines she and her sister are so brilliant, their mother is enjoying a quiet drink at the neighborhood social club, watching some new guy playing pool. She finds him interesting and moves closer to the pool table so she might have a chance to strike up a conversation with him.

Before long she's talking with him. He's apparently interested in her as well because when he misses an easy shot, he throws his cue stick on the table followed by a large bill. "Might as well stop playing, if I can't keep my mind on the game" he exclaims to no one in particular. With that said, he walks over to BJ and says, "You want something to eat?" BJ nods and they walk over to the other side of the club where it's a little quieter.

The girls have been out most of the day. They've found a place to cash their food stamps in for spending money and are ready to party. First, however, they have to dump their children with their mother. The children had all been crying from hunger, but exhaustion finally overtook them all and they were quiet when they reached their grandmother's house. The young mothers are both laughing as they walk into the little house the whole group calls home.

"Hey BJ. We gotta surprise for ya", yelled Leah.

Silence.

Misty followed her older sisters lead and hollers, "Yeah, surprise, surprise. Come out, come out wherever you are."

Silence.

Now Leah is getting a little angry. Her children have been in the same diaper all day so they needed changing and they hadn't been fed so they were hungry. She certainly wasn't going to change their messy diapers. Nor did she plan on fixing food and wasting all the time it takes to feed them. "Where in the hell are you", she screamed into the air.

Silence.

Misty says to her sister, "She ain't home."

"She has to be home. All these kids need changin', feedin' and bathin' and I ain't gonna do it. I got things to do and places to go."

Misty was a little quiet. She didn't know what to say to her sister when she was like this. So instead of saying anything, Misty just started taking her babies out of the crowded carriage and putting them in the bed they shared. Finally she said, "I'll do it for you. I know you don't like taking care of them too much." As soon as those words came out of her mouth, Misty knew she shouldn't have said them.

"Too much? I hate having anything to do with them. The only reason I had em was for the money. It ain't my fault we ain't rich and can't afford to have someone takin' care of em like it's supposed to be.

Misty said nothing. She just continued placing all the children in the bed and started changing them one by one. All of them were soaking wet from not being changed all day. Most of them had wet feces in their diapers. They all had fiery red bottoms.

"Leah, can you hand me that ointment on the dresser?"

"What?"

"Can you hand me that ointment."

"Why?"

"Because I need it for the babies and I can't reach it from here."

"Just walk over and git it yerself."

"I can't leave the baby on the top of the table. He might fall off."

Leah stomped over to the dresser, grabbed the ointment and slammed it into her sister's hand. "Waste of money buying this stuff. I bet it cost enough to buy me a dinner. She's always wasting my money that way."

"Whadda ya mean?"

"If'n it wasn't for me, she wouldn't be getting money for taking care of the kids. She didn't know how to do it. So I figure it's my money and she should be askin' me how to spend it. Besides, she's being paid for takin' care of the kids and here she is not even home. I oughta report her for leavin' my kids alone."

"Alone? Their not alone, we're with them. We've had em all day."

"So? She's paid to watch um and she ain't home to do it. So she should be reported."

"If we do that, then they'll take um away from her and they might give em back to us. Then what would we do?"

Leah thought about it for a minute and then replied, "Whatever. I can always find another man to take care of us all. A rich one this time."

While her daughters had to care for their own children, BJ wasn't giving them a single thought. She was having too much fun with the man she'd just met. Later that evening, Steven told her he had to go to work, but he'd call her when he got off. As she was walking home, she thought she should get around to getting divorced. She would have done it a long time ago, except she really didn't have the money and Bobby Ray wouldn't pay for it. She thinks this new man might be the one who'll take care of her, and maybe as good as her family did.

Every now and then she thinks of the big house and Sally. BJ wonders if she should have moved back to them when she and Bobby Ray split up. Too late now as she knows they would never want so many people in the house, especially all the babies. However, it would be nice to have someone like Sally around the house. BJ just sighed. If she ever told the girls about their grandparents and how they had money, there'd be hell to pay. Who knew what the girls would do? BJ didn't want to think about it any more. It was much too painful.

It was past dinnertime when BJ got home, but she'd already eaten so wasn't planning to cook.

As she walked in the door Leah started screaming at her. "Where in the hell have you been? There ain't no dinner on the table, ain't no food to eat in the fridge and we hadda clean up the kids ourselves."

BJ stopped, looked around and finally shouted, "I ain't your nigger. This is my house. I let you stay here and I don't need your permission to come and go. I also don't have to tell you where I've been or what I've been doing. You got that."

Leah and Misty just looked at her for a moment. Then finally Leah said, "Whatever. But we had plans and you ruined them."

"I'm not really sorry, cause you've ruined my plans for years."

"Whatever", Leah muttered as she stood there with her arms folded across her chest.

Then Misty quietly asked, "Well, what were you doing that you were gone so long. I was worried."

"Thanks. If'n ya must know, I found me a new man."

Both girls in unison said, "What?"

"Ya both heard me."

The girls were stunned. They knew BJ and their father hadn't even spoken in a very long time, but they were still married and the girls expected them to stay that way.

Misty finally said, "What about Daddy?" But before BJ could respond, Leah said sharply, "To hell with him. Does this one have money? Ya know what you're always tellin' me - be sure the next one has money."

BJ smiled, "I don't know much about him yet so I can't answer your questions. I'll tell you what I do know. He's not from around here. His name is Steven Boyd. He's from California and just moved here. He works over at the prison. He's got a federal job."

Misty squealed, "He's got money! All them federal guys got money. Hurrah! We're gonna be rich!" All thoughts of concern about her father were instantly gone.

Leah started asking more questions, but BJ cut her off. "I done told you all I know, except he's a sweet talker and he plays a good game of pool."

Both girls nodded their heads and sighed. They wanted all the details, but it was apparent to them that she was telling them nothing more.

Then Misty said to her mother, "We haven't eaten yet, have you?"

"Yes, but I'll fix you girls something."

"The kids ain't eaten either."

BJ exploded, "How many times do I have to tell you both that growing kids need food. I don't care if'n you don't eat all day, but ya can't do that to them little ones." Glaring at her daughters, she stomped into the kitchen and started banging pans.

Both girls hung their heads, just a little, and then plopped themselves on the couch and started watching the television.

BJ yelled at them, "Go and get them children cleaned up before they have their dinner. How many times do I have ta tell ya that I ain't ya're nigger."

Reluctantly the girls got up and went to see to the needs of their children.

This pattern continued over the next few weeks, until one day the girls came home and found their mother's new boyfriend was there. BJ was fixing dinner and he was in the kitchen talking with her while she cooked.

BJ introduced Steven to her girls and their children. Then she said dinner was ready, so all the adults sat down at the table.

A couple of months later, BJ filed for divorce from Bobby Ray. He didn't contest it so within 6 months both of them would be finally free from a marriage that never should have happened. Even though Bobby Ray didn't want to be with BJ any more, the finality of the action depressed him somewhat. BJ wanted alimony and child support for all of their children and their grandchildren. The judge didn't laugh, but he smiled when he was reading her request in open court. A series of snickers did come from the casual observers in the courtroom, but stopped when the judge peered over the paper-work at the audience.

"Mrs. Turnbull, are you employed", asked the judge?

"Yessir", was her reply.

"Are you making enough to support yourself and your youngest child?"

"Yes sir, but ...."

"No buts. You and the youngest child of the marriage are the only concerns of this court."

"How am I supposed to feed and put clothes on the backs of the other two girls and their children? They belong to him too so's he should be made to help."

"Are the oldest children still in the home?"

"Most of the time."

"Are they still attending school?"

"Hell, they ain't been in school in years!"

With that, the onlookers started laughing. The judge once again gave a hard look out on the audience and the noise stopped.

"Do they have children of their own?"

"Sure do and I has ta watch them all the time, so's he should be made to help."

"Do they work?"

"No."

"Is Mr. Turnbull the father of their children?"

"Hell, no!"

This time the courtroom burst into laughter. This time the judge said, "One more outburst and I will have the courtroom cleared."

"Then I suggest they get jobs and take care of their own children. As I said before, my concern is for the life style of you and the youngest child of the marriage."

"Lifestyle? I ain't got no life, much less style. I need money and free time for that. I ain't got either, so's I figure he has'ta at least give me money so's I can have it."

The judge looked over the courtroom. There was no snickering and no laughter, but there were a lot of faces covered with hands.

The judge looked over at Bobby Ray and said, "Mr. Turnbull, do you work?"

"Yes, I do."

"Do you ever see your youngest daughter?"

"Once in awhile."

"Why not more often?"

"I would see her every weekend if her mother would let me."

"Do you call her on the phone?"

"Not any more."

"Why?"

"If her mother or her sisters answer the phone, they always tell me Edna isn't there. If I leave a message for her to call me when she gets home, I never get a call back. I send cards for special days, sometimes with money for her to spend on herself, but I never know if she gets it or not."

"Ya never send much. Ya call sending a dollar or two spending money?" screamed BJ.

The judge's head snapped to look at the source of the screaming. BJ had been so quiet and polite up to that point. Then he asked Bobby Ray, "Do you pay child support now?"

"Yes I do. When we separated she went to court for a temporary support order. It was for her and the three girls. I stopped paying a portion of the support each time one of my daughters had a child and I knew they had moved out on their own or in with someone. I still pay half of what I was ordered to pay and when BJ calls and says she needs something for Edna, I send extra."

"Ya don't pay enough. Ya should hav'ta pay for everything so's I wouldn't hav'ta work no more. My mother never worked and they live in a big house and peoples respect them. Ya should hav'ta pay cause ya got me pregnant when I was so young," BJ screamed at the top of her lungs.

In the middle of BJ's screaming, the judge started banging his gavel to bring some quiet and order to his courtroom. The onlookers were no longer laughing. They were talking to the people sitting next to them and pointing at BJ. The judge kept banging and finally stood up and gave one final bang on his gavel.

"Bailiff, if this courtroom isn't quiet in 5 seconds, I want everyone moved out." The room got quiet immediately.

The judge put the paperwork that was in his hand down, took out a handkerchief and wiped his brow. He couldn't help but think back to his morning cup of coffee with his wife. He told her it was going to be an easy day, just two uncontested divorces to hear. He shook his head.

"All right now. I'm going to ask one or two more questions, and then I'm going to take a recess to ponder on my decision. Mr. Turnbull, how much do you pay in child support now?"

Bobby Ray told him and the judge made a notation.

"Do you live by yourself?"

"Yes, I do."

With that, BJ was up out of her chair screaming, "That's a lie. Ya lives with that Mexican and ..."

Before she could finish her screaming statements, the judge nodded to the Bailiff who swiftly grabbed BJ, pushed her arms behind her and forced her out of the courtroom."

"Whadda ya doin'? Ya can't touch me. I gotta right to say whatever I want, BJ was yelling at the Bailiff all the time he was pulling her through the back door reserved for criminals. Finally the door closed and it was once again quiet in the courtroom.

The judge looked at Bobby Ray who was now red with embarrassment and felt sorry for the man. "Mr. Turnbull, are you telling me the truth?"

"Yes your honor. I do have a friend who is a Mexican and we do have dinner almost every night, but I have my own place and so does she."

"That's fine. Thank you. Then he looked around the courtroom and said, "I've found I don't need to take a recess to make my decision." Once BJ was out of the courtroom his head had cleared so he could proceed. "I'm finalizing this divorce as of today. Your legal separation has served as the mandated cooling off period. I'm ordering you to continue paying your now ex-wife child support; however, the amount is lowered to $50 a month. I'd prefer to award custody of the child to you, but this I cannot do. I suggest you retain counsel who can guide you if you wish to pursue this further. Visitation is to be a minimum of two weekends a month. You will have joint custody of the child with your former wife. She will be the physical custodian until a time when a court changes this, the child is old enough to make her own decision, or she leaves her mother's home." Then he banged his gavel one last time and said, "Court adjourned!"

Bobby Ray couldn't believe his ears. He was finally legally free of BJ and the court says he's to have visitation. He felt he'd won.

CHAPTER 12

It's 1983 ......

Harry was devastated when Leah and the children left him. He'd call her every time he got a short break during the workday. After work he'd sit outside the duplex and wait for her to leave, then follow her, all the time trying to talk to her to find out why she left him. Sometimes when she went out without the children, he'd attempt to see them but BJ seldom allowed that. He stopped working his second job and was about to lose his job at the farm because his mind wasn't on his work.

Leah was furious with him. She'd left him and wanted no part of him anymore. All she ever wanted from him was money so she had a child with him to ensure she'd have income for a long time. Leah thought she'd be free of him when the divorce was final, but he was always hanging around. She was tired of him and wanted him totally gone from her life and didn't want him seeing the children either. Money was all she wanted from him; he paid, but only what the court had ordered and it wasn't enough for her to party on much less feed the kids and pay bills. She was tired of him bugging her all the time, so she decided it was time to play out the final phase of the plan she'd worked on for so long. She knew it would finally get Harry out of her life.

One day, when Harry had been extremely visible in his attempts to see the children, Leah stormed into the social club and announced to everyone there, "Can someone help me? I think Harry's gone crazy! He's been follerin' me everywhere and is tryin' to kidnap my chillrin. I don't know what to do!" Then she burst into tears and dropped into the nearest chair.

One of the ladies sitting at a table nearby rushed to her side. Leah didn't know this woman by name, but she'd seen her many times in the club. She dressed nicely and always had money to buy lunch and all the drinks she wanted.

"Now, now dearie, don't let some man get you down. I think there are enough of us unattached women here that can help you. Come over to my table and let's get you calmed down so you can tell us the whole story."

Leah didn't need calming down; she just needed some assistance in making her plan come true. Instinctively she knew that these fat, old women would be more than willing to help her.

"You look terrible. Would you like something to eat? Perhaps that would help calm you down."

"I don't think I could eat anything," replied Leah. "I'm too upset." However, she was thinking, "*I don't want food. I don't want to get fat like you old hens.*"

"You should eat something. You're so thin and pale."

Leah just nodded.

"How about a grilled ham and cheese sandwich and a few fries?"

"All right, I suppose I could try."

"That's the spirit! And how about a little drink to go along with it?"

"Sweet tea would be nice," crooned Leah. She really wanted a good stiff drink, but that wasn't part of her plan.

"Fine. Sweet tea and a grilled cheese sandwich with fries," the helpful lady said as she was snapping her fingers in the air to get the waitress's attention. "After you eat we can get you something stronger."

Leah was tempted to say she didn't drink, but she knew some of the people in the club knew she did. Instead she quietly replied, "Okay."

Leah wasn't one for eating. She preferred to drink very sweet tea and to munch on a cracker once in awhile, if the hunger pangs got strong; however, she knew she'd have to eat most of the lunch or she wouldn't be offered the drink. Leah also knew by their conversation these ladies were ripe for gossip. One drink would lead to another and she'd have them in the palm of her hand.

Leah correctly predicted what would happen and three hours later she walked slowly out of the club with her head slightly hanging. She turned, gave a small, forced smile to the woman, turned back and started walking towards her home. She was careful not to appear too happy for a couple of blocks. When she felt she was safe from their view, she stood up straight and smiled a very large smile. She had them right where she wanted them. Now if Harry would only do his part. She could hardly wait to tell BJ the plan and how well it was going so far. She was going to have to keep it from her sisters, however, as they would spill the beans and ruin it for her.

By the time February came Leah felt she had enough support to take the next step in her plan. Harry had just been to the house and caused a huge scene, even screaming at her from the front yard. Many of the neighbors had been outside and heard all he said. After he left Leah came out of the house, crying, and walking slowly in the opposite direction of where Harry had gone.

One of the neighbors said, "Honey, where ya goin'?"

"To the police. I cain't take this anymore. I'm scared. I'm scared for me and my chillrin'."

"I heard all he said, so if you need a witness – well you just tell them cops that I saw it all."

Leah turned to the old busy body and said, "Thank you so much. I've tried to keep this all quiet cause he always threatened to beat me again if'n I said anything."

"You poor dear. That's why you're so thin, isn't it. You're just worried sick and can't eat."

Leah nodded and walked on.

By the time she arrived at the police station she'd worked herself into a near hysterical state. Her acting was so good, the sergeant on duty called for a matron to assist him.

The matron could hear the commotion long before she walked into the reception area.

"What's the problem," she quietly asked the sergeant?

He whispered his reply. "Don't actually know. I've only been able to understand a couple of words but I think she's a victim of abuse."

The matron nodded and then quietly responded, "I can believe that just by looking at her. I'll take her in back to one of the interrogation rooms. Get Smitty to the viewing area. I'll see if I can get her calmed down enough to talk."

"Done," the sergeant said as he was picking up the phone to call for more assistance.

In the meantime, the matron had walked over to Leah, put her arm around her shoulder and started talking softly to her.

"Just come with me. Let's see if we can get you calmed down enough so we can find out what's happened. Okay?"

Leah just sobbed, but she let the woman lead her through the double doors that were labeled "NO ENTRY WITHOUT AUTHORIZATION". Leah had no idea where she was going but felt her plan was working. She really had to focus to keep the sobs and now hiccups coming. Leah knew this would be her only chance. If she blew it, she'd probably have to leave town. She kept her head down and stumbled along with the matron.

"Here we are, honey. Let's just sit in here awhile."

Leah looked up just in time to see bars on the windows. This time she screamed without too much acting. "I don't want to go ta jail! I didn't do anything," she wailed loudly. Now the tears were flowing for real. She thought they were locking her up because she was acting so crazy.

"Now, now," said the matron. "You ain't going to jail. All our doors and windows have bars on them. You have to get used to that working here. Even the bathrooms have bars all over them. This is just the quietest place we have."

"Really," asked Leah?

"Really," responded the matron.

Leah started to calm down some and allowed the matron to usher her into the room.

"You drink coffee?"

Leah responded, "Yes, but do you have anything cold?"

"Sure. Diet or regular?"

Leah made a face that caused the matron to laugh. "Okay, regular it is. I'll be right back. Just sit there and try to gather your thoughts so we can talk this situation out. Okay?"

Leah just nodded. The thought of her going to jail had scared the hysteria, even though it was faked, right out of her. She was exhausted. Leah hadn't realized how hard it was to keep up the act she'd designed. She didn't know if she should try crying again or just be quiet. Before she could make her decision, the matron returned.

"Feeling better?" the matron asked as she handed her a cold soft drink.

Leah just nodded her head as she took a small sip.

"Are you up to telling me why you came to the station and why you're so upset?"

Leah started to tear up again as she started telling the story she had been working on for weeks. She explained all the things Harry had done and said, but was very careful not to mention the word "crazy". She wanted them to say that word. Leah wanted them to be the ones to take action against him, not her. She tells how she's afraid for herself and her children as Harry keeps trying to steal them from her. When the matron asked if anyone else had witnessed him acting strangely, Leah smiled to herself and then said, "Everyone I know has seen him acting the way he does. My sisters, my mother and father, all the neighbors and probably anyone at the club we used to go to all the time could tell you something he said or did. The only thing that no one has seen him do is hit me." Leah was so proud of herself. She hadn't lied to the matron. Everyone she named could testify to something Harry had said or done and she hadn't lied when she said no one had seen him hit her, as he never had. Leah just never bothered to correct the implication.

The matron was writing as fast as she could. She hoped Smitty was outside the one-way glass and taking notes as well so they would get everything. The matron felt the family needed protection from the husband but she needed some assistance in deciding what kind of protection.

"Honey, wait right here. I need to get me another pencil. While I'm out would you like me to get you something to eat?"

Leah shook her head no and thought to herself, *"These fat pigs are always trying to get me to eat so's I'll look like them."*

Once the heavy door to the interrogation room closed, the matron started talking to Smitty. "What do you think?"

"I don't know," he replied. "There's just something about her and the story."

"Her story hasn't changed in all the time she's been here." the matron replied.

"I know. Maybe that's what bothers me. She was near hysterical when she got here, but she hasn't added a single detail since her first account of what's been going on. Seems to me if a person were really hysterical they wouldn't remember everything right then. Seems to me they would hit the most recent things at first and then start remembering all the other details after they calmed down a little."

"May be, but look at her," the matron said. "She's nothing but skin and bones. Her skin is pasty and it looks like someone took a knife to her hair."

"That's all true, but look at her eyes."

"What about them?"

"They're fixed on this glass but, her hands are fidgeting and her legs are shifting around, like she's nervous and upset."

"She is upset. You must have heard her scream when I first tried to get her in the room."

"I did. I wished I had been able to see her eyes then."

"Why?"

"Because even though her body language is saying she's upset, her eyes don't. If I had seen her eyes when I knew she was upset, I'd have a better idea of what's going on in her head."

"What's this all about? Isn't it obvious she's in an abusive situation?"

"Maybe."

"Maybe, nothing. She's scared to death. The poor dear can't eat and can barely talk."

"Ummmm, I just don't know."

"You're just taking sides again," the matron commented.

"Where're the children?" asked Smitty.

"What?"

"Where are the children?"

"What do you mean?"

"If she's so afraid of her husband, for herself and her family then where are her children now?"

While the matron and Smitty were talking, Leah was staring at the large mirror on the wall at herself. She decided she shouldn't have fixed herself up before going to the police. She looked a little too good. The longer she stared the more she got thinking about the mirror and how strange it was to have a mirror in a room where prisoners were normally kept. Then it dawned on her that it was probably a two-way mirror and someone had been watching her all the time. With that thought, she stopped staring at it and moved her center of focus to the back of the chair where the fat pig had been sitting. She didn't want anyone looking directly at her face. She was thinking about what the matron had been asking and what her answers had been. Then she thought about the story she'd been telling about Harry. She was trying to figure if she needed to add anything else or had she said enough. Just as she started feeling she had said enough, it dawned on her that she never mentioned the children. *"They're gonna wonder where the children are. If I'm so scared of Harry and what he might do to me and the children, where are the children? Damn! Where are the children?"* With that thought she turned her back to the mirror. She had to come up with some story about the children and come up with it fast.

"What's she doing," Smitty asked?

"Just moving around. What's wrong with that?"

"Normally nothing. But she'd been staring at the mirror when her eyes opened a little and she shifted to staring at the chair. Then her head moved up slightly and she shifted so her face couldn't be seen. I think she's up to something."

Just as he was about to tell the matron to get back in the room, Leah started to wail. It was a high-pitched, screech of a wail. The matron ran into the room and without waiting for the door to fully close, so the microphone would work properly, said, "My God, dearie, what's wrong?"

"My children. My children. Where're my children," Leah screamed at her.

The matron grabbed her by the shoulders and swung her around so her face could be seen via the mirror. "I don't know. Where are your children?"

"I don't remember. All I remember is leaving the house this morning after that last scene with Harry standing in the middle of the yard screaming, and swearing he would take care of me and the children – for good!"

The matron glanced at the mirror, giving Smitty a hard glare. She was furious with him for trying to protect the men all the time. She was going to get a warrant issued to lock this Harry up so he couldn't hurt anyone again.

"Honey, now don't you worry. I'm sending a car over to pick them up. You think you left them at the house?"

"How terrible a mother I am! I walked away and left my chillren' all alone," Leah wailed even louder.

"Now, now," the matron cooed as she held the near hysterical Leah. "We all understand. Sometimes a person can be pushed too far. I'm sure they're all right. Are you going to be okay for a minute?"

Leah nodded her head while gulping for air and wiping tears from her face. When the matron turned to walk out the door, Leah couldn't help but glance at the mirror one last time before turning her back to it. Once her face couldn't be seen, she smiled and started slowly heaving her shoulders. From the back, it appeared as if she were still sobbing; however, she was almost laughing. The heaving of her shoulders was simply the tension leaving her body. She'd stayed in character for hours and she was all tensed up from it. *I could sure use a cigarette and some ice tea – lots of sugar, if you please.* She almost laughed out loud, but caught herself, just in case they were listening.

"Smitty," the matron ordered, "send a car over to her house to pick up the children. If they ain't there, go to her mother's house. If she accidentally left the children alone, they might know enough to go to grandma's or grandma might have stopped by."

Smitty replied, "I don't think this woman has ever done anything accidentally."

"Just do it."

Smitty nodded and walked off shaking his head. In his heart he felt this poor shmuck was going to be railroaded and there was nothing he could do about it.

The matron was very diligent in her efforts to "save" the latest "victims" of spousal/child abuse – Leah and her children. She got an emergency hearing set for the following week. In the meantime she found a shelter where they could stay and be safe. The matron even obtained emergency funding so they could buy the necessities they left behind when they were "forced" into leaving their home so suddenly.

Leah was so pleased. She had a roof over her head she didn't have to pay for and she had someone to cook and clean for her – once again without having to pay for the services.

There were a few things she didn't like. She had to share a room with her children. She had to attend every meal and she had to eat and they all had to attend group-counseling sessions. The worst thing, however, was she couldn't go out at night nor talk on the phone. She didn't like being controlled, but she knew she had to submit to the rules or she'd lose all she was working for.

Harry had no idea what was going on. He'd been over to the house a couple of times, but never found anyone home. No one answered Leah's phone, nor her mother's or sister's. He'd tried talking to a couple of the neighbors but they couldn't or wouldn't tell him anything. One person just slammed her door in his face before he could even say anything. He knew Leah and he knew she wouldn't leave her party friends. Harry was concerned for the children, but didn't know where to turn.

After the weekend passed and he still couldn't find any trace of his wife and children, he went to the nearest police station. He hated going to the police, as he didn't know what they could do, but he didn't know where else to turn. He walked in the door to find it totally empty except for one officer who appeared busy doing paperwork.

"Ah, excuse me sir. Could I ask you a question?" Harry said politely.

The officer lifted his head to see who was talking to him. He was afraid it was one of the locals who liked to be part of the police scene. It wasn't, so he responded, "Sure. What do you need?"

"Well, my name is Harry Cauthern and I have a problem."

Before he could say anymore, Smitty leaned over the desk and said "You sure do. Don't say anymore. Sit right over there and don't tell anyone else your name. If anyone asks to help you, tell them you're already being helped. Got that?"

Harry was really confused, but said, "Yes sir." and went over to the chairs the policeman had pointed to and sat down.

Smitty picked up the phone and said, "Why aren't you here yet? I'm starving and I have someone waiting for me. Okay, five minutes and then I sign out and leave it to you to explain why the desk was left empty." He glanced towards the chairs to see the young man just sitting there. He thought, *"Either this guy has no idea what's happening or he's guilty as hell and a very good actor. I wonder why he came in here anyway?"*

About 5 minutes later, another officer came out of the back office and said, "Okay, okay. Here I am. Go get lunch. I sure wouldn't want to be the cause of you dying from lack of food or anything."

Smitty signed something on the desk, handed something to the other officer then muttered, "Thanks, I'll see you in about an hour." Then he walked from behind the counter, looked at Harry while nodding his head towards the front door and walked out. Harry stood up to leave just as the other officer said, "Can I help you?"

"Already taken care of, thanks", replied Harry and walked out the door as quickly as he could.

Once on the sidewalk, Harry stopped. He didn't know where to go next. He didn't see where the officer had gone. His impulse was to run – as fast as he could – away from the Police Station. Just as he was thinking of doing that he heard a horn blowing. He looked over his shoulder and saw a car double-parked a couple of cars away from where he was standing. Harry walked over to the side of the car and looked in.

"Get in and be quick about it."

Harry got in. "Do you mind telling me what's going on?" I don't know who you think I am, but I...."

"Did you say your name was Harry Cauthern?"

"Yes, I did, but what..."

"I have something to tell you but if anyone finds out I've done this, I'll lose my job."

Harry's mouth opened but no words came out. He had no idea what the man was talking about. If he weren't in uniform, Harry would have thought he was crazy and called someone to get him off the streets.

Smitty started talking as he drove. He told Harry what had happened the other day and how Leah and the children were in a shelter for battered women so he couldn't hurt them any more.

Every time Harry tried to say something in his defense, Smitty cut him off. Smitty had to get everything our before he let Harry talk.

All of a sudden, Smitty said, "I hope you like hot dogs cause that's what I'm buying us for lunch." Then he continued on with his story about what was going to happen if Harry didn't do something quick. Just about then Smitty turned into a parking lot and asked Harry if he wanted two or three hot dogs.

"I don't think I want anything. I think I'm going to be sick."

"You look like a two dog man to me so two it'll be. Be right back."

Smitty wasn't listening to Harry at all. Harry didn't know whether to laugh at what he'd been told or to be really afraid. Before he could count to 10, the officer was getting back in the car, tossing a bag in Harry's lap and pulling out of the parking lot. Then he said, "We can talk and eat at the same time, right over there in the park. I like it there cause it's quiet and I can think."

Once in the park Smitty said, "Okay, what's your side of the story."

Harry didn't know where to start, but as he forced the first bite of hot dog into his mouth, he found his words. Smitty was the first person to ever ask for his side. As Harry started talking, the words just poured out. All the problems, the lies, the children, the drinking and partying, the acting, all of it came out.

All the while Harry was talking; Smitty was quiet, except for his chewing. When Harry stopped, Smitty quietly said, "I knew something wasn't right. The story she told was too exact. It was the same every time she told it. Nothing ever changed. I was listening to a play. She was acting. Damnation! The bad part is everyone believes her." All of a sudden Smitty realized he hadn't told Harry the part about court. "Do you know there's a court hearing on Wednesday?"

"For what?"

"To have a judge decide if you're crazy."

"What? I ain't crazy – except with fear for my children."

"Well, you'd better get yourself an attorney cause come court day you'll need one."

"Don't they have to let me know about this in advance?"

"Technically, yes, but they'll mail you a letter as notification. You might get it the night before."

"That ain't right."

"Agreed, but legal."

"Ain't right and I ain't gonna play that stupid game. If I get a letter, I'll go to court but I ain't done nothin' to her so they can't do nothin' to me."

"Son, I'm telling you to get an attorney. I really do know what I'm talking about."

"I know you're tryin' to help, but I ain't got money for no attorney. Believe me when I say I've got nothin' to be afraid of cause I ain't done nothin' to her except yell some."

"I believe you, but she's so thin and looks so terrible. At least do me on favor."

"Sure, if I can."

"Is there anyone who knows how she is? You understand what I'm saying?"

"Yeah, there might be a couple of people but I wouldn't want to get them involved."

"Line them up as witnesses. Please, cause without anyone on your side, you're going to lose…big time."

"Okay. But how do I do that when I don't know when they're going to court?"

"Tough question, but valid. If I hear anything I'll call you, okay?"

"Thanks," said Harry.

Then Smitty asked, "Where can I drop you off? I'd like to talk to you more, but…"

"You've helped me a lot. I thank you for that. I got it covered from here. Drop me off on this next corner. I want to walk some. It might clear my head.

"Okay, son. But please take my advice."

"Bye. Thanks for the hot dogs. They were great. Never had any that good before."

Smitty waved goodbye to Harry and drove off. Smitty had done all he could. It was up to Harry now.

Harry looked after the car as it pulled away. He smiled a little at the thought of a total stranger trying to look out for him.

As Harry walked home he thought about all Smitty had told him. He tried to think of anyone who had really seen Leah acting like she does. He'd already tried talking to neighbors who might know something, but they apparently didn't want to be involved. He couldn't think of anyone else, right off. Even though he was late, Harry decided to go to work. He'd tell his boss the truth that he'd been looking all weekend for his wife and kids. That night, when he got home, there was nothing in the mail saying he had to go to court. He hoped Smitty had been wrong.

The next day, Harry still hadn't thought of anyone who could be a witness for him in court – if he ever needed them. He still didn't believe Leah would do anything like that to him. After all their problems, he knew she loved him. However, when he got home that night he found a letter from the District Attorney's office advising him there was to be a competency hearing the next day. Harry's heart stopped just a little. At first he thought he wouldn't go. He'd just pretend he didn't get the letter. He thought, *"What could they do to me anyway?"* Then he thought about what Smitty told him and wished he'd contacted an attorney to be with him even if he couldn't think of any witnesses. Then he thought, *"I'll just tell them I just got the letter and I'd like a little extra time so I can find an attorney. Leah gets extra time for stuff all the time. This will work. I'll go to court tomorrow and then I'll find me an attorney. "*

The next morning Harry was in court. The district Attorney was there, along with a policewoman, Leah's mother, her sisters and a couple of her neighbors. All of a sudden Harry was a little scared. When the judge asked him if he had legal representation, instead of saying what he had planned to say, he said "No". Then when the judge asked if he was representing himself, instead of saying no, he said, "I guess so".

The judge ruled the case could proceed. Harry didn't know what had just happened. He just sat there while the District Attorney called all the witnesses. He listened to all the stories they were telling. He was dumbfounded at what was being said. When the judge asked him if he had any questions, Harry always answered, "No".

After everyone was through giving their testimony, the judge asked Harry to rise. Harry believed he was now going to be able to give his side of the so try. Instead the judge said he found him to be insane and committed Harry to the Sunrise Asylum for an indefinite period of time. Two bailiffs appeared, handcuffed Harry and led him away. Harry had no idea how or what had just happened.

Smitty was at the front counter desk when the matron came walking in. "You look pleased with yourself," he said.

"I am. I just got that guy put away for an indefinite period of time."

"What guy is that?"

"You know, Cauthern. The one who was crazy."

Smitty just hung his head and said, "Mary, he isn't crazy. That wife of his is just a very good actress."

"Yeah? So you say, but the judge just declared him insane and committed him, so I guess your opinion don't count."

Smitty felt terrible. He should have done more. He should have gotten Harry an attorney instead of leaving it up to him. *"Maybe I didn't help Harry enough, but I can sure keep an eye out for his children and an eye on the wife,"* Smitty thought.

CHAPTER 13

March 1983 ......

Now that Leah has accomplished getting Harry out of her life, she goes to the welfare department and applies for full welfare benefits for herself and both children.

Leah's caseworker, Miss Meeks, had heard about the emergency sanity hearing. In fact, everyone in the city and county offices were talking about it, as it had never happened in Kenton County before. Miss Meeks had recognized the name so was not surprised when Leah made her appearance the day after the judge's ruling. She actually had expected her to come right after court concluded, so she was mentally prepared for the ordeal she was about to go through.

"I hasta see Ms. Meeks," Leah was shouting. I told her this kids father was crazy, but no one'd believe me. Now we got nuthin'. How we gonna eat? Where we gonna live? I got bills I gotta pay. How'm I gonna pay 'em?"

The receptionist was trying her best to talk to Leah to quiet her down, but was getting nowhere. Leah just wouldn't be still long enough to listen to her.

Miss Meeks knew it would be easier on everyone, if she just gave in and took Leah into her office – out of turn. Her other clients would be upset, but the sooner Leah was handled, the sooner peace would return to the whole department.

Just as the receptionist was once again telling Leah she needed to make an appointment, Miss Meeks came out of her office and said, "That's all right, Nancy, I'll take over from here."

"Bout time! I've been waitin' like forever out here and I got things to do," Leah boasted loudly.

The other women who'd patiently been waiting their turn just shook their heads. They all knew of Leah and her antics and were glad to have her gone, even if it meant they had to wait a little longer.

Once in the office, Leah jerked Andy into one of the chairs while she plopped into the other one. Miss Meeks didn't have to say anything. She pulled out a new interview sheet and started writing.

Leah saw this and said, "I ain't told ya nuthin' yet so's how come your writin' stuff down?"

Miss Meeks calmly responded, "I know your name and the date so I'm filling out the parts of the form with information I know. Would you rather have me ask you things I already know?"

"That'd be stupid. I's just checking."

"Okay, now that I have that done, I need to ask you what I don't know. Is that all right with you?"

Leah was furious. She just knew the bitch was making fun of her, but there was nothing she could do about it. This bitch was the way to her getting welfare money.

"Yeah", she quietly replied.

"What are you asking for in the way of benefits?"

Leah thought a minute and said, in a very sad, soft voice, "Well you know'd I had a man to take care of me and the youngn's until he gone an went crazy on me."

"Un huh."

"Well", Leah paused, trying to think of the words those bitches at the social club used. Then they came to her, "I've got a life I've gotten used to."

"Oh really", said Ms Meeks. "You mean a life style you've become accustomed to?"

'That's what I said", Leah replied, thinking she was being made fun of again.

"Okay, so let's see. How long were you married?"

The answer came very softly, "I wasn't."

"Sorry, but I didn't hear what you said."

"I said", shouted Leah, "that the bastard and I didn't ever get hitched!"

The light came on in Ms. Meeks head, "Oh, so you aren't drawing any Social Security for you and the children?"

"Right."

"Are both the children his?"

"What?"

"You heard me, are both the children his?"

"You know they ain't."

"No, I don't, you reported you didn't know who Billy Ray's father was."

"Ye're lyin'."

"No. It's right here in your handwriting on the form you filled out when you first wanted to start getting welfare."

Ms. Meeks was starting to enjoy this encounter. Leah, on the other hand, was starting to feel threatened.

"You whore!" Leah suddenly screamed. You done twisted what I told ya! Now ya throw'd it back at me when I'm grieving."

Ms. Meeks had jumped at Leah's sudden outburst. Leah saw that slight movement and once again felt in charge. Before Ms. Meeks could comment, Leah sat down, brushed her unkempt hair back and calmly said, "The first one was a gift from God. God's his father. The other one ain't God's, he's from Harry. So what?"

Ms. Meeks now began to think this woman was really insane and wanted her out of her office. Her response to Leah was, "Well, you can get full benefits for two years for your oldest child, but since your youngest qualifies for some benefits from Social Security we can't give you anything for him yet. The benefits for him from us will be based on how much you receive for him from Social Security."

"So's I get nothin' for the baby?"

"Not until we have proof from Social Security showing how much they're paying to you for the baby."

"How long's that gonna take?"

Ms. Meeks hated to tell her explosive client the answer for fear of her response; however, she replied, "Probably two to three months – or longer – from the time you file all the paperwork."

Leah was shocked. "Ya mean I get nothin' for the second kid til then?"

"Right."

"How about my benefits?"

"What do you mean?"

"For me. What do I get for me?"

Ms. Meeks paused to review her thick file and then responded, "You've used up all your possible benefits."

Once again Leah was shocked. "What do you mean, all used up?"

Ms. Meeks patiently explained that benefits for children were virtually unlimited; however, benefits for able-bodied adults had a limitation. She went onto explain to Leah that she had really exceeded the maximum benefits and given the right circumstances, the county could demand repayment for the amount she was overpaid.

"Ya mean, I ain't gonna get one penny for me, a single mom who can't work – ever again?"

"Why can't you work?"

"Cause I hafta take care of the two brats I have!"

"Do you have a condition that keeps you from working?"

A light bulb went on in Leah's brain. Ms. Meeks saw it and realized she'd made a mistake.

"I do. I hafta keep seeing my doctor. You need a note or somethin' from him?"

Ms. Meeks sighed, realizing she'd been beaten again. This time because of something she'd said. She wondered how long it would take for that bit of information to hit the street. After a long pause, Ms. Meeks said, "Yes. I need the Social Security paperwork and something from your doctor telling us of your condition."

Leah stood up and pulled Andy out of the other chair. As she was dragging him out of the office, she shouted back at the social worker, "And don't keep me waitin' so long next time. I told ya, I gots things to do."

Ms. Meeks walked behind the pair to her office door. As she watched them walk away, she shook her head. The child was cute, but very quiet and dull looking. The mother was extremely thin with very dark circles under her eyes. She knew from the file Leah was only 23, but she looked a lot older. Deep in her gut she knew something wasn't right in that household but she also knew she'd never know what it was. She was very concerned about the mother's outbursts. She didn't know if they were for real or if the girl was just a good actress. Maybe time would tell. However, she'd no more time to worry about them; she had 50 other clients to take care of, so to the receptionist she said, "Who's next?"

While Leah dragged Andy out, her brain was running at top speed, planning what she needed to do next. She wasn't going to be like other single mom's – going to work all day, spending her money on child care, cooking and cleaning all night and having no time or energy to party.

The next week Leah went to the welfare office to collect her benefits. She was disappointed at the little amount she received. The lady handing out the checks patiently explained she was only entitled to the minimum for one child, as Social Security hadn't notified them as to the amount they would be paying. The lady kindly asked if Leah had filled out all the paperwork yet."

"Ain't been there yet. Been too busy. Besides, I don't got a car to get there."

"You don't have to go downtown for that. We have a person in this office who can assist you in filling out all the forms and them submit them for you."

"Well, why didn't Ms. Meeks tell me that?"

"This is a different department and she may not have known."

"Well, how do I get ya to do this?"

"Come with me and I'll take you over to her – that is, if you have time."

Leah straightened her back, brushed her always unkempt hair away from her face, looked around at the other people standing in line, then responded, "Why, thank you. That would be fine." My other appointments aren't until later in the day."

The clerk looked at Leah, startled that her manner of speech had changed so dramatically, but to her said, "Good. I'm glad this'll work out for you."

Leah calmly followed behind the clerk into an office just out of sight of the waiting room. The clerk then said, "Ms. Hobbs, this is Leah Ramsey. Leah, this is Ms. Hobbs. She'll assist you with all your paperwork. Ms. Hobbs, here's Ms. Ramsey's file."

Leah walked into the room, said hello to Ms. Hobbs and then pleasantly thanked the clerk for her assistance. As the clerk walked away, she made a mental note to call Ms. Meeks to tell her about Leah's personality change.

The next month, just before it was time to collect her monthly benefits, Misty had her fifth child. So before she went to collect her monthly check, she went to see her social worker to add the new child. She again claimed the name of the father was unknown and, therefore, was eligible for additional welfare for the new baby.

When Leah heard her sister had no problem qualifying for additional welfare, she was furious. She realized if she'd only said she didn't know who Andy's father was, she'd have gotten all the welfare she felt she was entitled to – without messing with Social Security. She was embarrassed her sister, her younger sister, knew more than she did about how to get what's due her.

Misty, however, felt her sister was really smart to have found a way to get Social Security and welfare. She decided she'd have to find a way to draw both, just like her sister was doing.

Now both of BJ's daughters were living on welfare. She, on the other hand, was working full time as a clerk from Monday through Friday. In BJ's mind, she felt she'd always held a job and took good care of her children. She didn't understand them not wanting to work nor them feeling they shouldn't have to work. BJ was still dating Steven Boyd and in her spare time helping care for her 7 grandchildren. Even though her daughters were young, 22 and 23, and had money to take care of their own children, they didn't. All they wanted to do was party all night and sleep most of the day. She couldn't understand why they weren't better mothers.

Steven always got up early because the prison required him to be at work by 6am. After he leaves the house, Bobbie Jo always walks two doors down to the house her daughters and grandchildren share. Every morning is the same. She picks up the trash, washes the dirty dishes and baby bottles from the day before. Her next chore is to fix food and formula for the day. If she didn't she was afraid the grandchildren wouldn't be fed. Once she finished in the living room and kitchen she'd head into the dining room that was being used as a nursery to check on the babies. She knew those still in diapers would be lying in urine soaked clothes on soiled sheets.

One at a time, she picks the babies up, bathes them and dresses them with clean clothes she washed the day before. Her next step is to put the dirty clothes in the washer and dryer so they'll be clean and dry for the next day. After that she wakes up the two children who go to school. She gets them bathed, dressed and fed. After the children are all settled, she leaves for work dropping the two oldest off at their school along the way.

BJ does this everyday because if she didn't, the children wouldn't make it to school. Not that it would really make a difference, because they weren't doing well at school. She doesn't understand what's happened to them. They all used to laugh and cry and be very active. Now all of them, even the babies are very, very quiet and their eyes are dull. They don't even wake up when she comes in each morning until she shakes them. She's never heard of little babies sleeping so sound. BJ tells herself she needs to ask her daughters about it; however by now she's walking into the building where she works and the thought leaves her mind for another day.

Leah and Misty had been afraid that they were going to have to start taking care of their own children after their mother moved out of the duplex and into a house with Steven. They were pleased that not only did their lives continue to be the same, but also that things actually started getting better. This was due to the fact that both of them were getting welfare benefits; Leah was getting some Social Security for Andy, and BJ and Steven were working. They were quite content with things the way they were.

CHAPTER 14

July 1983 ......

One day Steven tells Bobbie Jo he has to go to California to get his son. She was somewhat surprised. She knew he'd been married before but he hadn't mentioned having any children. In reality, Steven had been married twice before and had 3 sons by two different wives. She also didn't know his second wife was also his first cousin. Of course, Steven wasn't aware that Bobbie Jo had married her first cousin, had three daughters and that she had sent her youngest child to live with Ethel in Crab Orchard so she wouldn't have to deal with her anymore.

"Why do ya have ta go?"

"He's had a bad accident and his mother wants nothing to do with him, so once again I have to fix the problem."

Bobbie Jo just nodded her head.

Steven's son did have a bad car accident and was in the hospital. He'd known about the accident before his ex-wife did as she had remarried and had a different last name so it took the police longer to notify her.

Since the accident, Steven had been checking with the hospital daily to find out when the boy would be released so he could be there before the boy's mother could get him. During the divorce from his son's mother it was proven that Steven had attempted to kill his wife and his sons. This caused the court to terminate his rights and deny all visitations. He'd moved from the state so he wouldn't have to pay the child support that had been ordered. Steven felt he shouldn't have to pay to support children that didn't live with him.

When Steven arrives at the hospital in Merced, California, the doctors advise him Jimmy will need a lot of therapy to have a full recovery. They ask him if he has insurance to cover all the treatment needed. Steven lies by telling them he's a federal agent and has wonderful medical benefits for him and his son. Upon hearing that information the doctor releases Jimmy to his father. The doctor has overlooked the notation on Jimmy's chart that says to check with the office before releasing the patient.

Jimmy's mother had also been in constant contact with the hospital and had provided them with a copy of the long-standing restraining order keeping Steven away from her and the children. When she arrived at the hospital to bring her son home, as previously arranged, she was told a mistake had been made and Jimmy had been released earlier – to his father. Jimmy's mother was devastated. The hospital said they were sorry, but mistakes do happen and it couldn't be that bad as the boy was with his father.

On the drive back to Kentucky from California, Steven discovers his son is no longer the strong-willed boy he was before his accident. He finds his son does whatever he's told to do. Steven likes the change. Once in Kentucky again, Steven doesn't see the need to waste money on taking his son to a doctor.

Leah and Misty are upset with Steven moving his son into the house, as they want their mother taking care of their children. They feel Jimmy's presence is going to cause them a change in their lives.

Each morning Steven wakes Jimmy and tells him to go to the bathroom and get dressed. When Steven leaves for work Bobbie Jo tells Jimmy to sit down and eat his breakfast. When she sees him eating, she walks out the door and her day proceeds as usual. The girls are pleased that their lives remain unchanged, even with another person for their mother to take care of.

One Saturday Leah stops by Bobbie Jo's for a cup of coffee.

"Where're the children?' Bobbie Jo asked.

"They're at home. They're about to drive me crazy so's I had to get outta there for awhile."

"Is Misty home?"

"Nope."

"She take her kids with her?"

"Some. The rest are asleep."

"Leah, I just don't know how you manage to get all the children asleep at the same time."

"Lucky, I guess."

Her mother just looked at her, but before she could ask any more questions Leah started talking.

"How old is Jimmy?"

"He's 17, I believe."

"Is he retarded or something?"

" Like you were told before, he was in a car accident and hurt his head real bad."

"Ain't he supposed to be going to a doctor or something?"

"Steven says it's a waste of money. He says the boy was always headstrong and it's better if he's this way. Less trouble for us all."

"But he just sits there," Leah points to the boy sitting on one of the kitchen chairs that had been placed in an empty corner of the room.

"Steven says he's not in the way."

"Yeah, but does he ever move?"

"Oh yeah, watch this. Jimmy," called Bobbie Jo. Jimmy's head moved slightly and his eyes that had appeared to stare at a spot on the floor, focused on Bobbie Jo.

"Jimmy, take that bag of trash outside, put it n the trash can, then come right back inside."

Jimmy got up slowly, picked up the bag and walked out the kitchen door with it. Leah jumped up to look out the window to see what he did.

As Jimmy turned to walk back in the house, Leah said, "He don't even look around. He just put the trash in the can and turned around to come back in."

Then Bobbie Jo whispered, "Watch this." Leah sat down to watch. Jimmy walked inside the door and stopped. Bobbie Jo started talking to Leah about the work she did at her office.

Leah said impatiently, "I don't care about your stupid office. What were you gonna show me?"

"I'm showing you. He's just standing inside the door, right?"

"Yeah. So What?"

"He'll stand there until somebody tells him to sit down."

"You're kidding."

"Nope. If I tell him to vacuum, he will, but I have to tell him when to stop. If I forget to tell him to stop, he'll vacuum all day. Pretty funny, isn't it? Steven says as soon as Jimmy gets a little better we can put him to work at a paying job. When that happens, I can quit work. Ain't that great?"

Leah nodded her head. This got her thinking about how maybe she could use a man like that in her life. She starts planning how she can get this moneymaker for herself. To her mother she says, "He's kinda cute."

He's only 10 years older than Billy Ray."

"Yeah, so what?"

"He's too young for you or Misty."

Leah just looked at her mother and said, "Whatever."

By the following Monday, Leah had a plan all worked out. That evening, when she knew Steven and Bobbie Jo were through with dinner, Leah showed up. She wanted to get their approval. "I got an idea", she announced as she walked in their door.

Bobbie Jo was afraid to ask her daughter as she felt she was up to no good. Out loud she said, "Let's hear it." Steven just nodded. He liked Leah and never minded her being around.

"Well, I was thinking how you two are having to work all day and Jimmy being the way he is and all – well I thought maybe I could help you two out. Ya know, cause he's kinda like a brother and all."

Now Bobbie Jo knew she was up to no good, but said nothing.

Steven responded, "How can you help?"

Well, since I have to stay home with me having kids to watch and all, I thought I could just come over here some."

Stevens response was, "And do what?"

"Well, you know, fix some lunch for him and make sure he don't just sit in one spot all day. You know, maybe get him talking a little. If'n you want him to get a job, he's gonna have to be able to talk a little."

Steven nodded, then looked at Bobbie Jo who had not said a word. "Okay, Leah. If you want to, I don't mind. The sooner he stops being a zombie, the sooner I can find him work. It's costing me a lot to feed him and he needs to be helping me out."

Leah smiled sweetly and said, "I'll start tomorrow. See ya" as she walked out the door.

"What brought that on?" Steven asked BJ.

"I don't know. I've never seen her volunteer to do anything," BJ responded, "but, if she does watch him, it'll take some of the load off me."

"That's why you have kids," said Steven.

"What?"

"That's what my daddy taught me. Look for a wife that'll give you lots of strong sons so they can take care of you when you get old."

"Are they supposed to help you out along the way to getting old too?"

"Yes, and if they won't, you get rid of them."

Bobbie Jo didn't ask him to explain any further. She knew it'd make him very angry. What she said was, "I only got girls."

"Yep, and they're nothing but trouble. At least they're having boys. So some good will come of it."

Tuesday morning, Leah heard BJ and the children moving around downstairs. She was anxious to start putting her plan in place, but she didn't want her mother to hear her moving around. She couldn't stand the smell of those kids when they were all wet and she sure wasn't going to bathe and feed them all, much less wash all the sheets and clothes every day! It was too much smelly work for her. That's all her mother did – work. She had better things to do with her time than waste it taking care of other people.

She and Misty liked to go to the many neighborhood clubs in the area and they sure couldn't drag all the brats along but they couldn't afford to pay someone to watch them all either. BJ wouldn't watch them all the time so she found a way to make them go to sleep early and stay asleep all night.

He mother didn't know it but every night Leah put a few drops of Kahlua in each of the bottles for the babies. It was sweet and had a chocolate like flavor. The older children were given Grape Pucker mixed in with nighttime cough medicine. If any of the children dared to ask why they were getting medicine if they weren't sick, her response was a larger dose accompanied by the words, "You need this to give relief." After a few times of getting double doses, the children never questioned her.

Right after Leah heard the door close, she got out of bed, dressed, grabbed her cigarettes and slipped quietly out her back door and walked the few doors down to her mother's house. As she walked in the door she shouted, "Hey, Jimmy, where are ya?" No response. "Jimmy, where'd ya go?" No response again, so Leah started walking around the house. Finally she found him sitting on the bed in a bedroom upstairs.

"What's ya doin'?"

No response.

"BJ said ya didn't talk much. Well, we're gonna work on that. Come with me and I'll get ya somthin' to eat."

Jimmy stood up and followed Leah out of the bedroom and to the kitchen.

Leah was getting a bowl down for cereal when she noticed he was just standing in the middle of the room.

"Well, for heaven's sake, sit down." Jimmy obeyed.

"I'm gonna do this for ya for a couple a days, but then you'll be doin' it for yourself cause ya needs the practice. Now, watch what I'm doin' so's ya can get the idea."

Jimmy didn't move his eyes from the invisible spot on the table he was looking at.

"Well, that's okay for today. We'll practice you follering directions a little later. Now eat the breakfast I worked hard on fixing for ya." She pushed the bowl of cereal in front of him.

Jimmy didn't move.

Leah was getting frustrated with him.

"You're more stupid than my kids. Now pick up your spoon and eat."

Jimmy did.

As he was eating Leah pulled out her cigarettes. As she struck a match to light up, Jimmy's head popped up and focused first on the flame and then on the glow at the end of the cigarette.

"Ya like that, don't ya?"

Jimmy just stared.

"Well now, when ya get better, you can have one. Okay?"

Leah worked with Jimmy for a few more hours without much progress. When it was lunchtime she brought him back to the kitchen.

"I'm gonna fix ya lunch but ya need to be paying attention so's ya can do it yerself next time. Are ya listening?"

Jimmy didn't say anything but he did sit down at the kitchen table without being told to. Leah fixed him a baloney sandwich and pushed it in front of him.

"Now ya eat this lunch I worked so hard on."

Jimmy picked up the sandwich and took a huge bite. When he was done, Leah said, "I think that's enough for today. You better go to the bathroom and then go lay down on your bed. You look tired."

Jimmy's response was to yawn wide as he stood up and walked away. Leah put the dirty dishes in the sink, lit a cigarette and sat down. She heard the toilette flush and then a door shut. She waited until she'd finished her cigarette then went to check on her student. He was sound asleep. She closed the door and left her mother's house to go back to her own. As she walked away she thought, *"This ain't going to be easy."*

Later that night, before she left for the club, she stopped in to talk to BJ and Steven. She wanted them to know how hard she was working. She didn't want money from them; she wanted them to be grateful so she'd be able to come back on them later on.

After she'd covered her bases with them, she went back to her house expecting to get Misty and go out. When she got there Misty wasn't ready.

"What's the hold up?"

"Brian has a temp."

"So?"

"So, I can't leave a sick kid home alone."

"He ain't sick, he just has a little temp."

"Leah, that means he's coming down with something."

"So give him some more medicine."

"That ain't helping him."

"Whatever. I'll see ya later." *God, I hate kids!"* she thought as she picked up a fresh pack of cigarettes and walked out the door.

Each day Leah spent time with Jimmy, teaching him and bringing him out of his near vegetative state. When he got to the point where he could function a little on his own, Steven found him a job at a nearby tobacco farm. Each day Steven dropped him at the farm on his way to work and picked him up on his way home each night. At first Jimmy was totally exhausted by the end of the day and could barely eat dinner. As time wore on, his strength returned and eating was no problem.

The farm paid the employee's every Friday, but not for the first week of work. When Steven picked his son up the first Friday he asked, "Where's your check?"

"Didn't get one."

"You're a liar. They pay every week," his father screamed.

Jimmy recoiled, "They didn't give me nuthin' – really!"

Steven quickly turned the car around and went back to the farm's office. "Stay here. I'll take care of this," Steven said as he slammed the car door.

When he came out he looked angry, but said nothing then or during the whole ride home. As he entered the house BJ said, "Where's the money?"

"What money?"

"You know, the money we talked about."

"Go get cleaned up for dinner," he yelled at Jimmy. To BJ he said, "Those bastards hold back a week."

"I was counting on that money!"

"Me too, but I can't do nothing about it."

"He's costing us a lot of food now and he ain't putting anything in to help," cried BJ.

"It's just another week and he does help around the house and yard," replied Steven.

"Can I tell the grocery store it's just another week? I don't think so," screamed BJ.

"You got paid today, didn't you," asked Steven?

"Yeah, so?"

"So where's that money," asked Steven?

BJ responded, "Now that he's working, that money's mine, so I spent it."

"I said you could quit when he started working but as long as you're still working, you gotta give it to me – just like always."

"Well, it's gone, so I can't," BJ snapped.

Steven just stormed off thinking, *"You can't trust women. You just can't."*

Just then Jimmy came into the kitchen and asked, "Where's dinner?"

BJ yelled, "We ain't got no money so there's no dinner. You wanna eat, make yourself a baloney sandwich." Then she stomped out the front door and down to her daughter's house. When Misty and Leah heard their mother's story, Leah said, "Eat with us. We got plenty of chicken cookin' in the oven."

BJ's response was, "Great" and went back to get Steven and Jimmy. Steven's car was gone. She knew he was furious with her but she didn't care. She got Jimmy and together they shared the pan of chicken and loaf of bread Misty and Leah had put out for dinner. The rest of the week went about the same. Steven would drop Jimmy of at the house and then leave. BJ and Jimmy would go to the girls' house, eat and go home. Steven would arrive home around 11PM and go directly to bed.

The following Friday when Steven picked Jimmy up at the farm, Jimmy had a smile on his face.

"What's the smile for," Steven asked?

"I got some money," was the response.

"Good, now give it to me," Steven directed. Opening the envelope he said, "Well, let's see how much there is." As Steven counted it, Jimmy watched with fascination. When he was done counting, Steven said, "There's just about the right amount."

"For what," asked innocent Jimmy?

"To start paying me back for all you've cost me and for your room and board."

Jimmy didn't respond, but his smile disappeared. Once home he went directly to his room and cried. When he hadn't come out to eat dinner, Leah went to check on him.

"What's wrong?"

"Sad."

"'Bout what?"

"He took all my money."

"Who did?"

"My dad."

"Why?"

"Said I owed him."

Leah hugged Jimmy and said, "I'll bring you what's left over from dinner. Ya need to eat so you'll get strong."

She walked into the kitchen and, pointing to Steven said to her mother, "He took all the kid's paycheck."

"Did you, BJ asked Steven accusingly?"

"Sure. Why not? We need it and besides, what's he gonna do with it? Whatever brains he had are gone now. He's got no use for money."

Leah responded with, "He ain't as dumb as you think. It's just taking him some time to heal that head of his."

"You don't know what you're talking about. I seen him as a little kid. He was stupid then and he's stupid now."

Leah started to answer but Steven cut her off when he said, "And you can just shut up. I ain't taking any lip from some skinny assed girl."

Leah was furious, but when she looked at her mother and saw the look on her face, she decided not to argue with him anymore. Instead she replied with her sarcastic, "Whatever," and walked off. She'd find some way to get back at that old man.

As she left the room with the small plate of food she'd picked up for Jimmy, she heard Steven say to BJ, "You need to teach her what her place is or else I will." BJ just nodded.

Leah spent as much time as she could with Jimmy. She coached him on how he could keep some of his paycheck and how he could get more to eat. She became the person Jimmy depended on for everything. She soon found her way into his bed. He was 17 and she was 23. Now Leah felt Jimmy was totally in her control and loved the feeling.

During the day, while Jimmy and Steven were at work, Leah's bored. Her mother, who now is home all the time, pretty much takes care of her two sons so Leah's free to socialize. She runs into a young man she used to see when she went to school. Before long she's meeting him every afternoon for a quick moment of passion.

He's the son of a wealthy farmer and he always has money in his pocket he's willing to spend on her. He has a nice truck and clothes. He promises her a big house and a car of her own if she'll marry him.

Leah likes Jimmy but Jerry Kilborne has money. Leah believes life with Jerry would be easy so in late September 1983, Leah and Jerry are married in a quiet ceremony. He's promised her a long honeymoon after the crops are in.

Jerry moves Leah into a small cottage on his father's farm. She leaves her sons with her mother "temporarily", explaining she needs time to adjust to being married and living in a new place.

BJ didn't mind keeping the boys. In fact, she preferred it because she felt Leah didn't take care of them the way she should. Besides she thinks she might be able to find out why they sleep so much and for so long.

A few days after the boys move in with Bobbie Jo, Jimmy and Steven, Billy Ray tells his grandmother, "We like living here."

"Why's that?"

"Because you make us dinner and you forget to give us our medicine."

"Doesn't your mom make dinner?"

"Sometimes," Billy Ray responds quietly. He was afraid he'd said something wrong. "But she always remembers to give us our medicine," he said smiling.

Bobbie Jo knew she had to be careful in asking her next question or he'd stop talking. "I guess I need to go to the store and get your medicine. Your mom must have been in such a hurry to pack, she forgot to put it in your bag of stuff. I don't know what you take so I need to know what you take the medicine for?"

"To give relief," he said brightly.

"Oh, you mean to get relief."

"No, mom always says we have to take it to give her relief."

"Oh, my mistake. What does it taste like?"

"Terrible. It's grape."

Bobbie Jo knew she'd better not ask anymore of the child. Instead she said, "Oh dear, I don't know what it is. I'll just ask your mom."

Billy Ray shouted, "Oh no, don't do that! She'll be real mad at me if she knew I told. She told us it's our family secret and we couldn't tell anybody."

"Well, I'm family so it'll be okay."

Billy Ray started sobbing, "No, no, please don't. They'll take me away and never let me see her again!"

"Okay. I won't say anything," BJ said as she held him and stroked his head. "Stop crying. Just help me find the medicine in the store. Okay?"

Billy Ray nodded his head and wiped his eyes.

Then BJ asked the little boy, "Do you know what store she buys it in?"

"Yep! I go with her when she gets it."

"Great! Tomorrow you and I can go get it. Okay?"

The little boy smiled and said, "Okay, grandma. I'll help you."

The next afternoon BJ and Billy Ray walked to the bus stop so they could go downtown. As they were waiting Billy Ray said, "This is going to be fun. I've never been on a bus before."

BJ looked at him and said, "How do you get to the store?"

"We walk or ride our bikes."

"Where's the store your mom goes to? I thought it was downtown."

"Oh no, it's just a couple blocks away."

"Here comes the bus. Let's go downtown first and go to the other store on our way home, okay?" BJ said to her grandson.

"Okay. This is going to be so much fun!" the little boy squealed.

BJ really had no need to go downtown, but she didn't want to disappoint her grandson, so downtown they went. Billy Ray's eyes were bright with excitement as they walked from store to store looking in the windows. Finally BJ said, "Well, even though I didn't find anything I needed, wasn't this fun?"

Billy Ray was hopping up and down, laughing as he did it. "Yep! It sure was. Do we have ta go home?"

"Sorry, but we do. I have to fix dinner or Steven will be mad. Plus we have to stop at the other store to get the medicine. Remember?"

Suddenly, the little boy got quiet. "Oh yeah, I forgot."

Even when BJ said, "Here comes our bus," he didn't brighten. He got on the bus, sat down but didn't say a single word for the rest of the ride home. As they got off the bus BJ said, "Which way is the medicine store?"

Billy Ray still said nothing. He just started walking. BJ walked with him as he led her to a neighborhood corner store about three blocks from their house. Once there he walked up to the counter and pointed at a shelf filled with bottles sitting behind the clerk.

"Hi Billy Ray. How are you today?" asked the clerk.

Billy Ray didn't respond.

BJ said, "Oh we're all just fine. He's a little tired cause I've been dragging him all over town. I need to get some of that stuff my daughter Leah buys all the time. All I know is its grape flavored."

"Here's the stuff she gets buys. Grape Pucker's the name. Does she need some of the cough medicine too?"

"Does she normally get it at the same time?"

"Yes'm, she does."

"Well, I guess we need both, don't we Billy Ray?" The little boy just looked at BJ with a blank stare."

After the purchase the two walked home in total silence. Once at home, BJ started hurriedly fixing dinner so it would be ready when Steven and Jimmy got home. She was just putting the potatoes in the pot as the front door opened. "My timing is perfect today. You both have just enough time to clean up before dinner's ready."

"Good, cause I'm hungry. How about you, Jimmy?" Steven asked his son.

Jimmy nodded and said, "Yes, very hungry," and walked towards his room at the back of the house.

"Gee, Steven, working seems to be doing Jimmy some good. Everyday he's talking a little more and doing things without being told."

Steven replied, "I guess that's good. What's for dinner?"

"All your favorites. But I found out something today and I need your opinion."

"What?"

"Can't talk now. After dinner when all the kids are where they can't hear."

Steven just shrugged his shoulders and walked towards the bathroom.

Moment's later BJ yelled, "Dinner's on. Everybody come and eat."

After dinner, BJ was doing the dishes and Steven was enjoying a cup of coffee. "So what's so important that you couldn't talk in front of the kids?

"Remember the boys asking about their medicine?"

Steven nodded.

"Billy Ray and I went downtown to find it today."

"You told me you were going, so what?"

"We didn't find it there. Leah's been buying it at that corner store – you know, Minter's."

"So," Steven said as he sipped his coffee.

"So, she's been buying grape cough syrup and something called Grape Pucker."

"So," Steven repeated.

"So, the cough medicine is 25% alcohol and that pucker stuff is 15%."

"So?"

"So, Leah's been mixing the two of them and giving it to the children – every day before dinner and again at bedtime."

Now BJ had his attention as he sat up straight and said, "Why?"

"Billy Ray said it was so they'd give relief. When I told him he meant get relief he told me, No – mama said give relief."

"Why? What's wrong with them that she thinks alcohol's the cure?"

"I don't know that anything is wrong with them and I can't think of anything that drinking alcohol cures – especially in children."

"You'd better set her straight!"

"I agree, but do you have any idea how?"

"She's your kid. Just tell her."

"She won't listen. She's selfish and self-centered. I don't know why she had kids. She doesn't like them."

"Tell her she either stops giving that crap to the kids or I'll go to the welfare people, tell them what she's doing and get her money stopped."

"She's married now so it's going to stop anyway."

"Well somebody better be paying us for taking care of them. Kids ain't cheap to feed and keep in clothes. I think we ought to be collecting money as foster parents or something."

BJ nodded, but said no more. She'd just make sure the boys got weaned away from the alcohol their mother had been giving them.

In early October BJ and Steven fill out an application to be married. On the application Steven checks the box showing he had been married before. Next to the question asking how the marriages ended he wrote, "#2 ended in divorce and #1 ended when spouse died." BJ checked the box showing she had never been married before. Neither one told the truth.

Then in late October 1983, just before Halloween, when BJ and Steven go to the courthouse in Covington and are married in a civil ceremony.

The next day BJ quits her job as Steven told her, "No woman of mine will ever work." BJ had never really liked working so she jumped at the chance of staying home.

CHAPTER 15

It's 1984 ......

Leah had been married less than 4 months when she started showing up at BJ's everyday to have coffee or to drop the children off. At first BJ didn't say anything to her, but finally she asked, "Leah, what's wrong? You have a husband who really cares for you, a nice place to live and rich in-laws. Why're you hanging around here every day? Don't get me wrong, I like the company, but I'm worried!"

"I'll tell you what's wrong. Jerry hasta work all day or he don't get no money. His cheap father don't give him nothin' if he don't work. Then if that ain't bad enough, he comes home smelly and tired and not wanting to do anything but eat supper and relax."

"Leah, that's life."

"Not my life! I like to sleep late and party at night. I thought he liked that too."

"He probably does, but the fact is you can't party all the time. You have to work, make money and be responsible. You have two children. Isn't it about time you start thinking about them and settle down?"

Leah just stared at her mother for a minute then said, "Ya know what? That old man expects me to work on that dirty farm too."

"So?"

"So, why should I? It ain't mine! If'n he needs help he needs to hire him some niggers!"

"Doesn't he provide you and your children a home?"

"Yeah, but it ain't much of a house."

"Doesn't he get someone to drive you wherever you want to go if Jerry is busy?"

"Yeah, but I have ta ride in a smelly truck."

"Doesn't he pay any medical bills you and the children might have?"

"Yeah, but I don't get any spending money."

"Maybe if you helped out around the farm some, he might give you some money."

"It wouldn't be enough."

BJ saw she wasn't getting anywhere with her daughter so she asked, "Does Mrs. Kilborne work on the farm?"

"Dunno. Don't care. I ain't nobody's nigger, I told ya that once already!"

BJ just looked at her daughter and shook her head. She knew she never won an argument with her daughter and this time was no different.

At the same time, Leah was looking at her mother and wondering, *"What's come over her? She's talking different and acting like she never slept late and partied all night. Hell, she's the one who taught me how to party. Just because she's married to a government worker she thinks she's better'n us."*

In December Misty gives birth to her 6th child. She had a difficult time during this pregnancy and had barely hung on to the child long enough for it to survive the birth. She and the child had to spend more time than normal in the hospital.

While Misty is in the hospital BJ and Steven watch her other five children as well as taking care of Leah's two during the day. Leah's told Jerry she's out looking for work, but in reality she's either at the social club in the old neighborhood or just out running the streets.

Steven isn't happy with the situation but deals with it by staying out late each night. He's even less happy when Misty moves in with them after she's released from the hospital. BJ tries to smooth over the situation by telling him Misty couldn't afford the house she, Leah and the children had shared now that Leah wasn't there to help.

When Misty feels well enough she goes to the welfare department with her newest baby and qualifies for additional welfare again; however, she's told if she continues having children they won't give her anymore financial assistance.

"Doesn't matter cause I can't have anymore." Misty put her hands over her eyes for a few seconds and then wiped them. The social worked didn't know if she was truly upset or just acting. She knew Misty and her sister were very good at getting what they wanted.

"How old are you now, Misty?"

Misty popped her head up and said, "I'm almost 23."

"What are you going to do with the rest of your life?"

"I got kids to take care of."

"What about a job?"

"Job? Are you crazy? I just told ya, I got kids to take care of."

"How are you going to live?"

"We'll get by."

"Where do you live?"

"What do ya mean?"

The social worker was getting frustrated with Misty.

Misty, on the other hand, was getting tired of all the hassle. She knew the social worker was trying to trick her into saying something wrong so she could cut her welfare and she wasn't going to fall for it. "Look. I got six kids. I don't got no edecation so's I can't go to work. Why are ya giving me such a bad time?"

The social worker didn't say anything. She just looked at Misty. About a minute went by with no one speaking. Finally the social worker started writing. When she finished, she handed a card to Misty. "Here's your temporary card for the new child. I've noted your records that you've been informed about being cut off from any additional welfare for any more children you might have. Good bye Misty."

Misty took the card, nodded her head, picked the baby up and left. Once in the main office she immediately got in the line for emergency assistance.

When she arrived back at the house, Misty told BJ what had transpired at the welfare office.

"I think we need to find a more dependable way for you to get your welfare money. You know, so you don't have to worry about being cut off."

"What can we do? It's the system. They don't care about me and my gifts from God."

"I know it's the system, but Steven and I've been talking. He's got what I think is a pretty good idea."

"What's that?"

"Let's wait until tonight and let Steven explain it to everyone at the same time."

Misty was curious, but just nodded her head.

Then BJ said, "I think I'll call Leah and see if she can come for dinner tonight. I think she needs to hear this too."

"I'll call her," said Misty. I know you're busy fixin' dinner and all."

Misty called her sister and told her what BJ had said.

Leah's response was, "I don't want no food. I already ate once today. Everybody tries to make me fat."

"No, that isn't it, but we thought you might be able to get Jerry to give you a ride over here if he thought we needed a family conference over dinner."

"I have been stuck here for over a week. He don't believe me anymore when I tell him I'm looking for a job so's he won't let anyone give me a ride to town."

"You ain't looking, are ya?"

"Hell, no, but it's the only way I can get out of this dump."

"Well, what about dinner?" asked Misty.

"No, I told ya I don't want no food, but I'll come over for some cold tea and listen to what the old man hasta say. It ain't gonna be anything to help us. That old man just looks out for his self."

"Don't be that way. He's a nice person."

Leah snapped, "Whatever. You'll find out sooner or later, but I'll see ya after dinner. The kids are already asleep so's I don't have ta worry about them."

Misty hung the phone up and told her mother what Leah had said, except the part about Steven.

"That Leah never eats. And how can the boys be asleep already? She couldn't have fed and bathed them already."

"She don't feed them at night. She says food dilutes the medicine." With that she stopped short, knowing she'd said too much already.

"About that medicine, just what's wrong with them boys anyway? I never heard of such small children needing so much medicine."

"I don't know," Misty truthfully told her mother and then walked away before she was asked anything else.

BJ was actually happy her oldest child wasn't coming for dinner as Leah always caused problems when she was forced to eat. BJ and Steven liked having a peaceful dinner and it would be that way only if Leah weren't around.

True to her word, Leah showed up, cigarette in hand, right after dinner. She walked in the house and plopped down in the most comfortable chair. Then she hollered, to no one in particular, "Hey! Is there any sweet tea out there?"

BJ cringed but shouted back, "I'll bring you some."

"Well, make sure it's good and sweet, not sour like ya usually have."

BJ made no comment. Steven, however, said, "Why do you let her get away with talking to you like that?"

"She's my child, so I have to. Besides, it must be my fault she acts like she does."

Steven just glared at her.

"Be nice when you explain what you have in mind. Misty will agree right away when I tell her it's better, but Leah ain't and is gonna argue – no matter what. This ain't gonna help her so she's gonna be mad. She might help us out like we want, if we're real nice to her."

Steven just looked at his wife. BJ was wife #3 and not too bright, in his opinion. However, she didn't question his decisions or ask him about money. He didn't like her daughters. He could tolerate Misty as she was dumb and would do as he said, but he could no longer stand Leah. Leah didn't have much formal education but she was street smart and picked up quick on things. She was always arguing with him and he didn't like it. He was the man in the family and what he said was not supposed to be questioned. He didn't like the fact that all the kids were in his house eating his food and spending his money without ever contributing anything or even offering to contribute. He didn't mind the young kids being there as he could train them in his way of thinking, just as he has trained Jimmy that they need to contribute. The kids are too little to help yet, but he expected the mothers to give him some compensation for BJ's time and what he had to lay out to take care of them all. This is what he hoped to get straightened out once and for all.

Steven walked into the living room to find Leah had taken his chair. Just as he was about to say something to her, BJ walked in and said, "Leah, here's your tea. It's real sweet just like you like it." She followed that comment with, "Steven, why don't you sit right next to me on the couch. We hardly ever do that anymore, not since you got that fine chair."

Steven glowered at Leah, but to his wife said, "That's a good idea." After they were seated Misty burst into the room.

"Sorry, I'm holding you all up. I had trouble getting all the kids down."

Leah chastised her sister by saying, "I don't never have a problem getting the kids down. You must not know how to do it right."

Just as Misty was going to engage in an argument with her sister, BJ interrupted them by saying, "Girls! We're here to have Steven tell us his plan for us getting more money. I won't have any of this bickering tonight."

Both girls stopped their talking and looked strangely at their mother. She never talked like that before. Steven, however, was looking at his wife, smiling and nodding. BJ appeared to be very proud of herself for speaking up.

With that, Steven started laying out what he thought would be the perfect plan. Misty thought it sounded wonderful and said so. Leah, on the other hand, didn't like the sounds of it at all. Her response was, "So what's in it for me?"

Steven chuckled, "Nothing. You're married and tied to the farm your husband's family owns. You're just here cause you'll have to talk to the welfare people if they come checking up on your sister and her kids."

"Ya called me all the way over her for that? Damn, I could have been out having a good time and instead I had to come all this way for nuthin'. I can't believe ya done this to me," Leah screamed.

They all looked at her with surprise. They all thought she'd argue or give suggestions, but neither Steven nor BJ thought she'd be mad.

Finally Steven spoke up, "Sorry you feel that way Leah, but we did want you to know what we were planning to do. I'm sorry if you're married and you won't be able to be a part of it, but that's not our doing."

"So give me a ride home. I'm tired of listening to all of ya. I'd rather be in that old farmhouse than sittin' here."

Steven got up and walked to the door. He opened it then said, "Well, you coming or are you walking back to your place?"

Leah wouldn't dignify his question with a response. She just got up and walked out the open door.

BJ and Misty were left looking at each other. Then Misty said, "Well, I'm gonna turn the TV on and watch my favorite show before Steven gets back and changes the channel."

CHAPTER 16

It's February 1985 ......

One Friday, Steven came home from work in a foul mood. When BJ simply asked where Jimmy was, as Steven always brought his son to and from work, Steven exploded.

"That lazy half-wit needs to start taking care of himself. I got better things to do than go outa my way to get him all the time."

"But he doesn't drive and he doesn't know how to catch a bus"

"Then he can damn well walk."

"It's 5 miles. He'll miss dinner."

"That's all right. It'll save me some money on food."

"Steven, what happened to make you so mad at the poor boy?"

"Are you telling me how to handle my half-wit kid?"

"No, I'm just concerned about you getting so upset. It ain't good for you to get so mad. If your blood pressure gets too high you might have a stroke and I'd lose you," BJ said strongly.

"Well, I do need to calm down. My pressure is probably too high. I just don't like people stealing from me – especially when it's my own child."

"Jimmy stole from you? I have a hard time believing that sweet boy would steal from anyone, much less you, his own father."

"You calling me a liar?" screamed Steven.

"Not at all, Steven," BJ said softly. "I'm just needing to know what he did so I can help."

"All right then. Why didn't you say so to begin with? I called the boss man over at the farm today to see why Jimmy hadn't ever gotten a raise in all the time he'd been working there. Even if the kid is a half-wit he does good work. I didn't want them taking advantage of him."

"So what did . . .?"

"Don't interrupt me!" snapped Steven.

BJ hung her head as she whispered, "Sorry."

Steven glared at her then continued, "So I started telling him all the reasons Jimmy deserved a raise, but before I could say too much he interrupted me."

"He didn't"

"Yes he did and you know how I hate to be interrupted."

"Yes, I do."

"I hate being lied to even more."

"Right!" agreed BJ.

"But when I'm made a fool of and lied to, I'm really mad."

"What are you talking about?"

"What part of being made a fool of and lied to don't you understand?" Steven yelled at BJ. "Are you going to let me finish?"

BJ just nodded in response.

"That boss man interrupted me to tell me how Jimmy got off to a slow start, but never had to be told twice how to do anything. Plus he said he's always careful with the tobacco leaves and all the equipment they have all over the farm."

BJ let a "Wonderful," escape from her lips.

Steven shook his finger at her accusingly and continued with his story. "Then he says Jimmy's even driving a truck around the farm making pickups for him."

Before BJ can say anything, Steven shakes his head at her.

"Then he tells me he's given Jimmy four raises since he started." Now Steven's so angry he's pacing around the small kitchen floor.

Now that Steven had stopped talking and appeared to be waiting for BJ to make some comment, she didn't know what to say.

"So after I hear what the boss man said to me, I had to think quick of something to say to him so I didn't look like a fool!"

"What did you say?" asked BJ.

"I laughed and told him I was glad he knew he had such a good worker."

"Good for you," BJ said encouragingly.

"Then I told him I'd have to have a few words with you cause you never told me."

"Me?" I don't know anything about how much Jimmy makes, so's how's it my fault?"

Steven ignored her comment, and then said, "The boss man laughed and told me his wife was about as bad with remembering to tell him important stuff too."

"You're so good at talking with people," BJ complimented Steven.

"Yeah, but my own son never told me he was getting more money each week."

"True."

"He's just been giving me the same amount each week."

"True."

"So he's been lying to me."

"Not really," BJ said.

"You calling me a liar again?"

"No, but did you ever ask him if he got a raise?"

"You saying it's my fault?"

"Of course not. It's just that Jimmy can't think too good on his own."

"Well, that's right."

"So he didn't really lie to you, he just didn't know enough to tell you any different."

Steven looked at his wife without responding to her logic. Then Steven asked BJ, "So how'd he know to keep the extra and what's he doing with the money he's keeping?"

"I don't know, but I bet Leah had something to do with it."

"You know I don't like her!" Steven growled at his wife.

"I know but I have to love her – she's my first born. I just don't always trust her."

"Besides all the money I didn't get, who said he's allowed to drive?"

"He's just driving old trucks on the farm. That ain't like real driving."

Steven didn't respond to his wife's comments this time either. He just stared at her for a moment. When he did speak he shouted, "So where's my dinner. I'm starved!"

"Ain't we gonna go look for Jimmy?"

"Hell no. If he's such a good worker and sneak, he should be able to find his way home."

"Steven," BJ cajoled, "don't be so hard on the boy. He probably don't know no better."

"If he ain't home after we finish our dinner, I'll go check on him."

"He's probably still waiting on the bench outside the office at the farm."

"Ain't gonna hurt him to wait."

"He hasn't eaten since breakfast."

"He ain't gonna die. I'll go after I eat."

BJ started putting dinner on the table for Steven. She'd fed Misty's children earlier as she usually did so they wouldn't upset the breadwinner of the family.

After dinner Steven was having a cigarette and a second cup of coffee when BJ asked if he was going to check on Jimmy.

"Look, if the kid ain't home by 8 o'clock, I'll go check on him."

BJ was concerned but couldn't force Steven to go looking for his son.

About 7:30 Jimmy walked in the front door.

Steven yelled at him, "Where you been? You missed dinner."

BJ looked quizzically at Steven and then at the exhausted Jimmy.

Jimmy, almost in tears, answered, "I was waiting for you just like always."

"Well, I found out you been lying to me so, I figured I'd better teach you a lesson."

"I don't lie," Jimmy said as he started crying. "Can I eat? I'm so tired and so hungry."

"You missed dinner so go fix yourself a bologna sandwich," Steven shouted at the exhausted boy.

Jimmy was tired, dirty and his feet hurt so badly from the too short shoes he wore. He didn't know what he'd done wrong and was very confused.

BJ tried to cheer him up by saying, "Why don't you go clean up, take your shoes off so your feet can rest and then come to the kitchen. I'll fix us all some sweet tea while you fix yourself a sandwich or two." She knew she couldn't make the sandwiches for the boy or give him any of the leftovers. If she did, Steven would get angry and take it out on her, but she'd learned how to do things for people without getting him angry.

When Jimmy finally padded into the kitchen in his bare feet, BJ had the tea made and all the sandwich fixings laid out. She'd also found some potato salad left over from a few days before.

Jimmy quietly asked, "Can I have milk? I don't like tea too much?"

"Just one glass, otherwise you Dad will notice and get mad at both of us."

"Okay. Why'd he say I lied?"

"He found out you've been keeping the extra money from your pay."

"I only did what Leah told me to do."

"What'd she tell ya?"

"Leah told me to count my money each time I got paid and if there was ever any extra, I was to keep it. That's all I did. Did she tell me to do something bad," asked Jimmy as he was gobbling down the second sandwich?

"I'll talk to your father. He won't be mad when I tell him why you took the money."

"Okay. You sure?"

"Yes, I am," BJ, said very softly. What did you do with the money you kept?"

"Most of it's in the box under my bed. I kept some for cigarettes, but that's all."

"I didn't know you smoked."

"Leah showed me how. She told me it would keep me from being hungry and give me relief?"

"Does it?"

"Not really, so I don't always buy cigarettes. Please don't tell her cause she'll be mad at me."

"No she won't."

"Please, please," Jimmy begged, nearly in tears again. "She'll be so mad if she knew I bought candy and sandwiches and not cigarettes. She told me if I didn't do as she said she'd never come to my bed and sleep with me again!"

BJ looked at the man boy in front of her, then got up, took his now empty milk glass over to the refrigerator and refilled it with milk.

"Won't Dad be mad?" Jimmy asked as she handed him the glass.

"I'll talk to him. Do you want another sandwich?"

"I don't like bologna much."

"Hmmm, I've got a couple of slices of ham and a little cheese left over. Would you like that better?"

"I like ham," Jimmy said brightly, with all the signs of tears now gone.

"Okay, ham and cheese it is."

As Jimmy wolfed down two more sandwiches, BJ thought how silly it was to make him eat sandwiches when she had plenty of leftovers just waiting to be heated up. However, she also knew she didn't dare cross Steven more than she already had.

Finally Jimmy sat back and rubbed his belly.

"You full now," asked BJ?

"Yeah. I really like milk."

"It's late. You'd better get ready for bed. You have to get up early."

"Okay. I am tired," Jimmy said yawning wide, "It's a long walk from the farm to get home."

After Jimmy padded out of the kitchen, BJ rinsed his glass and went to the living room to talk to her husband.

"So what did the dummy eat? I know you gave him more than bologna."

"You're right. I gave him those dried up pieces of ham and some of that old cheese."

"That it?"

"Nope."

"Didn't think so."

"Gave him some milk."

"He ain't no baby," Steven chided.

"Not in years, but mentally he ain't too far from it."

"Why'd he steal from me like he did. It ain't like him."

"You're right about that. It ain't like him, but it's like Leah."

"What's she got to do with it?"

"Everything! She told him to do it. She also has him buying cigarettes and telling him he should be smoking instead of eating."

Steven shook his head. He didn't want the boy lying to him, but he didn't want him spending money on cigarettes either, especially when Leah probably took them from the kid. "I don't like her influencing him."

"You ain't heard the worse part."

Steven didn't say anything to BJ; he just turned towards her with a scowl on his face.

"Leah's been sharing his bed."

"What? That's it! I don't want that bitch around him or around here any more. Got that?"

"Yeah, I got it, but you'd better start talking to him about her and how bad she can be. He's afraid she told him to do something bad and that he's in trouble with you so you'd better be careful how you do it."

"You telling me how to talk to my kid?"

"No, I'm just telling you how impressionable he is and we don't know how deep her hooks are into him."

Steven looked at his wife. He couldn't believe he heard her right. She never talked like that before. He began to wonder if she wasn't smarter than she acted most of the time. "Don't worry, we'll be out of here soon. That'll break their connection."

"When are we leaving?" asked BJ.

"I'm not sure, but soon. I've got some offers of a better job. I just don't know which one I'm going to take."

"Where are we going?"

"I just told you I didn't know which job I was going to take, so how would I know where we're going? Besides, you know they don't let me know much ahead of time where the job is going to be. That's why I've been telling you we have to be ready. We might only have a couple of days notice."

"How're we gonna move all our stuff? You gonna get us a truck?"

"Nope. If the old wagon can't haul it, we don't need it."

BJ's eyes popped open. "Steven, there's 10 of us, not counting Leah and her boys."

"Leah and her rat's ain't coming with us. I told you I want her out of our lives."

"Okay, but that still leaves 10 of us. We can hardly fit into the station wagon when we got no luggage so how are we going to fit with luggage?"

"Well, I figure there's us three and Misty and the three youngest babies that fit fine. That leaves us plenty of room for the stuff we need."

"What about Misty's three oldest kids. We can't just drive off and leave them!"

"We won't. I figure we can leave them with Leah until you and me can come back to get them. Shouldn't take more than a month."

"Do you think she'll take them in?"

"She owes us for all the babysitting we done for her. Besides, it's been part of the plan from the beginning, remember. I told her that night when I told them my plan.

"She never agreed."

"I didn't ask her to agree. I told everyone what we were going to do. It wasn't a discussion."

Steven started thinking about what BJ had said and realized Leah probably wouldn't help willingly. If she started her screaming and acting she could cause the plan to fall apart. He also realized Misty would never leave any of her children behind. He had to rethink his plan to account for the extra people.

"I'm going out for awhile. Start packing some stuff, but keep your mouth shut about what's going on."

BJ, as usual, just nodded her head. She didn't want to move, but Steven kept telling her it was the only way he could get more money coming in. He was working at the prison so he had to make pretty good money and Jimmy was working at the tobacco farm bringing in a check every week. Plus they got the food stamps and most of the welfare money Misty got. They were getting along just fine. She didn't understand why they needed to move.

Steven was always hinting at how he used to work undercover and how he wanted to get back into it again, but she liked him being at home most of the time. Now he was talking about them moving where it was warmer and where he could get a better job. She'd always lived in Kentucky and wasn't sure she wanted to move. He never asked her opinion about anything, he just made a decision and everyone was supposed to accept it. BJ did go along with Steven because she was getting what she wanted - money to spend and a roof over her head without her having to work. What she didn't like was not being able to talk to anyone. BJ had always liked talking things out with her friends at the social club and with her daughters.

BJ started packing, just as she had been told. She never mentioned how she felt to anyone, especially not to Steven. He had told her from the beginning of their relationship that he expected any wife of his to stay at home and be a good mother. BJ realized if she wanted Steven to take care of her and all the children and grandchildren, she was going to have to play by his rules.

The following Friday Steven and Jimmy were a little late arriving home. When they walked in Jimmy said, "We got a surprise!"

BJ laughed and said, "What?"

"We got us a little trailer."

"What kind of trailer," BJ asked?

"The kind the wagon can pull," Jimmy said strongly.

BJ looked over at Steven.

"Pack up the rest of our stuff. We're out of here Sunday."

"But we just paid the rent."

"All part of the plan, now when's dinner going to be on the table? We're hungry and Jimmy and I have lots to do to get the wagon and trailer ready for the long trip we're all taking."

"All of us," asked BJ?

"Yep. That's why we have the trailer. I decided it was cheaper to buy a little trailer than to make a second trip."

BJ nodded her head, and then said, "Dinner's ready now. I've been holding it just waiting for you two to get home."

After dinner Steven and Jimmy started loading the trailer that had been backed up to the rear door of the little house where it couldn't be seen. His plan was to start out late Saturday night so none of the neighbors would see them leaving with a trailer. He hoped to leave without anyone knowing about it at all, not even Leah.

He'd quit his job at the prison the week before telling them he had gotten a permanent job in the plant on the other side of

Covington so if anyone started asking about him they'd say he was still around town somewhere. He'd collected his final check that day. Steven was just a contract janitor at the prison so his co-workers were pleased to see him get a better job. They'd even thrown him a little going away party.

Jimmy didn't know they were leaving town and that he wouldn't be going back to work the next week. If he had known he would have told his boss man and Steven didn't want anyone knowing they were leaving town. Jimmy would lose the first week of pay the farm held back, but that was the price Steven had to pay in order to have his plan work.

Misty had just received her yearly re-certification for herself and her 6 children from the welfare department and had gotten her monthly check and food stamps. Steven was disappointed they wouldn't be able to use them all before they left, but planned on going shopping the next day with Misty to stock up on things that didn't go bad like baby formula and canned meats and drinks. It was going to have to last them until he found work.

He had his check, Jimmy's check, Misty's welfare money and Jimmy's stash of money. It wasn't a lot of money but it would have to do.

He also had his stash of money that no one knew about, but that was in case things got really bad and he needed to leave quickly.

Saturday morning he left Jimmy and BJ to pack the trailer and watch the little kids while he and Misty went to the store to get supplies. Misty was surprised at how much Steven was buying. When she questioned him he told her it was cheaper to buy it at home rather than while they were traveling. Misty thought they were going on a vacation.

Once back at home, Steven checked what had been packed in his absence, and began taking some items out and adding others. He had BJ busy doing laundry and cooking most of the day. Finally the trailer and wagon, which was now behind the house as well, were both packed except for the people who would occupy all the seats. The rear of the wagon had been converted into a holding and sleeping area for the babies with their little blankets and pillows. The remaining space was filled with the full sized pillows and blankets as well as an ice chest for the few perishables they were taking.

The extended family sat down for a dinner of beef stew and biscuits for what would be their last meal in that house. When they'd finished Steven said, "Okay, everyone get a bath and into bed. We have to get an early start on our vacation tomorrow."

Once everyone had been put down for the night, BJ went to the kitchen to wash the dishes. She didn't know if they would be back or not, but she couldn't stand the thought of leaving dirty dishes to get smelly and moldy. As she was wiping the table off for the last time, Steven came walking through the kitchen towards the back door carrying a large brief case. BJ had never seen it before and asked about it.

Steven stopped and thought about telling her to mind her own business, but decided to show her what was inside. He thought she'd been getting a little nosey and this might help him keep her in line. Steven laid the case on the now clean kitchen table. Taking a ring of keys out of his pocket he unlocked the case and turned it so when it was opened, BJ would see what was inside. Then he slowly opened the case to expose the contents to BJ. Her eyes went wide with fear.

"Now, don't ever cross me or you and all your kids will pay. I will hurt you all. Got it?"

BJ nodded her head ever so slowly.

With that Steven continued walking to the back door and disappeared outside. When he returned BJ was still standing with the wet dishrag in her hand.

"Go to bed. We'll be leaving in a couple of hours. I'll wake you when it's time."

BJ nodded her head and went up the stairs to the bedroom she shared with the man she now realized she knew nothing about.

CHAPTER 17

November 1985 ......

Steven, Jimmy, BJ and Misty's six children have been in Florida less than 8 months but have moved four times.

Steven had a difficult time finding a job; however, he'd found Jimmy a job almost immediately at a ship repair yard working a minimum of 50 hours a week. Just like at the tobacco farm, Jimmy worked hard and progressed from being just a gopher for all the workers to being an apprentice welder. Jimmy was a good all around fix-it person as well, and the boss recognized that in him.

When it came time to send a ship up the East Coast on a trial run, Jimmy was asked if he wanted to go along. Jimmy, who had been mentally progressing very quickly while working at the challenging job, said yes. He knew he'd be paid for all the hours he was gone, not just the usual 10 to 12 he worked each day.

Jimmy was tired of having to depend on his father for a ride to and from the shipyard and had found an old junker he could buy for $600. Even though his father insisted he turn over most of his hard earned money to keep the family fed and a roof over their heads, he had saved some. This one trip would give him the extra money to buy the car and get the tag for it.

Steven's plan that sounded so wonderful and so easy when they were in Kentucky wasn't working in Florida and BJ was worried. One day she confronted her husband. "Steven, what happened to the job you were transferring to? Why aren't you working?"

"Stop nagging me!"

"I'm not nagging! If Jimmy wasn't working we wouldn't be eating or have a roof over our head."

"You saying the half-wit's the man of the house now?"

"Well, I hadn't thought about that, but come to think of it, he is the one putting food on the table. That and the food stamps I've been able to get."

"That's cause we didn't get here soon enough. The company had an opening but by the time I got you and your kid and her brats here and all settled in, they'd given it to someone else. They don't just wait on people, you know, so I lost out!"

"If that's the case, why'd we stop in North Carolina and stay in that motel for a month?"

"I had a job to do there and it took time to scope it out."

"I never saw any money come in while we were there."

"They welched on how much I was to get cause it took me so long to set it up. The rest I used for expenses."

"What was the job and why did it take so long to set up?"

"It was just a job. Sometimes it takes longer than expected to find a pattern, plus I had to always be looking out for this whole damn family, so it just did. Now, shut up!" Steven raged.

BJ had no idea what Steven was talking about but decided she'd better keep quiet. While they were in North Carolina, Jimmy had gone to work at a fast food place. It wasn't much money, but he could eat for free and sometimes they let him bring leftover food home. Steven didn't ever want them leaving the shabby motel and would continually call them to be sure they were still there. Poor Jimmy had to lie on the application to get the job as Steven didn't want anyone knowing where they were living. What confused BJ even more is the fact that Steven hardly spent any time at the motel. He'd paid the rent on the motel for adjoining rooms for two weeks, hurriedly emptied the wagon, unhitched the trailer and left. They didn't see him for a week. Then, with no notice, he came back with a big bucket of chicken for them to eat and a couple of bottles of soda. While the large family was eating, he took a shower and left again. That pattern continued each week for the entire month.

The last time Steven came back he didn't have the food. He'd just walked in and announced they were leaving so they packed the wagon, hitched up the trailer and got back on the highway heading south. BJ never asked him about the absences.

Eventually Steven found a full time job working as a janitor. That evening he came home and announced, "Well, the good job finally came through. I'm working for the county and before long we'll have benefits and everything. Have you talked with Leah lately?"

"Yes. She says she's freezing up there and that Jerry won't let her go anywhere."

Steven just grumbled a response, then said, "Call her and ask her if Misty and Jimmy can stay with her awhile."

"Why?"

"Because, I told you to," Steven said angrily.

"No, not why should I call her, but why would Jimmy and Misty be staying with her?"

"Misty doesn't drive so Jimmy will have to take her back to Kentucky. I just started my job, so I can't go. He's getting a car so he can drive her."

"Why does she have to go to Kentucky?"

"Don't you remember the plan? We get Kentucky to give Misty the welfare for her kids for another year and we get Florida to pay us for keeping them as foster kids."

"Isn't that cheating?"

"It's either that or you go to work!"

I thought you said I'd never have to work again!"

"Right, but we need income to feed all these kids. The half-wit's pulling in good money but he's gonna have a car real soon that's gonna need gas and oil and such."

"All right, I'll call her. When will they be going?"

I'll have to see when Jimmy gets some time off. I don't want him losing that job, but I don't want them going up over the holiday either."

"Why?"

"The welfare office needs to be open so Misty can get all the interviews and paperwork done. Can't you figure anything out on your own?"

"Okay, I'll call her. You know she doesn't like surprises, but she'll probably love to see her sister again."

Steven just glared at her.

In reality BJ and Leah had been talking all along. BJ knew Leah and knew she wouldn't like this one bit.

"How ya doin' baby?" BJ crooned when her oldest daughter answered the phone the next day.

"Ya know how I'm doing. I have ta get these kids up to meet the school bus and then I have to watch them when they come home. I have no way to go to town during the day and I can't go ta any clubs at night. This whole place smells like pigs and hay plus I'm freezing my ass off. Thank you very much for askin'."

"Want to move to Florida?"

"Yeah and that'll happen when pigs fly."

"How'd you like company for a week or so?"

"Who?"

"Misty and Jimmy."

"Them two together now?"

"No, Misty needs to check in with them welfare people so's they'll keep sending her a check for the youngins."

"So?"

"So she needs a place to stay."

"Ain't got no room."

"Come on, you're living in that fine house with only four of you. There must be some room for her."

"What's in it for me, other than having to cook for two more people?"

"Maybe a ride to visit us?"

"Visit? If I ever get to leave this dump, I ain't coming back."

"Didn't say you had to, did I?"

"Steven know about this?"

"Not about you moving here with us. I don't see the need to tell him, at least not yet."

"I'll think about it. When would they be coming?"

"Not sure. We have to see when Jimmy can get some time off."

"Steven's him drive now?"

"Yep. He's getting his own car and everything. We're doing great here and it's always warm."

"Like I said, I'll think about it."

After Leah hung the phone up, she started planning how she'd leave. Misty would have to give them welfare people a different address and find someone else to mail her check to her in Florida. That might be a problem, but Leah knew she could think of someone who wouldn't rat her sister out. Misty and Jimmy could stay with her and the boys. She was sure Jerry wouldn't mind a short visit. Then her mind went back to moving. She wouldn't be able to pack much but since BJ and Steven were doing so good they could afford to buy them new stuff. *"Hmm, this might work out fine. All the checks from welfare and the Ramsey's have stopped so all I've got coming in for me is the little Social Security check from that crazy Harry. If I can get to town, I can get the address changed so Jerry would never need to know where we moved to. He can take care of all the bills that come in. Ain't my fault it costs so much to keep kids and run a house. He'll find out after I'm gone and then he can deal with it. Hmm, this might work out just fine."*

With that Leah decided she'd make a hot dinner for her family. She knew Jerry and if she just started keeping the house up a little more and cooked a meal now and then, he'd think everything was fine. Now that she had the beginning of a plan, she could work the situation to her advantage.

When Jerry came in from working in the family fields, he was greeted with a wonderful aroma coming from the kitchen.

"What's in the oven?" he asked pleasantly.

Leah's first reaction was to say something sarcastic, but thought better of it.

"Just some chicken and taters and carrots," she said smiling sweetly.

"Smells great!" said Jerry while he was really wondering what she wanted. He'd learned early on to survive on bologna sandwiches for lunch and dinner. He knew if he was tired of sandwiches for dinner, he could eat with his mom and dad.

"Hurry and get washed up. Ya don't want the biscuits to get cold do ya?"

"Biscuits too? Wow! What's the occasion?"

"No occasion. I just felt like cooking. You complaining?"

"Hell, no!" Jerry said as he walked into the bathroom to wash the dirt of the fields off his hands. On the way to the kitchen he looked in on the boys. Finding them fast asleep he shut the door so as not to wake them and went into his bedroom to get his slippers. As usual, he'd left his dirty work boots by the front door just as his mother had taught him to do.

As he walked into the kitchen he said, "I'd thought the boys would have wanted some of this great food. You fixed enough for us all."

"They were so tired after they come home from school, they could hardly keep their eyes open."

"What did they have for dinner?" expecting to hear the normal response of bologna sandwiches.

"Nuthin'."

"What?"

"Nuthin', I said. Can't your hear?" said Leah getting a little upset with Jerry. "They was tired out so they went to bed."

"Wake them up."

"What?"

"Are you the one who can't hear now? Wake them up. You do it or I will."

"Why?"

"They need to eat."

"They had lunch at their school. That's enough for anybody for all day. They don't' need no more."

Jerry slid his chair back, got up and walked to the room the boys shared. He had to shake them each a couple of times, but finally succeeded in getting them up.

"Come on now, sleep heads. Go to the bathroom, wash your hands and come out to eat with me."

The boys looked dazed and confused, but they complied. When the three were seated at the table, Jerry started putting food on each of their plates. Leah just glared, first at Jerry, then at the boys.

"Don't you give them that kind of look. They need to eat and as long as they live in my house, they're going to."

Leah just said, "Whatever!" and got up from the table. All she'd eaten was the skin off one chicken leg.

As the boys ate, they got livelier. They started talking with Jerry about school and about how much fun they had. Then Billy Ray asked, "Can I do my homework now?"

"You have homework?"

"Yep, but I ain't been doin' it and my teacher's mad at me."

"Why haven't you been doing it? Don't you know how to do it?"

Before Billy Ray said anything, he looked towards his mother. She was staring hard at him.

"I been tired," Billy Ray said meekly.

"Well, school can be awful tiring," Jerry said understandingly; however, he realized Leah was controlling what the boy said and didn't press any further. Instead he suggest to the little boy, "When you're done eating, go get your homework and we'll do it together. Okay?"

"Okay," Billy Ray said enthusiastically. He grabbed another chicken leg from his plate and devoured it. Then he ate all the potatoes, carrots and biscuit Jerry had given him.

Leah was still glaring at the boy, but Billy Ray never turned his head towards her until his place was clean. When he finally did, the smile he'd had on his face immediately disappeared.

"Go get your homework. We can do it while your mom washes the dishes," Jerry said staring at his wife. He knew she didn't do dishes every night and she'd be mad. The fact was, he usually wound up doing them when they started to smell the house up. He didn't care if she was mad. From now on he was going to see that the boys were fed each night.

Leah was furious and showed it in the way she was slamming dishes around while cleaning off the table.

"Ain't nuthin' left," she complained.

Jerry's response was, "Good. You don't like leftovers anyway. Does she boys?"

Billy Ray and Andy just shook their heads no while their little eyes bounced from Jerry to their mother and back. They'd enjoyed dinner, but they knew their momma was mad. They hoped she wouldn't take it out on them.

Jerry helped Billy Ray with his homework and spent some time with Andy helping him read.

Then, as they were heading off to their room, Jerry asked, "Did you have your bath already?"

Both boys stopped in their tracks. Before they could think of anything to say, Leah jumped up and said, "Water and soap are expensive so they don't take baths but once a week."

Jerry didn't know how to respond to his wife's statement, so he kept quiet.

The boys, however, sighed a silent sigh, scurried into their room and shut the door.

When Jerry heard the door snap shut, he turned to Leah and said, "We have three deep wells on this farm, one is for the animals, one is for the main house and one is for us. Water is not a problem! And soap is pretty cheap. I want these boys to bathe everyday. Got it?"

Leah gave her normal response, "Whatever."

Normally BJ called her daughter, but this time Leah called her mother first. "So when're they coming? I can't wait to get out of this place," is how the conversation started when BJ answered the phone.

Later that week, over dinner, Steven asked BJ, "So did you make that call I asked you to?"

"BJ looked a little puzzled, but then figured out what he meant and responded, "Yes and she said it's okay with her."

Steven glared but responded, "Well, I talked with the half-wit. He's going on a test trip on one of them ships they been working on. When he gets back, he'll have a week off. So that's when they'll be going up there. It'll work out good cause the county offices will be open every day. Misty will be able to get all her paperwork done and be set for at least another 6 months. Speaking of Misty, tell her to get the kids birth certificates out for me."

"What for?"

"Cause I said so, that's why. But if you must know, I'll be needing them to apply for foster parent status while she's gone."

Jimmy and Misty had an uneventful trip on the drive to Kentucky, stopping only for gas, to make small engine repairs and to sleep a little.

Arriving near dark at the house Leah was living in they were surprised to find no lights on.

Sitting in the car, looking at the large house, Misty said, "Sure doesn't look like the little dump Leah talks about."

"Sure doesn't. Didn't she know we were coming?"

"Momma called her just before we left, so I know she was. You sure we're at the right place? There was lots of different driveways."

"Yeah there were, but I turned on the one that said Kilgore Farms and had a sign over the driveway that said the same thing. So I know we're in the right place. I just don't know if it's the right house. I only see two houses and the other one is huge so this has to be the one.”

“Guess you’re right,” Misty said. “Let’s go knock on the door. Maybe they’re in the back where we can’t see the lights.”

“Okay,” Jimmy said tentatively, and the two of them got out of the car and walked up on the porch of the darkened house.

“Knock on the door,” Misty whispered to her companion.

“You knock, she’s your sister,” he replied.

Just then Misty spotted the doorbell button and pushed it.

“I didn’t hear anything, did you?” asked Jimmy.

“No,” she replied pushing it a second and a third time.

All of a sudden the porch light came on and the front door was yanked open.

“What the hell’s so important you can’t wait for a body to get to the damn door?” screamed Leah.

Jimmy and Misty jumped back. Neither one of them expected a greeting like that.

Equally surprised was Leah. “What the hell you two doing here already?”

Misty and Jimmy still didn’t know what to say. Leah appeared to have been drinking and was in a very foul mood.

Misty softly said to her sister, “We drove right through cause we didn’t want to waste money on a motel.”

Leah’s response was “Well, come on in. Wasn’t expecting you till tomorrow so don’t have anything ready.”

“That’s okay. We don’t need anything special, just a bathroom and someplace to sleep. We been on the road a long time,” said Jimmy.

“Well, the bathroom’s down that hall and there’s a bedroom back there we don’t use. Just move the stuff off the bed. I’m sure the two of ya don’t mind sharing a bed.”

“You crazy or somethin’? Jimmy’s my brother. We don’t sleep together,” Misty, scolded her sister.

“Whatever!” Sleep where ya want,” Leah responded as she stomped off towards the kitchen. She needed to put her bottle of Vodka where her nosy sister couldn’t find it. Just as she’d shut the cupboard where she kept her liquor, Jimmy walked in.

“What do you want?”

"Got anything left over from dinner we could eat? We've just been eating crackers on the way here."

"So?"

"So we're hungry. Dad only let us bring enough money to get gas with a little left over, in case. And we already needed the in case money on repairs for the car."

"Ya should have bought a better car!"

Jimmy hung his head a little, "Didn't have the money. I bought what I could afford and it done pretty good", Jimmy added proudly.

Leah just looked at Jimmy for a second. "I ain't nobody's nigger. If'n ya find anything in there," pointing to the refrigerator, "you can have it but ya gotta cook it and clean up after yourself." With that said, she walked out of the kitchen to the living room. Just as she sat down, Misty walked in.

"The bed seems nice and comfortable."

No comment from Leah.

"Where are the boys?"

"Asleep."

"Leah, what's wrong with you? I know momma talked to you about us coming up, so why you acting like you are?"

"Wasn't expecting ya till tomorrow. I already told ya that."

"Are you drinking again?"

"I don't never drink nuthin' but sweet tea. Ya knows that so don't be spreading lies."

Misty just looked at her sister. She knew she used to drink Vodka or that awful Grape Pucker. Somehow she didn't think she'd changed all that much.

"So where's your husband?" Misty asked.

"Off with his father looking for more pigs or chickens or something else smelly."

"When will he be back?"

"Why, ya think ya can steal him from me?"

"No, I was just asking to be polite. Did you tell him we were coming?"

"Not really."

"Well either you did or you didn't."

"I told him you guys might come up sometime and he said he didn't mind."

"Leah, why are you like this? You got a fine house and a man who loves you. He takes good care of you and your kids that aren't even his. You got it made!"

"So you say. You ain't seen him shake and shake my boys, forcing them to get up outta bed just so's he can force them ta eat and talk to him."

"When was this?"

"Happens when ever I give them their medicine so they can be put down early."

"Do you feed them before you given them their medicine?"

"Like I told him, they done ate at school so they don't need to eat when they get home."

Misty shook her head.

"Plus, I gotta pay for them to get their breakfast and lunch there!"

"What?"

"They says we got too much money so If'n I want them to eat there, I gotta pay."

"So what?"

"Jerry gives me money for me, not for them to be wasting it eatin'. They want me to give it to them at that damn school. That's what we pay taxes for!"

"I think taxes are to pay teachers and buy books, not to pay for food for children who have parents who can afford to feed their kids at home."

"I don't feed them at home cause the school's supposed to do that."

"But you can afford to feed them. You just don't want to."

"Look, ya want ta stay here or not?" Leah shouted at her sister.

Misty shook her head yes, realizing her sister was getting very angry.

"Fine then, shut up. Them's my kids and it's my money, not theirs."

Right then Jimmy came out of the kitchen and announced, "Dinner's ready! We got mac and cheese. We got burgers. We got pickles and tomatoes. What we don't got is buns, but we got bread I toasted." Then he noticed the two girls standing nose to nose.

"Oops, did I interrupt something?"

Misty was the only one to respond, "No. I'll be right there."

"Okay, but don't take too long or it'll get cold."

Leah sat back down on the couch with her glass of tea as Misty walked into the kitchen.

"Jimmy, this looks great! How do you do it?"

"Do what?"

"Make good things from not much of anything."

"Is that what I do?"

"Yep," Misty said taking a huge helping of the macaroni and cheese.

Leah walked to the kitchen doorway and stood there looking at her sister and stepbrother.

Jimmy noticed her and invited her to eat with them.

"Ya trying to make me fat like BJ?"

"No, just trying to be polite since we're eating your food in your house. That's all."

"Polite, huh, well enjoy it. I ain't goin' ta get fat. So eat it all or I'll have ta throw it out tomorrow," Leash shouted over her shoulder as she stormed into her bedroom and slammed the door.

Misty looked at Jimmy and shrugged her shoulders. "She's always been like that."

"She don't like food?" Jimmy asked.

"Nope."

"Nothing?"

"Nothing but sweet tea and hard candy."

"Her teeth will rot out."

"They already have."

"What?"

"Most of her teeth are rotted or broken off. That is, those that haven't fallen out."

"Hell, she couldn't eat a burger with bad teeth. She ought to drink milk and eat cheese. Maybe it would help. My mom always had us drinking lots of milk and eating cheese. She said it helped our bones be strong."

"She won't do it. She's always thought milk was too fattening and cheese, well cheese is pure fat."

"Maybe they have pills, like vitamins she could take."

"Jimmy, don't waste your time on her. She's a very mean person. She doesn't even like her own kids."

Jimmy looked strangely at Misty while still chomping on his burger. In his mind all people were good. He knew Leah was because she helped him so much when he was sick. Misty would see. Once Leah got to Florida with the rest of the family, she'd be happy and nice again.

Misty looked at the boy-man sitting across from her wondering if Leah was going to use him up and throw him away like she had every other man in her life.

After they ate they washed all the dishes in the sink, even though most of them had very apparently been sitting there for quite awhile. Neither of them said anything more to each other while they washed and dried them. As Jimmy washed he hummed and whistled. As Misty dried, she thought, *"How can she leave so many dirty dishes sitting in the sink? What does she do all day?"*

When they were done washing, drying and putting away all the dishes, Misty said, "We're finally done! That took long enough. I'm off to take a bath and go to bed. I've got the bed for tonight. You can have the couch. Okay?"

"Sure."

"Tomorrow, we'll switch."

"That's okay. I'm used to sleeping on a couch. You keep the bed."

"You sure?"

"Yep."

"Okay, but I got the bathroom first."

"That's okay too. I'll clean it when I finish."

"You don't have to do that."

"I always do it at home, so why not? Besides, it's kinda dirty in there. You should clean it a little before you take your shower."

"I was thinking of taking a bath instead."

"I wouldn't. The tub is very, very dirty," Jimmy said shaking his head.

"Really?"

"Really. Take a shower, okay? Too much dirt."

"Okay, I will, but you shouldn't have to clean up after me."

"That's okay. I'll scrub it real good and then tomorrow you can take a bath."

"Thanks. You're a good guy."

"Thanks. See ya tomorrow. I'll fix us some pancakes in the morning. I saw all the stuff I need in the cupboard."

"Sounds good."

CHAPTER 18

It's December 1985 ......

Misty and Jimmy had arrived on a Saturday night so she decided to visit her father on Sunday instead of waiting until Monday after he got off work. She wanted to ask him if he'd be willing to forward her mail and talk to the social workers if they ever showed up on his door looking for her and her children. Misty needed an address in Kentucky she could give the welfare people on Monday.

True to his word, the next morning Jimmy had the batter ready for pancakes when Misty got up.

"Ain't Leah or the boys up yet?"

"Nope. Ain't heard a peep from anybody, so I guess it's just you and me eating these," replied Jimmy.

After they finished eating, they cleaned up the dishes but left the batter so Leah could fix pancakes for the boys when they got up. While Jimmy was finishing up in the kitchen, Misty wrote her sister a note so she wouldn't worry. Then the two of them drove over to see Bobby Ray.

When they pulled up in front of the building where Bobby Ray lived, Misty said to Jimmy, "I don't want to be mean, but I think it would be best if you waited in the car."

"Okay. I just might catch me a few more winks. I'm still a little tired from the drive."

Misty nodded her head. As she got out of the car she turned to Jimmy and said, "I'll try not to be too long."

"Take your time," was the response she got and with minutes he was fast asleep.

When Misty returned, Jimmy was still sleeping. He jumped at the sound of the door opening, saw her and then settled down asking "Everything okay?"

"Yes, it is."

"Okay then. Where to now?"

"Let's go to a grocery store, if you can find one. I'd like a good dinner. We know Leah ain't gonna be cooking and there ain't much in her house to eat."

"You'd think living on a farm and all, she's have a lot of good stuff to eat."

"Told ya, she don't like food."

"Oh yeah, I forgot," said Jimmy. "I saw a store right on the way back to the house. We can stop there. Okay?"

"Fine. We don't got a lot of money, but I think we can get enough to last us the time we'll be here."

"What about our trip home?"

"What about it?"

"We'll have the kid's with us, so we'll need to stop to eat or have something in the car for them. I don't need to eat, but kid's do."

"Don't worry about that. I'll make sure Leah has money to get food for them on the trip."

"Okay, if you say so," said Jimmy as he turned into the driveway of the little grocery store he'd seen. It didn't take them long to buy the meager groceries they could afford and then they were on their way back to the farm.

As they pulled up in front of the house they'd left only a few hours before, Misty commented, "It looks like nobody's home. Wonder where she and the boys went?"

"Dunno, but I bet we can still get in."

"Hope so," Misty said as she carried one of the three bags of groceries from the back seat up on the porch and to the front door. Jimmy was only a couple of steps behind her carrying the other two bags.

As Misty tried to open the door she found it was locked. "Jimmy, Leah's locked the door on us."

"Why would she do that when she knew we were coming back?"

"Don't know. She's a crazy bitch," Misty said frustrated.

"Don't say that. She probably just forgot and did it out of habit."

To Jimmy she said, "Right," but she knew her sister. She didn't mind sitting on the front porch, but she didn't want the groceries to spoil. They couldn't afford to replace them.

"Hold on to these, please," Jimmy said as he handed his bags to Misty. "I'll get us in."

"Can you?"

"Sure. Wait right here."

Misty smiled at his comment, and wondered where Jimmy thought she could go.

About a minute later she heard a click and the front door opened to reveal a smiling Jimmy standing in the doorway.

"How'd you do that?" asked Misty.

"I come through the back door. It ain't got no lock on it. I figured I could get in there," he said smiling proudly. "Of course, I was right!"

"Of course," Misty replied while walking in the house with all the bags.

Several hours later Misty and Jimmy were sitting in the living room watching television when the front door opened.

"Leah, I'm home," shouted Jerry.

"She's not here," replied her sister. "We've been waiting for her all day."

"Who are you two?"

"I'm her brother Jimmy and this is her sister Misty," responded Jimmy standing up to talk to his brother-in-law.

"Where's Leah?"

"Dunno," said Misty. "I had business to take care of this morning. I don't drive so Jimmy and me left early. When we come back Leah and the boys weren't here."

"Did she leave a note?"

"No, and on top of that, she'd locked us out. It woulda been okay except we'd spent about all we had on groceries and they woulda spoiled."

"There's no lock on the back door," Jerry said smiling.

"Jimmy found that out."

"When did you get here?"

"Yesterday."

"I'm sorry I wasn't here. My dad and I were off to an auction to get some new breeding stock, but I could have left early, if I'd known."

"No problem. This is a great farm and it's your job. Bet you gotta work hard to keep it up," said Jimmy.

Jerry smiled while thinking, *"They sure don't talk or act like Leah."* "Well, Leah doesn't drive so unless she got one of the hired hands to take her somewhere, she couldn't get too far."

"How come she don't drive?" asked Jimmy.

"Don't know. I've tried to teach her but she just doesn't seem to be able to get the hang of it. Say, it's about time for dinner. Let me call my mom and ask her if we can join she and dad tonight."

"Why can't we eat here? We don't want to put you out."

"I don't cook."

Misty proudly said, "Jimmy and I can cook and we did go shopping today."

"You both know how to cook?"

"Sure, it ain't hard," Jimmy answered.

"Well, okay then. Let's do it! How can I help."

Misty said, "Get washed up and report to the kitchen. Jimmy will tell you what needs to be done."

Jerry headed to the bathroom to wash up while Jimmy and Misty went to the kitchen.

"He seems nice. Not at all like Leah described him," Misty commented to Jimmy.

Jimmy picked up her thought and added, "Not at all. How many people would have been so nice when they found strangers sitting in their living room?"

"Not many, that's for sure. So what are we having tonight?"

"That's what I'm asking," said Jerry as he walked into the living room.

"Depends," replied Jimmy.

"On what?"

"On if you have a grill or not."

"Nope. Don't have one anymore. Used to, but Leah threw it out."

"Okay, doesn't matter. Instead of bar-b-que, we'll have chicken and rice."

"Really? Just like that you can change?"

"Sure, why not?"

"Nothing, I guess. It's always been a big deal if Leah was missing something."

"Nah, I just wish we had some veggies."

"You guys eat vegetables?"

"Of course, don't you?"

"Not lately. Leah keeps saying we're not rabbits and don't let us have any."

"That's silly," Misty responded.

"Sure is. Say. Let me run over to my mom's. She has tons of onions, garlic, lettuce, tomatoes – well, lots of stuff."

"That'd be great! We couldn't afford to buy all the stuff we needed for the time we'll be here, so we mainly got meat."

"What about breakfast?" asked Jerry.

"What about it?" Jimmy asked.

"Want some bacon and sausage?"

"We don't want to take too much. Aint' polite," was Jimmy's answer.

"We raise pigs. My mom and dad have tons of it."

"How come you don't?" Misty asked.

"Well, Leah always threw it out, so I stopped bringing it home."

Jimmy responded enthusiastically, "Wow, some fresh sausage would go great with the pancakes."

"Pancakes? Leah fixed pancakes?"

"Oh no," Misty said laughing, "Jimmy did. He left her enough so she could fix them for the boys, cause they weren't up yet."

"She probably didn't."

"Sure she did. The pitcher wasn't here when we got back, so she must have."

"Wait here, let me check the garbage can." A few minutes later Jerry came back to the kitchen carrying the plastic pitcher that had contained the batter.

"She threw out the batter and the pitcher?" asked Misty dumbfounded. "Why'd she do that?"

"So she didn't have to wash the pitcher," Jerry calmly responded.

"Really?" was Jimmy's comment.

"Oh yeah," replied Jerry. "Happens all the time." Then he brightened and said, "How about I invite my parents over for dinner? I think they'd like to meet you both."

"Great, as long as they don't mind sharing what we have."

"They'll love it. Let me call them," and with that Jerry left the room.

Misty said to Jimmy, "Will we have enough for the rest of the week if we feed us all?"

"Somehow it'll work out. Don't worry. I'll just add some more rice and stuff."

Right about then Jerry walked back in the kitchen. "Don't worry about side dishes. Mom's making cracklin' corn bread, a tossed salad and her green bean casserole."

"Wow," Misty exclaimed. "We're only doing chicken and rice."

"They said they haven't had that dish in a long time and looked forward to eating with us."

"Well, I'd better get moving," said Jimmy as he started chopping the chicken into pieces and dropping them into the frying pay to brown. "Jerry, can you find me a casserole dish?"

"What's it look like?"

"Kinda like glass and about this big around," Jimmy said as he spread his hands apart.

Jerry started searching each cupboard. As he opened one of them he said, "My, my, what do we have here?"

"A casserole dish, I hope," laughed Jimmy.

"Not hardly! How about a couple bottles of booze."

"What?" Misty and Jimmy said in unison.

"Booze – vodka, grape pucker and, let's see what this one is," Jerry said as he turned the last bottle around. "This one is peppermint schnapps."

"That's probably what Leah calls her medicine."

"It's not medicine in my book."

"Not mine either," said Jimmy. "Don't care about that crap, I need me a casserole dish."

Right them Misty said, "Got it. Will this one do?"

"Perfect! Now, if you would please set the table for us."

Jimmy put the casserole in the oven and a couple of minutes later Jerry's parents knocked on the door.

Mr. & Mrs. Kilgore breezed into the kitchen talking and laughing. "Jerry, I don't think you've ever asked us over to dinner before."

"You're right and I didn't this time," he said laughing. "Misty and Jimmy did and Jimmy's doing the cooking. If it was me cooking, we'd all be poisoned."

"Well, how about a little cornbread and salad to go with whatever you fixed that smells so good."

"Nothing special, but thanks."

"Smells wonderful. How long before it's done?"

"About 20 minutes. Sorry I'm so slow."

"Just enough time to catch the evening news on TV. That okay with you, Jerry?"

"Fine. I'll turn it on. You coming Jimmy?"

"Sure. Let me set the timer so I don't burn this. I'd feel terrible if I ruined it with your parents here and all."

"We'd all eat it anyway and it wouldn't be the first time. Don't worry about them."

Before long the news was over, the casserole done and everyone was sitting in the kitchen eating, laughing and having a good time.

As they were finishing their meal, they heard a noise outside. Seconds later Leah and her boys burst through the front door. When Leah saw the group sitting in the kitchen of what she considered her house, she started screaming.

"What the fuck you doing in my house when I'm not here?"

Jerry yelled back, "It's my house and you ain't been here all day."

"Don't you be yelling at me. Next thing ya know you'll be shaking my kids again."

"The only time I shake them is to wake them up to feed them and you know it."

"You lying bastard!" Leah screamed. "You hurt them all the time, just like ya hurt me."

"I've never touched you."

"Lies, that's all ya tell is lies."

Jerry just shook his head and turned away from her.

"Ya'll get outta my house. Ya got no right eating my food without me saying it's okay."

Misty stood up, turned to her sister and started towards her. "None of this is your food. Jimmy's money bought the chicken and rice. Mr. & Mrs. Kilgore brought everything else. Jimmy's cleaned your dishes, your kitchen and your bathroom and you ain't even been nice to him or me. Where do you get off screaming at all of us?"

"This is my house and I didn't invite none of ya here," was Leah's reply.

Right then Mr. Kilgore stood up and helped Mrs. Kilgore out of her chair. To Misty and Jimmy he said, "I've had a great time. Better than I've had in a long time. Jimmy, you're a good cook. Misty, you're fun to talk to. Jerry, you're crazy to continue living with that woman." To Leah he said, "You're wrong. This house isn't yours. It isn't even Jerry's. It's mine. I've worked very hard for a lot of years to have all of this. None of it will ever be yours and as long as Jerry's married to you, none of it will ever be his."

Jerry looked at his father and as tears started rolling down his face he said, "I'm sorry dad."

"Me too, son. Me too." Then he and Mrs. Kilgore said good night to Misty and Jimmy and walked out the door.

Leah screamed at Jerry, "So why don't you leave too? Ya ain't no good. Ya ain't done nothing ya promised me ya would."

Jerry just shook his head. He'd known this marriage was over for a long time. He knew it had been a mistake from the beginning, but he'd taken an oath and he'd keep his end of the bargain.

Leah grabbed her two sons by their thins arms and pulled them towards their bedroom. She opened the hollow cored door, almost ripping it off the hinges and shoved them inside. "Get in bed and shut up. I'm tired of all your whining." Then she slammed the door shut and turned the button on the door know, locking them in.

"That ain't right," yelled Jerry. "I told you not to turn that knob around. What if they need to use the bathroom?"

"They'd better not. They already went once today."

"You're crazy!"

"See how ya treat me and the boys. I'm only protecting them from you."

"Me? What the hell are you talking about? I ain't never hurt you or them boys."

"Almost every day you shake the shit outta them boys."

"Only because they need to eat and you don't feed them!"

"I feed them!"

"You're a liar. You don't ever feed them."

"They're alive, so I must!"

"They're nothing but skin and bones. They're always hungry and there's no need cause we have access to plenty of food."

"We ain't got no good food here. All we got is crap – pig crap."

"Pigs are a good source of food."

"Pigs are, well they're pigs! I ain't gonna talk about it anymore."

"Fine, cause I'm right. You're lucky them boys ain't dead."

"Why do ya say that?"

"If they were dead, you'd have to work to support yourself and you sure don't want that to happen."

"I work all the time!"

"Doing what?"

"I take care of the house."

"I clean the house more than you do."

"Oh yeah?"

"Sure, and I'll prove it. Tell me, where's the vacuum?"

"What?"

"You heard me, where's the vacuum?"

"What kinda trick question is that?"

"No trick question, just making a point. You don't cook. You don't clean. You don't have sex with me."

"Why should I? You heard your father. I thought if'n I married you, I'd be rich, but I find you don't got nothin' to give me."

"I have a lot, but you ain't getting any of it."

"I'm your wife. I'm supposed to get it all."

"What are you talking about?"

"When we get divorced, I'm supposed to get everything you got."

"Why do you think that?"

"Cause I'm an abused wife with children so's I can't work and you got lots and can always get more."

"You're crazy. Dad's right."

"I'm smart. I married ya fer money but so far I ain't got none, but I will. And I ain't even got a car."

"You don't drive."

"Ya won't teach me right. My lawyer said he can get me half the farm cause you been beatin' me and starving me and my poor boys."

"Your lawyer? What do you mean, your lawyer? What do you need a lawyer for?"

"To get me the money I married ya for and deserve. He says he can make you give me money for food and everything else I need."

"You get money for groceries every week and you spend it on what you call medicine."

"Gotta get medicine. My lawyer says you gotta pay for food and medicine for me and my boys."

"Does your lawyer know your medicine is just booze?"

"I gotta note from a doctor saying I gotta take it and I gotta give it to the boys."

"Like hell! Let me see it."

"I gave it to my lawyer," Lead said, all the while knowing the lawyer she saw told her she needed to provide him with the prescribing doctor's name.

"Like hell. No doctor would give you a prescription for booze."

"It ain't booze, it's medicine! Boy, when I own this place, I'm gonna make sure ya don't set foot here ever again."

"You're totally crazy. Nothing you say even makes sense. I'm staying with my mom and dad tonight. When I come back in the morning, you'd better be gone."

"Go to hell!" Leah shouted after Jerry as he walked out the door of his own house.

Once outside, Jerry saw Jimmy and Misty standing on the porch.

"Sorry about you having to hear all of that."

Misty responded first, "Me too. We ain't got enough money to get a place to stay and we got business that'll take a couple of days to clear up."

"You can stay with us at the main house."

"That's so nice of you, but she's my sister so I can't accept your offer."

"She might kill you in your sleep."

"She would if she got mad enough at us or if it would get her something. We got nothing for her to get so she'll leave us alone, that is unless we talk to you for too long."

"Really?"

"Yep, so forgive me but I gotta protect me and Jimmy."

"Sure, but…"

"What the fuck you talking about?" screamed Misty at Jerry. "I seen them bruises on her so ya can't fool me."

Jerry looked surprised then realized what Misty was doing. He responded as he knew he had to, "You're just like that crazy bitch inside."

Misty picked up a stick and threw it ineffectively towards Jerry and screamed, "Get your lying ass out of here." Then she turned towards a wide-eyed Jimmy and said, "Let's go inside."

Jerry had turned his back to the duo and was walking towards his parents home as Jimmy looked first at Misty, then Jerry's back, then to Misty.

Her response was, "You coming in with me or you goin' with that asshole?" She pleaded with Jimmy with her eyes to come with her. She knew it was the only thing she could do.

Jimmy realized she was acting to pacify her sister, who was peaking at them from behind the living room curtain. He responded with a simple nod and followed her into the house.

The rest of the night was relatively calm and quiet in the house they would share with Leah for the next few days.

Misty took her shower and then went into the kitchen with her sister so they could talk. Jimmy took his shower and then started cleaning the bathroom as he felt it was still too dirty. After he got done, he grabbed the pillow and blankets he was sleeping with, made up the couch and laid down.

He heard the sisters talking and laughing. He really wanted to join them but knew if he did, they'd start fighting. He didn't want to hear any more fighting so decided just to go to sleep. Soon after he put his head on the pillow he was in a deep sleep.

Leah and Misty talked late into the night. Misty knew she'd have to get up early in order to get to all the welfare people, but Leah was very talkative and Misty didn't want to anger her by saying she was going to bed.

Finally Leah said, "You'd better get to bed. It's 1:30AM and the boys have to be up at 6AM in order to catch the school bus."

"The welfare office doesn't open til 8:30AM so I'll be okay if I get up by 7:30AM."

"I just old ya, the boys gotta be up by 6AM."

Then it dawned on Misty, her sister was expecting her to get the boys up. "So why do I have to get your kids up?"

"Cause I'm going out to party now and I might not be back in time."

"This late? No place is open now."

"Sure there is. Ya just gotta know the right people," Leah said with a wink. "See ya sometime tomorrow," she called over her shoulder as she walked out the back door.

Misty was left sitting at the kitchen table with a look of shock on her face. She couldn't believe what her sister had just done. Slowly she stood up, washed the glasses they'd been drinking out of and headed off to bed.

The next morning Misty was up early so she could get breakfast ready for the boys. Right at 6AM she lightly knocked on their door and then opened it a little while asking softly, "You guys awake?"

She heard no response so she walked in and said louder, "Wake up, sleepy heads." When she still didn't get a response she walked over to Billy Ray's bed and touched the blanket covering his little shoulder.

Billy Ray jumped and cried out, "Don't hit me. I'll take my medicine, I promise!"

Misty gently said, I don't have any medicine for you. I just wanted to tell you breakfast is just about ready and to ask you if you wanted to take your shower before or after you eat?"

Billy Ray finally uncovered his head and looked at his aunt. "Is it Friday?"

Misty thought he'd asked a strange question but answered, "No, it's Monday. Why?"

"We take our showers on Friday night and we don't eat breakfast," Billy Ray said with an arrogant tone to his voice.

Misty was quiet for a moment not knowing how to respond to the little boy. Then she said, "Okay, but today's a special day."

Now she had two little boys staring at her not saying a word.

Misty continued saying, "It's special because I'm getting you ready for school today and I like to cook."

Billy Ray quickly responded, "My mom likes to cook."

"I didn't say she didn't. I just said I like to cook and I'd like to have someone eat it so it doesn't go to waste."

"We eat at school," Andy offered.

"Why? There's all kinds of good stuff to eat here."

"Because mom says we're entitled," Andy answered.

Billy Ray looked at his younger brighter and told him to shut up.

Misty wondered why both boys were acting like they were, but decided not to address the issue with them. Instead she chose to try something different.

"I'm sorry if I don't know how your mom does things, but I really don't want the food I cooked to go to waste. Could you do something different today and eat the breakfast I cooked?"

Andy looked to Billy Ray for the answer.

Billy Ray thought for a moment and then said, "Okay, but just for today. I don't want mom to get mad at us."

"I'll tell her. She won't be mad."

Both boys sat up straight and cried, "No, don't! She'll be really mad at us."

"Why?"

"Cause, we're entitled!"

"Okay. I'll have the dishes done before your mom gets up. I promise."

Both boys seemed to relax so Misty took that as her cue and said, happily, "Get those covers off and get dressed before your food gets cold."

The boys tossed the blankets off and jumped out of bed, already dressed. Misty wanted to ask them whey they slept in their clothes, but decided against it. They two little boys headed towards the bathroom as Misty went to the kitchen.

When the boys got to the kitchen, they saw glasses of milk and orange juice sitting on the table and their eyes went wide.

As they sat down Misty spoke. "The pancakes and bacon are in the oven keeping warm. How do you want your eggs cooked?"

Silence. The boys looked at each other but said nothing.

Misty asked again, "How do you want your eggs?"

Still she heard no response so she turned to look at the boys and saw they were just staring at her. "Why aren't you answering me?"

Each boy smiled slightly but said nothing.

Misty was confused, but she persisted. "Does your mom cook them sunny side up, over easy or scrambled?"

Billy Ray finally answered quietly, "We eats them how she cooks them. She don't ask us."

"Okay, so do they have a runny center?"

"Sometimes," Billy Ray said quietly.

Then Andy joined in, "But not hardly ever. She says that's bad and takes that long handled thing and turns them over til' they ain't runny no more."

Billy Ray looked at his brother and once again told him to shut up.

"Billy Ray, your brother was just answering my question so I'd fix your breakfast right."

"He's telling family business. He knows he ain't supposed to be telling family business."

As Misty was cracking the eggs in the pan she told Billy Ray, "No, he wasn't. He was just telling me how he wants his eggs. No big deal."

Billy Ray glared at Misty and Andy.

The boys quickly devoured the fried eggs, pancakes and bacon that were put on the table. Misty sat with a fresh cup of coffee watching them eat and thought how fast they ate.

As she was taking the dishes off the table she told the boys to brush their teeth and get their book bags and jackets. "I'll walk with you to the bus stop, but you'll have to show me where it is."

"Why?"

"Why, what?"

"Why you gonna walk with us?"

"Cause I promised your mom I'd get you to school."

"She never walks with us," Andy commented.

Billy Ray told his brother to shut up for the third time that morning.

Misty let it pass, only saying, "Come on, let's go or you'll miss the bus. If that happens, I'll be in trouble."

The boys shuffled out the door with Misty falling in behind. She tried talking with them as they walked down the long driveway, but they never responded. As the little group neared the main road Misty saw a school bus coming towards them. "Is that your bus?"

"Suppose so," responded Billy Ray.

"Well, is it or not?"

"Have ta wait to see if he tells us to get on," Billy Ray said sounding irritated.

Misty would have said more, but the bus stopped and the doors opened. The two boys just stood by the bus. Finally the driver yelled, "Billy Ray! Andy! Are you coming or not?"

The two boys responded by getting on the bus. They never turned to say goodbye or to even look out the window.

Misty waved and said goodbye. The driver waved as he shut the door.

Walking back, Misty couldn't help but wonder at how strange the boys were acting; however, she didn't have too much time to think because she heard a car coming up the driveway behind her. As she turned to see who it was, Leah jumped out of the front seat.

"Glad I got here in time! I thought I was gonna be too late."

"Late for what?" Misty asked.

"Late for walking back from the bus," Leah laughed. "Boy, am I tired. God, I hate this walk!"

Misty just looked at her sister.

They walked in silence for a few moments before Misty said, "I fixed us all breakfast and made sure they got off okay to school."

No comment from Leah.

"Did you hear me?" asked Misty.

"Yeah, so what? Don't matter if they go or not. I told you I was tired, so shut up. And when we get to the house, be sure you and the dummy keep quiet so's I can get some sleep."

When the sisters walked in the house they saw Jimmy was up. He said to Leah, "You guys were really quiet this morning. I never heard anybody at all."

Leah glared at him. To Misty she said, "Clean up your mess in the kitchen and get rid of the awful smell you caused. Its' enough to gag a maggot." With that, she walked to her bedroom and slammed the door.

"What did I say?" Jimmy asked Misty.

"Nothing. She's just tired from being out all night."

"Did she just get home?"

"Yep. She made it look like she'd walked the boys to the bus stop.

Jimmy shook his head.

"Want some pancakes for breakfast?"

After Jimmy finished eating, they cleaned the kitchen and left the house so Misty could be first in line at the welfare office. She knew from past experience how long the lines could get. Unlike her sister, Misty always waited her turn. Jimmy stayed in the car, as Misty didn't want the social worker to have any reason to with hold any benefits.

By the end of the day Misty had filled out all the paperwork for her address change. She explained she and the children were living in a kind of boarding house and gave the name and phone number of the landlord in case they needed to get in touch with her. What she didn't say was the so-called landlord was her father. The social worker thanked her for letting them know she'd moved.

When Misty opened the car door, Jimmy jumped a little.

"Sorry. I didn't mean to startle you."

"That's okay. You finished?"

"Yep, totally finished. I don't have to check in with them for another six months. So we can leave whenever we get everybody ready."

Arriving back at the farm, they discover the front door again locked. This time both Misty and Jimmy went to the back door. Once inside they found Billy Ray and Andy sitting in the kitchen.

"Didn't you hear us at the front door?" asked Jimmy.

"Shh! You'll wake momma," said Billy Ray.

Misty laughed, "That's okay. She's been asleep all day so it's time she got up. Besides, I need to talk to her. Let's get dinner started. That'll get her up and complaining about the smell before long."

The boys stared at their aunt like she was crazy.

Jimmy asked, "You guys like burgers?"

No response.

"Well, will you eat burgers?"

Billy Ray quietly spoke up, "We ate breakfast here and we had lunch at school."

"So what?" asked Jimmy.

"So we can't have no more food."

"Sure you can," Misty responded.

"Nope. Mom says it costs too much."

"Well, your mom didn't buy this food, I did and I say we all eat. Okay?" asked Jimmy.

The boys looked at each other and finally said, "Okay."

Just as they were finishing their meal, they heard Leah hollering, "What's that awful smell?"

That's all it took for both boys to run to their bedroom.

Misty was starting to wash the dishes and Jimmy was wiping the table when Leah stumbled into the kitchen.

"Oh, you're up! Good, cause I need to talk with you," said Misty.

"Make me some coffee," she ordered no one in particular.

Jimmy moved to the kitchen counter and started making coffee while Misty sat down with her sister at the table. She told Leah what happened at the welfare office and how they were ready to head back to Florida.

"Are you and the boys coming with us?" Misty asked her sister.

"Dunno."

"Why?"

"Why, what?"

"Why don't you know?"

"I ain't said goodbye to all my friends."

"Well, Jimmy has a little work to do on the car so we're planning to leave early Wednesday morning. If you and the boys are coming, you need to be ready by then."

Jimmy put the coffee in front of Leah, walked to the living room and turned on the television. He didn't want to be a part of their conversation.

Leah sipped her hot coffee and stared across the room, saying nothing.

Misty went back to washing the dishes.

Leah poured herself another cup of coffee and walked back to her bedroom.

Later, as Misty and Jimmy were watching television, there was a knock at the door. Jimmy opened the door to see Jerry standing there.

"Leah here?"

Jimmy pointed towards the bedroom as Jerry walked in and shut the door.

"Is she leaving?"

Misty answered, "Don't know. We're leaving Wednesday. We asked her if she was coming with us, but she said she didn't know yet."

"Wednesday, huh?"

Now Jimmy spoke up, "It'd be tomorrow, but I gotta do some work on the car. Sorry."

"That's okay. You're welcome to stay. I'd just like her gone, but I need her to sign some papers before she leaves. I'll see if I can get them to her by tomorrow night."

Misty and Jimmy nodded.

Opening the door, Jerry said, "Well, good night. If I don't see you before you leave, have a safe trip."

"Thanks," Jimmy said. "You've been real nice to us."

"Let me know if you need any help with the car. We have lots of tools in the shed. We've even got gas and oil you can have, if you need it."

"Thanks, again. Maybe I'll see you in the morning."

Jerry nodded as he walked out.

"He's sad, Jimmy."

"Yep, he is."

Tuesday was a busy day for Misty and Jimmy. Right after he ate breakfast Jimmy drove the car over to the shed Jerry had talked about to so he could work on it. His eyes lit up when he saw all the tools on the walls, each one in it's own spot so they were easy to find.

"Pretty nice place, isn't it?" asked Jerry.

Jimmy jumped at the sound. He hadn't heard anyone come in. "Oh yeah! Someday, maybe I'll have something like this."

"My dad fixed it like this. He told me he was tired of hunting though all his tool chests so he built this shed. Now anybody can find the tool they need just by looking on the wall."

Sounding amazed, Jimmy said, "They're all so shiny."

"Yeah, well its kind of hard to leave anything dirty when you have to put it back on the wall where everybody can see it."

Both men laughed. Then Jerry said, "I talked with dad."

"'Bout what?"

"You know how I told you there's gas and oil here."

"Yeah."

"Well, dad said to fill your tank before you leave."

"I can't take that much. Ain't right. We been staying here for nothing as it is."

"Please do. We'd all like to help you out some."

Jimmy thought a minute, and then said, "Thanks. It'll ease my mind a little." He reached to shake Jerry's hand, "Tell your dad thank you for me."

"I will," Jerry said. Then looking at Jimmy's hand asked, "How do you keep your hands so clean? I thought you worked on your car all the time?"

"I do. It's a trick I picked up working at the ship repair yard. I wear gloves. You know, like doctors wear."

"Rubber gloves?"

"Yeah, tight ones. You can still feel things, but you're hands stay clean. You can buy them by the box pretty cheap."

"We got to get some. Mom's always complaining about our dirty hands. Thanks for the tip! I'll be on the other side of the farm tomorrow, so I won't see you leave."

"Thanks again for the gas and the loan of the tools and, well, for everything."

Jerry waved and walked away without looking back.

That morning, Misty walked with the boys to the bus stop after breakfast and was back in the house cleaning up when she heard a car stop outside the house. Then she heard Leah shouting and laughing. However, as soon as Leah opened the door and saw her sister standing there, her laughing stopped. "You still here?"

"You know we planned to leave tomorrow."

"Whatever. I'm tired. I'm going to bed."

"Wait a minute!"

Leah stopped. "What? I said I was going to bed."

"Are you and the boys coming with us?"

"Dunno yet."

"Well, if you ain't, we're leaving after Jimmy's done working on the car."

"It's a hunk of junk."

Misty didn't respond, instead she just stared at her sister.

Finally responding, Leah said, "I suppose we are. Ain't got nothin' to stay here for."

"Okay, then you're going to have to pack a few things for you and the boys. But it all has to fit in the trunk."

"Yeah, I'll do it after I get some sleep," Leah growled as she walked towards the bedroom.

Misty didn't want a fight so she just went back to the kitchen. She'd finished making her plans for the food still in the house and went into the boys' bedroom. She knew Leah wouldn't pack anything for them, so she would.

Misty had been in the room before, but the window shades had been closed and no light turned on. So when she pulled the curtains open and put the shade up, she was startled. Clothes were thrown everywhere, on the bed, under the beds, on the floor, on the one little dresser, everywhere except where they should have been.

The dresser drawers were empty, except for a few crayons, pencils and crumpled sheets of paper. Some of it looked like unfinished homework. The rest was simply paper that had been ripped in pieces. The closet had nothing hanging on the rod except for a few empty hangers, while the floor held a couple of threadbare blankets, torn living room pillows and three empty cans of bug spray.

It looked as if no one had ever cleaned the room. Misty started sorting the clothes into separate stacks. Those worth keeping were laid on the bed. Those that were either too worn or looked too small were thrown in a pile on the floor.

When finished, she brought the worn out items to the trashcan outside the back door. The remaining clothes were taken to the outside washhouse. It was a little cool there, but she thought what a good idea it was to have the washer outside. Misty was surprised, however, to see a big dryer in the washhouse. Her sister had always complained about the clothes not getting dry so Misty had assumed the wet clothes had to be hung on a line.

While the washer was running, Misty took the opportunity to look at the farm her sister had told her was so terrible. She could see a couple smaller sheds on the other side of the driveway, the big house where Jerry's parents lived and what was probably their wash shed. She also saw some fences beyond the small sheds and assumed the pigs were kept there. As she walked, she saw there was a big barn a little farther out, with fields beyond it. She was looking in amazement at how big the farm was and so was surprised when she heard a female voice say, "It's a pretty view, isn't it."

Misty jumped at hearing the words and hurriedly said, "I'm sorry. I didn't mean to trespass. It's so pretty and so quiet. Not at all like the city."

"Don't you worry none. You didn't do nothing wrong," replied Mrs. Kilgore. "I was just sweeping when I saw you walk by and wondered if you wanted some fresh vegetables."

"I didn't know you could grow them at this time of year."

Mrs. Kilgore laughed, "Didn't used to be able to, but we built us a small hothouse so now we can. Of course, this means we get to work the dirt all year long."

"In that case, I'll take some, but we're leaving tomorrow, so just enough for tonight. I don't want to waste anything." As Misty followed Mrs. Kilgore to the hothouse they talked about the farm and the family. Misty could have talked with her all day, but finally told Mrs. Kilgore she had to go so she could fix lunch for Jimmy and finish the laundry so she could pack for the trip. Misty thanked her for everything. Mrs. Kilgore thanked her for inviting them to dinner.

As Mrs. Kilgore watched Misty walking to her son's house, she couldn't help but think Jerry had attached himself to the wrong sister.

When Misty reached the laundry shed, she turned and waved to Mrs. Kilgore and thought, *"What nice people they are."*

Misty kept busy all day and by the time the boys got home from school, their room was clean, beds were made and the now clean clothes folded and put away. However, the reaction of the boys was not what she'd expected.

She was walking behind them as they entered the now clean and bright room. First they stopped and looked around, then Andy started screaming and Billy Ray ran to the window. He pulled the shade down and the curtains shut. His face was contorted with fear.

Misty was attempting to quiet Andy and trying to find out what was wrong, when Billy Ray started to cry too. She finally got the two of them to settle down when she told them they were going to wake their mother up. They were both very upset, but wouldn't tell her anything. She finally got them to come to the kitchen with her.

"Okay. I know you're upset but I don't know why," Misty said as she put a glass of milk in front of each of them and a big plate of cookies on the table where they both could reach them.

Neither boy moved.

"Go ahead. Eat some cookies and drink your milk, then we can talk."

Andy looked at Billy Ray who finally said, "Don't drink milk."

"How come?"

"Mom says we ain't babies no more so's we gotta drink sweet tea."

"Well, I can't put it back in the bottle and I don't want to waste it by throwing it out, so will you drink it for me?"

"Can't. She'll be mad," was Andy's response.

"She won't know."

"She'll find out."

"Eat some cookies and drink the milk real fast. I'll wash the glasses and fill them with tea. I promise she won't know, unless you tell her."

The boys looked at each other, gobbled a couple cookies each then drank the milk right down. Misty hurriedly washed the glasses and, as promised, re-filled them with tea.

Soon after the glasses had been re-filled with tea, Leah walked into the kitchen. "Want some cookies?" Misty asked her sister.

"Hell no. Just came to get some tea. She poured herself a glass and asked her sister, "Where'd all the milk go?"

"Jimmy and I drank it with our lunch. We didn't want it to go bad and we can't take it with us."

"Whatever." Turning to the boys she said, "We're leaving this dump tomorrow so get a sack and put some of your stuff in it." To Misty she said, "I'm goin' our fer awhile. Pack some stuff for me." Leah shut the refrigerator door and walked back to her bedroom with her glass in her hand.

Misty hollered after her, "We're leaving at 7 tomorrow morning."

"Whatever!" was Leah's response.

Early the next morning, Jimmy, Billy Ray, Andy and Misty had a big breakfast of eggs, sausage, pancakes and the last of the milk. Misty washed the dishes while Jimmy and the boys finished packing the car.

At 7AM, Misty knocked on Leah's bedroom door, but got no response. Next she slowly opened the door a crack, calling her sisters name, but still got no response. When she fully opened the door she saw the bedroom was empty. "Leah, are you in the bathroom?" Misty called.

Silence.

Disgusted and angry, Misty slammed the door shut and stormed back to where the children and Jimmy were patiently waiting.

"Where's Leah?" asked Jimmy.

"I don't know. She ain't in the house anywhere."

Right about then they all heard a car coming up the driveway, radio blaring. Leah had apparently stayed out all night partying again and was just getting home.

"Now, ain't that cute? All a ya just standing in the middle of the yard waitin' fer me," Leah said when she got out of the car. Then turning to the two young men in the car, "Thanks for the lift. Maybe I'll see ya tonight."

The men waved back, made a u-turn and drove off.

Misty was so angry she screamed at her sister, "Where have you been? I told you we were leaving at 7AM. I told you there was packing to do. You knew there was laundry to be done before we could leave. You said you were going out for awhile. All night is not awhile!"

"Whatever. I gotta get some sleep. We can talk later."

"No," said Misty. "We're leaving now, with or without you. Make up your mind – right now."

Leah turned to her sister and stared. She didn't want to stay, but she wanted to leave on her schedule, not anyone else's.

"I gotta pack for my boys."

Billy Ray answered, "We done that already momma."

Leah glared at him and the boy shrunk back.

Next she said, "I gotta get my stuff."

Andy responded this time, "Misty, Billy Ray and me done it for ya, momma."

Leah glared at her youngest son and Billy Ray pulled him away from her.

"I gotta get some sleep so's I can clear my head to think about this."

Quietly, Jimmy said, "You can sleep in the car. We put pillows and blankets in the back seat. It's a long drive and we're leaving - now."

Leah just stood there.

"Okay, last chance for everybody to go to the bathroom before we get on the road," Misty ordered. The little boys and Jimmy headed into the house.

"You coming or do I take all your stuff out and we leave the three of you here?" asked Misty. "This is going to be our only trip up here, so make up your mind. We ain't coming back to get ya."

"Take the brats. I'll stay."

Misty looked dumbfounded at her sister. "What?"

"You heard me. They cramp my style so's you take um."

"No. Either all three of you go or you all three of you stay. We ain't just taking your kids."

Leah started at her sister and thought for a minute. Then, as the boys were coming out of the house, Leah called out, "Well, hurry up. We got places to go. We can't keep waitin' on you brats all the time."

Misty shook her head and said, "I gotta pee. I'll be right out. Get in the backseat." Leah didn't like sitting in the back seat, but decided not to argue with her sister for once.

As Misty walked in the house she passed Jimmy on his way out. "Be careful of her. She's in a strange mood." Jimmy nodded his head.

Moments later, Misty exited the house, shutting the door behind her. She paused for a moment to look at all Leah was walking away from.

"Ya coming or not?" screamed Leah breaking Misty's moment of peace.

As Misty got in the car, Leah asked her, "What was ya looking at?"

"Nothing. I was just wondering if I should lock the door or not."

"Hell no. Nothin' in there a body would want." As the car slowly moved down the driveway, Leah looked around and thought, *"Nope. Nothing here I want."*

The trip was taking them longer to get to south Florida than it did to make the drive to northern Kentucky. When it was just Misty and Jimmy, they would use the restroom when they stopped for gas and they were happy with eating whatever they had packed. Leah and the boys needed or wanted to stop more frequently.

As the scenery started changing, Misty noticed the boys glued to the windows looking at all the things along the highway. Before long, Billy Ray and Andy forgot their mother was in the car and started talking and asking questions about things they saw. Pretty soon they were laughing and talking about everything they saw along the side of the road. They were having fun and the time was passing quickly for all of them.

Suddenly Leah started yelling, "Why the hell can't you young'ns keep quiet. And you two," waving her finger at Misty and Jimmy, "are worse then these brats. Don't ya ever shut up?"

The boys sat back down on the seat they shared with their mother. Leah pulled Billy Ray close to her, holding him by the throat and whispered something in his ear. His eyes went wide and he shook his head no. Then she grabbed Andy, holding him and whispering in his ear just as she had his brother until he shook his head no.

"All right, then. Remember what I told ya," Leah said in a vicious voice.

Misty started to say something to her sister but swallowed her words before they came out. The rest of the day dragged by as they rode in total silence, as no one wanted to hear Leah screaming again.

Since the drive was taking longer and they had no money for a motel, Jimmy stopped to rest for the night at truck stops. He wanted to be some place safe for his passengers. He also wanted to be somewhere they could get something to eat, get gas as well as have bathrooms available. The truck stops filled all his requirements.

Each night, Leah left her children with her sister and half-brother to sleep in the car. She told them she was bored and was going to find some fun people to party with. Each night she stayed gone, returning just in time to get back in the car for the next day's drive.

Each morning, as she entered the car, she'd tell them to shut up so she could sleep. Then she'd say, "That smell of bacon is enough to gag a maggot, Billy Ray. Hold your breath and count to a million." Then she'd laugh at her joke, put a pillow under her head and go to sleep.

Finally the little group arrived in Fort Lauderdale at the house Jimmy's father had rented. It had 3 bedrooms, and 2 bathrooms with a small living room and kitchen. It also had a large enclosed patio they called the "Florida" room that served as a bedroom for Misty's children.

BJ greeted her children and grandchildren warmly. She had missed Leah and the boys and was very happy to have them with her once again.

Leah, on the other hand, was not happy at all. "This place is a dump and it's so small." Compared to the house she shared with Jerry in Kentucky, it was small.

BJ responded brightly, "Well, Steven says when all the money starts rolling in we can move to a bigger place. This is just temporary."

"Better be. Where's my room?"

Misty responded to her question by saying, "You're in with me. It's right over here," as she walked to a small hallway off the living room.

Leah looked inside the open door, but didn't say anything.

Misty continued with the tour of the little house, "That door's to Mom and Steven's room and that's Jimmy's room," she said pointing down the hall. "The boys are gonna be in the Florida room with my kids. The bathroom's right over there and, of course, you seen the kitchen already."

"As I said before, kinda small." She didn't like the idea of sharing a room with her sister, but decided she would keep quiet until she figured things out.

Not long after they were settled in, Steven arrived home from work. He didn't like the idea of having three more people in his home and he didn't trust Leah. He felt she was trouble. After they ate dinner, the children were put to bed and Jimmy excused himself. He wanted a long hot shower before he dropped into his own bed. Steven had no intention of spending too much time with all the women. He told BJ he had an errand to run and would be right back. He wouldn't return until everyone was in bed.

The next day Steven and BJ took all eight of their grandchildren to meet the social worker. They needed to finalize the paperwork for them to become the children's legal foster parents. The social worker made arrangements for them to receive immediate assistance for caring for the children and advised them a check would be mailed to them on the first of each month. Steven asked if he could pick it up in person, as he didn't trust the mail. He was told they could not arrange for that as the check was sent from Tallahassee, not from her office. Steven didn't like that answer, but knew he could do nothing about it.

Later that evening, Steven informed Jimmy he'd gotten his son a part time job on the weekends, cleaning the floors of the county buildings, the same place Steven worked. Jimmy told him he was already working many weekends at the shipyard and probably wouldn't be able to do it.

"I told them you'd be there so don't argue with me," Steven yelled at his son.

Jimmy persisted, "I'll lose that good job if I tell them I can't work on the weekends."

"Wouldn't be no loss. They take advantage of you anyways," Steven told his son. In reality, Steven didn't like his son's attitude since he'd been working there. He was becoming too independent. Steven wanted to be able to control him again.

Jimmy didn't respond to his father. He just looked at him and went to his room and cried. He liked the job at the shipyard. It was hard work, but he made enough so he had money for himself after turning over give most of it to his father for what his father called upkeep. Of course, Steven didn't know Jimmy was holding back some money and Jimmy wasn't about to tell him. He remembered how angry Steven got the last time.

While Jimmy was crying in his room, Steven was talking to BJ about all the things he was going to do with the money they were going to have rolling in. "Yep, BJ, in a couple of weeks we're going to start seeing the welfare checks from Kentucky, the Florida money for taking care of our foster children, Jimmy's ship yard paycheck and his county job as well. Then we can find us a nice, big house for all of us and maybe a newer car for me."

BJ was smiling and then added, "Don't forget the Social Security Leah gets for Andy and your check too."

Steven bristled and said, "My check is my money. My money isn't to take care of your brats, remember." However, he had forgotten about the Social Security Leah received for little Andy. He had to figure a way to get that money each month too.

While Steven and BJ were scheming ways to cheat the system and their children, Jimmy was in his room. He was sad. Deep in his heart he knew he used to feel happy, but he still couldn't remember any details. It bothered him to know he had forgotten so much.

Jimmy started looking through the little red address book he'd found in the bag of things he'd brought with him from the hospital in California. As he looked at each of the names, he would try to picture them. He still couldn't bring his memories clearly to his mind; however, he was starting to get flashes of things in his past. He now remembered his mother, what she looked like and how he felt when he was around her. He couldn't totally believe she didn't want to see him anymore. He'd started thinking he'd like to write to her. Steven had told him she didn't want him around anymore, but he didn't believe his father. He was positive he'd written her address in this red book, but somehow pages had been torn out and it wasn't there now. Every time he looked at the little red address book he cried a little. He knew there was so much he couldn't remember and he didn't know if he ever would.

He was startled by a knock at his door. No one had ever knocked on it before. Before he could say anything, the door opened and Leah was asking him, "Say, you look real sad, would you like a little company?"

CHAPTER 19

It's September 1986 ……

It hasn't been a full year since Leah and her boys moved in with Steven and his extended family in Florida. It had been 11 long months of too many people in a house that was too small.

Even though Steven and BJ were receiving money from many different sources, the move to larger quarters never happened.

Misty and BJ were content with the situation.

Leah was not.

One day as Jimmy was heading to the kitchen to eat some breakfast before going to work, Steven said to him, "Give me your car keys."

"Why?"

"Because I said so."

"No. I have to get to work."

"I'm your father so you have to do what I say, so give me your keys."

"I'm grown. I paid for my car. As a matter of fact, I've paid for almost everything in this house. You ain't getting my car."

"It's only your car, if I say it is, and I say it's mine," said Steven as he lunged at his son.

Steven was surprised when his feeble minded son grabbed his arm and twisted it behind his back immobilizing him. "Don't mess with me, old man. I told you, you ain't getting my car."

As he let go of his father's arm Jimmy said, "Cool down, old man. We can talk tonight, but for now I'm taking my car and going to work. So back off."

Steven stared at his son for a moment, finally responding softly, "This ain't over yet."

Jimmy laughed a little and replied, "Probably not. Nope, probably not."

As Jimmy drives to his new job at the warehouse he thinks about what had just happened. He'd lost his job at the shipyard when he could no longer work weekends. Now the old man was trying to take his car away from him. He just wasn't going to let it happen.

Jimmy remembered how he'd accidentally discovered he wasn't working for the county. His thoughts went back to that evening, several weekends after losing his main job. He was buffing the floor of the lobby of the county building where he worked when a courier arrived with the paychecks. He signed for them and after the courier left, he thumbed through them, looking for his. He'd realized it would be a short check because they'd hold back a week's pay but he knew he had one coming. However, none of them has his name on it.

When he asked his father about the missing check, Steven gave a long explanation about how bookkeeping was having a problem with the duplicate last names. He told Jimmy both their wages would be combined until he could get it straightened out. Steven also told Jimmy not to worry, as he would take care of it.

Jimmy remembered how he thought how wrong that was but how he didn't say anything more to his father, instead deciding to investigate the problem on his own.

He remembered how he felt when he called the county personnel office on following Monday morning and discovered there was no bookkeeping problem. The problem was the county didn't allow related people to work the same job on the same shift.

Jimmy was stunned when he realized he wasn't being paid. He was just doing his father's work while his father disappeared.

Jimmy remembered how bad he felt and how he had to find another job so he could take care of Leah and her children. He'd been desperate. He called the shipyard hoping they would take him back. Kevin, his old supervisor was sorry, but there was nothing open; however, he did tell Jimmy about a new warehouse he'd heard was opening over by the highway.

Jimmy thanked Kevin for the information. He still remembered the fear he felt as he was driving to the warehouse and how nervous he was as he filled out the application. Jimmy didn't read and write well but the man didn't seem to mind that the handwriting was terrible. He barely looked at Jimmy as he told him to report for work the next day. The job didn't pay as well as the shipyard, but he was happy he had a job again. He had people depending on him.

When he arrived home that night Jimmy excitedly announced he'd found a new job. Leah immediately asked how much he was making and when was he paid. Steven was red with anger, but said nothing more to his son that night.

Since that day, Jimmy and Steven had been fighting almost continually, with Leah quietly feeding the arguments each night by telling Jimmy what Steven said during the day and during the day telling BJ what Jimmy had said. So, it should have been no surprise when that evening, Steven asked Jimmy, "You gonna give me your car or not?"

However, Jimmy was surprised. Things had been pleasant over dinner so he thought he father had calmed down. Apparently he was wrong.

Jimmy's response was, "Old man, I told you this morning, I paid for this car and you ain't getting it."

"Then you and your whore girlfriend and her kids can get out," Steven shouted.

"What?" Jimmy questioned.

"You heard me. Get out – now."

"Old man, I've given you my paycheck each week so I don't got no money to move. I lost a good job so I could work weekends like you wanted. I wasn't paid for doing that job. I done your work while you were off doing whatever it is you do. I contribute enough to keep this house up and all the people in it fed. This is more my house than it is yours."

"My names on the lease, so that don't mean jack."

"Maybe not, but we ain't leaving until we have a place to go. I ain't making Leah and the boys live on the streets just because you got a wild hair up your butt. We'll leave, but only when I find us a place." With that, Jimmy took his dirty dishes over to the sink and stormed into the room he shared with Leah.

Steven watched his son leave. As his chest was heaving with anger, he looked at his wife and yelled, "Get them dishes washed," as he stormed out the back door.

Leah looked at her mother. "You gonna let him call me names like that?"

"Now honey, you know I ain't gonna get in the middle of the men fighting. You need to tell Jimmy he has to do what his father says. Steven gets really mad when somebody doesn't do what he says."

"But Jimmy's right. He's been paying for almost everything ever since I got here. All he's got is that junk car. That old man can't take it from him cause he'll lose his job again." Leah whined. "What'd we do then?"

"You have to understand. Steven's under a lot of pressure with that undercover job he has and he don't need us making things harder on him."

"If'n he has such a wonderful job, why don't we see any of the money he makes? How come we're still living in this dump? And how come Jimmy's gotta turn over his whole paycheck?" Leah asked her mother.

Ignoring most of what Leah asked, BJ responded, "Children are put on this earth to take care of their parents. That's why Jimmy's supposed to turn over all his money. It ain't really his, it belongs to us."

Leah was surprised at what her mother had said and before following Jimmy into their bedroom, told her, "You're as nuts as Steven. We ain't gonna be taking care of you and Jimmy ain't turning over our money to you no more."

The next day Jimmy started looking in the paper and talking to people at work. Soon he found an apartment they could afford and talked the landlord into holding it until he was paid.

The following Saturday, the day after payday, Jimmy moved Leah her boys and the little bit of clothing and furniture they had into the apartment.

Steven has not softened in his feelings at all.

As Jimmy was moving the last box of clothes out of the bedroom he's shared with Leah, Steven cornered him and said, "If I ever see or hear of you talking with anyone in this house again, I'll kill you. I should have finished you off years ago along with your mother and brother. You ain't been nothing but pain and misery in my life."

Jimmy held his tongue but remembered what his father said. Some of the words started coming together in his head, like he'd heard them before.

Jimmy said goodbye to BJ and Misty and left the house.

He was really terrified. He was only 21.

He'd never been on his own before and now he not only had to take care of himself, but he had Leah and the two boys to take care of. Jimmy decided he'd just have to address each challenge as they came, one at a time.

In his heart, he felt he'd done the right thing, but he was scared. Jimmy knew he wasn't the smartest person in the world, but he felt he deserved to be treated fairly. He'd have to work hard to take care of his family, but he'd do it.

He liked the sound of the words, his family. Smiling a little, he drove the last load of possessions to the apartment and the start of his new life.